Sailing to Jessica

By Kelly Watts

Author's note
Owners of smartphones can scan the 26 QR codes within this book to easily connect to the Sailing To Jessica website which contains additional material, per chapter, and includes maps, photos and e-mails.

Download the free Microsoft Tag app at http://gettag.mobi then hold your phone's camera about 4 inches away from the code and it will take you directly to the related supplemental material.

Get the free mobile app at
http://gettag.mobi

If you don't have a smartphone, you can still access the material by visiting www.sailingtojessica.com

Front Cover:
Paul hanks a line at the mast while Kelly and Paul sail to the Yasawa Islands, Fiji. Photo: Kelly Watts.

Back Cover:
Cherokee Rose at anchor in Tarawa's lagoon, Kiribati. Photo by Kelly Watts. Inset photo: Paul and "Bucket Babe" Kelly show off the lobsters they caught on Minerva Reef. Photo: Enchante.

This edition published in 2012
Copyright ©Kelly Watts, 2012.
All Rights Reserved. No part of this publication may be reproduced, stored in a retrieval system or transmitted in any way without written permission from the author. No representation is expressed or implied, with regard to accuracy of the information contained in this publication and no legal responsibility or liability can be accepted for omissions or errors.
ISBN 978-0-9874548-0-5

To Paul who makes everyday an adventure
and to Jessica and Nick,
who bring such love and joy to our lives.

Table of Contents

Double Maiden Voyage 7
Meaning of Life 14
No Regrets on Rosie 24
Surviving Cape Fear 32
Life with No Means 37
Beginners on Board 43
Provisions, Preparations and the Harmonica 51
Woman Behind-the-Wheel in the Bahamas 64
Chickentown 75
No Emergency Exit 88
Transiting the Panama Canal Twice 94
Storms, Pirates and the Galapagos Islands 101
Land Ho! after Twenty-two Days at Sea 112
Buddy-boating to Black Pearls 124
Tahiti to Bora Bora with our Cat 133
John and the Sharks of Suwarrow 145
Spin Cycle to New Zealand 159
Boat Work and Body Work 170
Misadventures of Howie and the Engine 186
From Soggy Suva to So So Bay 199
Celebrations in Tuvalu 212
Sorrowful Goodbye, Sudden Hello 220
Oh baby! 230
Killer Kiribati 237
Lurking Hazards and Insufferable Delays 250
Final Passage 261
Glossary 265
Acknowledgements 284

What would I say if my daughter told me she wanted to sail around the world? That's easy. Heck, no. I know the perils of such a journey: the relentless, formidable strength of Mother Nature; the predatory habits of sharks, sea snakes and orca whales; the lurking threat of pirates. And yet, I wouldn't have a daughter if my parents had told me no when I presented them with the same proposition.

Mind you, they tried.

My dad, a retired Commander in the US Navy, shook his head disapprovingly and said, "Kelly, you and Paul are foolishly risking your lives. Neither of you knows how to sail!"

My mom was more blunt.

She told Paul, "You will get my daughter killed."

She was nearly right.

Double Maiden Voyage

Atlantic Ocean, off South Carolina coastline, April 2001

 A deafening, high-pitched alarm pierced the still night that had descended over the Atlantic Ocean. Startled, the three of us leapt up from our seats in the sailboat's cockpit. Bruce, our friend and the only sailor on board, poked his head into the cabin. Red bars glowed ominously on one of the navigation station's instrument panels.

 "It's the high temperature alarm on the engine," he said. "It's overheating!" Bruce flew down the ladder into the cabin, followed closely by my husband, Paul.

 Over his shoulder, Paul ordered, "Keep watch, Kel."

 Gulp.

 What was I supposed to do? This was my first watch. I recalled the sailing books I had read before this trip. While the boat was sailing, someone had to be on watch at all times to monitor the weather and to make sure that the boat didn't hit anything. I glanced nervously around the horizon.

 The lights of Sullivan's Island and the Isle of Palms glittered in the distance on our left; otherwise the vast Atlantic Ocean surrounded us. I looked forward, across the deck of the 1980 42-foot Tayana cutter-rigged sailboat that Paul and I had purchased two days ago. The sails were rolled up. Without even a whisper of wind, we hadn't bothered to set the sails. We were motoring north across the glossy, flat sea. There wasn't any sign of the gale that was expected to cross our path in 2- 3 days.

Maybe the weather forecast was wrong, I thought, unaware of the truth behind the expression "the calm before the storm."

I surveyed the water. I didn't see anything that we could hit or, equally important, that might hit us. I stepped behind the wheel because it seemed like the right thing to do on watch. But it was a pointless gesture; because the autopilot was steering us, I couldn't turn the wheel. The alarm continued its shrill cry. Anxiously, I looked into the cabin.

"Turn the engine off!" Bruce shouted to me over the alarm.

The two guys looked up expectantly.

I hesitated as I looked at the controls mounted on either side of the wheel; there was a red-handled one and a black-handled one. Which was the gear shift and which was the throttle?

Paul saw my indecision and hollered, "Pull the black one toward you, then put the red one straight up."

The alarm blared relentlessly as I shifted the engine into neutral.

"Push the black button," Paul barked, pointing to a small control panel mounted on the side of the cockpit bench, next to my shin. "And flip off the engine switch."

I did.

Then there was silence.

Absolute, eerie silence.

"I bet it's the impeller," Bruce said, adding, "With a little bit of luck, this will be the only problem we have on our shakedown cruise."

According to him, the purpose of the ominous-sounding "shakedown cruise" was to familiarize the crew with the boat and 'shake out' any problems that needed to be fixed. Paul and I preferred to call this our maiden voyage – or double maiden voyage, as the case was. This was our first time sailing Cherokee Rose. And aside from a five-day sailing course, this was our first time sailing. Ever.

Despite the gale warning we were sailing the boat from Charleston, where we purchased her, to Philadelphia where we lived. The 600-mile passage was expected to take six days. If the storm approached, we would seek shelter in the Intracoastal Waterway, a strip of protected water that ran along the eastern seaboard.

"What makes you think it's the impeller?" Paul asked.

Bruce explained how, as an impeller ages and deteriorates, it becomes less efficient at pumping coolant through the engine. "Then the temperature rises and you get a situation like this." He paused and asked, "Do you have a spare impeller?"

"All of the spares are under this seat," Paul said, as he removed the seat cover and started rummaging through the locker. Bob, the previous owner, had collected an impressive assortment of spares which we inherited with the boat. Luckily, there was another impeller.

It took them 45 minutes to change the impeller. Then they ran the engine to test it. While the temperature still registered higher than normal, it was not red-bar critical.

"Because it's possible that some rubber pieces of the impeller might be lodged in the heat exchanger, I think we should only use the engine if absolutely necessary," Bruce said.

Paul agreed.

"Why don't we turn around and go back?" I suggested, thinking that this was an obvious and sensible solution. We weren't that far from Charleston Harbor.

Paul and Bruce nixed that idea. They had both taken time off from work to sail the boat to Philadelphia. It was now or never.

"It is a sailing boat, Kel," Paul reasoned. "We don't need the engine,"

I shrugged, deferring to their decision. What did I know about sailing?

The next 48 hours passed very slowly. By the second morning of our trip, the skies had become overcast, the wind had freshened and the waves had steadily grown. They were three feet high and coming at us from the side. Everything was gray; the heavy low clouds, the frothing waves, and my mood. Even a school of playful dolphins flitting and jumping around our boat didn't cheer me up.

For the first time in months, it wasn't the emotional roller coaster ride of fertility treatments and the prospect of a childless future that made me glum. Today it was the very real roller coaster ride of Cherokee Rose's up-and-down motion that got me. Despite the seasickness patch behind my ear, I felt queasy.

I vaguely realized that I hadn't slept on this trip.

The combination of the see-saw motion and my fatigue was overwhelming. After I lost my battle with seasickness, Paul coaxed me into the cabin and tucked me into my sleeping bag on the salon couch. Cold and exhausted, I wished that everything – the boat, the sea, and oh, please god, the motion -- would go away.

I drifted asleep.

Hours later, Paul woke me with his excited cry, "Kelly, I see land!"

His hands were frozen popsicles and I jerked away from his touch.

"We're approaching Cape Fear."

Due to the declining weather, they had decided to tuck into the Intracoastal Waterway at Cape Fear, which was located at the southern end of North Carolina's coastline. I was elated at the thought of being on calm water again. I sat up quickly, then instantly regretted it as nausea swept over me. The boat's rocking had grown worse while I had slept.

"Come see," Paul said encouragingly before he climbed into the cockpit.

I stood up gingerly and then fell unexpectedly against the dining room table as the boat lurched. Ow! I steadied myself against the table, then grabbed for the desk, the kitchen counter and finally the handrails on the ladder to the cockpit.

Halfway up the ladder, I stopped climbing and poked my head outside. Looking forward through the mist and drizzle, I saw land.

Hallelujah!

"How quickly can we get there?" I eagerly asked Paul and Bruce, who were standing in the cockpit and analyzing the waves and wind. "Let's go!"

"I don't know," Bruce said slowly.

"What?" I demanded, not pleased with his tone.

"Look, it is almost 4 o'clock; it's going to be dark soon. We won't be able to see where we are going." He looked at the sky. "And the weather is getting worse." He glanced at Paul. "I think we need to turn around and head out to sea."

"What?" I protested, glaring at the two men, "But we are so close!"

Paul shifted his weight from one foot to the other, thinking. "Kel, Bruce is right. It's too dangerous to go in. Remember what we read? Boats can survive most storms at sea; but land can sink us. Especially if we can't see it in the dark."

I stomped my foot and threw Bruce the meanest look I could muster before another wave of nausea forced me to retreat to my bed. Helpless to change my plight, I escaped it by falling asleep again.

Bang!

Startled, I woke up and wondered what had crashed on deck. I dimly heard Paul and Bruce shouting at each other outside. It was hard to hear them over the sound of water rushing past the hull and the racket inside the cabin. With each rock of the boat, cans of food and spare parts rolled, crashed and banged inside the dozen mainly empty lockers.

I must have dozed because it was dark when Paul nudged me.

"Kel, I'm in a bad way."

It wasn't his arctic touch as much as his distressed tone of voice that jolted me out of my semi-conscious state. I looked at him. Water dripped off his hair, his jacket and his pants, creating a puddle around his soggy tennis shoes. His blood-shot eyes were sunken in his sheet-white face. His body shivered incessantly.

Then it hit me; he had hypothermia.

Alarmed, I sat upright. "Okay, strip," I ordered. "We have got to get you out of those wet clothes."

While Paul clumsily unzipped and shrugged off his coat, I climbed out of my sleeping bag. Standing, I pulled off his wet shirt before the boat's motion pitched me to the floor. I unlaced his saturated shoes. Nausea overcame me and I threw up in the bucket by my bed.

"Kel, you've gotta help Bruce." Paul struggled to speak as if even his tongue was frozen. "The staysail and the mainsail ripped. And the GPS died."

I nodded grimly.

Once he was out of his wet clothes, Paul half-climbed while I half-pushed him into the bed that was adjacent, and above, my couch. Swapping my still-warm sleeping bag for his cold one, I zipped him into its snug embrace. Without a doctor to consult, getting him warm seemed like a logical remedy. I just hoped it was enough. I latched the bed's side rail into place so that Paul wouldn't accidentally fall out of bed – a real possibility in this sea – and looked for Bruce.

Where was he?

I stumbled to the companionway, hastily put on my jacket and harness and tethered myself to a U-bolt next to the door. I opened the slatted doors just to have the wind rip them from my hands and slam them against the cabin. The wind howled, startling me with its ferocity, and icy rain pelted my face.

Bruce was hunched over in the cockpit. As I stepped outside, a wave slammed against the side of the boat, causing her to heel over sharply and throwing me against the companionway. I steadied myself and warily scanned the vicious sea.

Other than the meager cone of light that shone down from our mast-head, we were engulfed in darkness, suspended in a black world without sea or sky. Behind Bruce, a ten-foot frothing wave materialized out of the black void and crashed into our boat, dousing us with frigid salt water.

With rapt horror, I watched another wave magically roll into our little arena of light.

Frightened, I tore my eyes away from menacing spectacle and looked at Bruce for reassurance. His head was tucked against his chest. Beads of water glittered on his wool cap and streams of water cascaded down the folds in his yellow foul-weather gear.

"Bruce?" I asked.

He lifted his head, revealing bloodshot eyes and blue lips on a white face. He, too, was shivering uncontrollably.

With a sinking sense of déjà vu, I said, "Bruce, go down below and get warm."

"I'm on watch," he said, slurring his words slightly and stubbornly shaking his head. Then he tucked his chin back into his coat collar and hunched his shoulders.

As the waves continued to assault our boat, I assessed our situation. We were stuck in a gale at sea, somewhere off Cape Fear, with 40-knots of wind and scary seas. We had an overheated engine, ripped sails and a broken GPS. Paul and Bruce were suffering from hypothermia.

The gravity of our situation hit me.
Our survival depended upon me.
But I'm not a sailor, a panicked voice inside of me screamed. How did I get here?

Meaning of Life

Philadelphia PA, seven months earlier, September 2000

Paul called it a rough patch. I thought it was a depressing funk. Psychologists term it a "life crisis" - except we didn't know that. We weren't seeing a psychologist; why would we? Neither of us screamed, smashed wine glasses or had an affair. Neither of us had the urge to buy a shiny red Porsche. Our life crisis didn't cause us to do anything *that* dramatic. We just quit our jobs, sold our house and hopped on a boat.

I first realized something was wrong when Paul stopped bouncing. Paul's buoyant personality and zest for life had earned him the nickname of "Tigger" in my family but it had been ages since I had seen a bounce.

Paul was a software engineer and a project manager for a major pharmaceutical company. Together, he and his work colleagues had designed and written a control system for the first fully-automated mail-order pharmacy in the world. That was great for his career, but not so great whenever the pharmacy went down as my husband was on call 24/7.

When the problems reached Paul, who was the final line of support, they were always critical – and urgent. Every minute of down-time cost the company thousands of dollars. To compound matters, these calls always seemed to come at inopportune times, like when Paul was carving the turkey for Thanksgiving dinner or while we were windsurfing in Aruba on vacation. Paul never had a break and after four years it

14   Sailing To Jessica

showed.

While watching TV or working on the computer, he would unconsciously gulp breaths of air, as if he were drowning; and during the night, he had begun grinding his teeth so viciously that he frequently woke me up. Even the colorful shirts he typically wore looked garish against his pallid face. I blamed his job for these involuntary distress signs until our doctor diagnosed us with a bigger problem.

We apparently couldn't get pregnant. I say apparently because our doctor couldn't find anything wrong with us despite the fact that we had been trying to conceive a baby for five years. We were an "unexplained" case of infertility. At his recommendation and at the age of 35, we started down the rather unpleasant path of fertility treatments, which consisted of popping pills, getting shots and removing any spontaneity and romance from our love-making. Yet Paul and I endured them willingly, because they gave us hope. This might be *the* month.

But it was never the month.

Instead, every month found me sobbing at another failed attempt. My stubborn "perfectly healthy" body had betrayed me again, snatching away the prospect of a baby – and my very breath, it seemed. Bitter disappointment and grief nearly suffocated me; yet whenever I gasped for air, I inhaled anger. Damn my body. Because there *wasn't* anything wrong with it, there wasn't anything concrete to fix. And damn this situation; it was so unfair. Having children was practically a human right. Why were we repeatedly denied it?

And, as if dealing with my own raging emotions wasn't difficult enough, I still had to tell my beloved husband. Paul wanted a baby as much if not more than me. Being the bearer of bad news, I got to karate-chop his heart. Every month.

This cycle of constantly trying and constantly failing battered any positive outlook on life we could muster. And yet we weren't ready to quit treatment. So here we were, torturing ourselves in this wretched holding pattern, waiting for good news that never seemed to come. A depressing gloom settled over us as tangibly as thick fog.

Then one evening the fog lifted. Paul smiled for the first time in months. We were at a party my friend Diane was giving. Paul was chatting with her guests of honor, Phil and Christine. From across the room, I watched his smile broaden and then he became animated as their conversation continued. What had captivated my husband?

When I joined him, Paul explained that Phil and Christine had just sailed across the Atlantic Ocean on a friend's yacht, and that they intended to sail around the world in a couple of years. Fascinated with a lifestyle so foreign to ours, we chatted with Phil until it was time to leave. Paul continued to discuss their trip as we walked home. Well, I walked; Paul bounced.

The bouncing lasted as long as our conversation and then the fog descended. After two more nights of teeth-grinding, Paul went to work on Monday morning with slumped shoulders and a big sigh. Tomorrow he had to fly to Las Vegas for a major software installation. The mail-order pharmacy was located there, but Paul worked long hours and rarely saw the glittering sights.

I sat in my office and stared absentmindedly at my computer screen. I worked from home as a freelance food journalist and regional contributor for house-and-garden magazines. I sighed at the blank word document in front of me and tried to focus on writing. But it was futile. I was worried about Paul. How would he survive another 100-hour work week in Vegas?

That afternoon as I drove home from yet another doctor's appointment, I passed a bookstore. With sudden inspiration, I swerved into its parking lot. Maybe I could find Paul a book about sailing that would take his mind off work and baby-making. Thankfully, the boat section in the Philadelphia store was small, so it didn't take long to choose two books.

That night as Paul packed for his trip, I gave him the books. "They might cheer you up," I explained.

Paul smiled tiredly, examined the books and handed them back to me. "Here, you keep one. I won't have time to read two books. I doubt I'll even have time to read one."

"Okay, pick one," I said. "After all, it's your gift."

Paul's choice surprised me. He kept "Maiden Voyage," a book about an 18-year old girl, a New York City bike messenger, whose father gave her an ultimatum: either go to college or sail around the world. He handed me the book written by Peter Goss. It looked like a chest-pounding, man-against-nature book based on the cover photo, and one that I thought Paul would have jumped at. I took the book unenthusiastically and put it in my office upstairs.

The next morning, Paul left the house before dawn for his early flight.

Later that morning as I was brewing a cup of tea, the phone rang. I glanced at my watch. Paul's flight wasn't scheduled to land yet.

"Hey, Kel."

It was Paul.

"Where are you?" I asked, concerned. "Are you okay?"

"I'm fine. We had a tail wind and our plane arrived early in Vegas. I gotta run but, Kel, I had to call you," Paul sounded breathless. "That book was so good, so emotional. I've almost finished it.

"Oh, Paul, you should've slept. You are going to be so tired."

"I know. But I couldn't put the book down. This girl, Tania, didn't know how to sail – like us. She just loaded up the boat with sailing books and learned along the way." He rushed on, "Kel, I think we should do it. I think we should sail around the world."

I opened my mouth to respond but nothing came out. I was speechless.

"I love you," he said. "I'll try to call later."

Then there was a click and he was gone.

I stared at the phone in disbelief as I placed it back on the kitchen wall. What had I done? My gift had backfired. I wanted to cheer him up. I did not want to sail around the world.

As I trudged up the stairs to my office, I listed my reasons for not wanting this particular adventure. It was dangerous. I got seasick. And, oh yeah, we didn't know how to sail.

I picked up the Peter Goss book on my desk. If Paul was serious about this – and by the dread I felt in the pit of my stomach I knew he was – I had better read up on it so I could change his mind. I needed ammunition. Perhaps it was fortunate that I had been left with the man-against-sea book; the one whose cover showed a boat battling treacherous seas and epic waves. If there were ever a reason not to go sailing, that had to be it.

The next night, Paul phoned me from Vegas; as usual, he didn't have much time to chat.

"What do you think about sailing around the world?" he asked. He sounded weary from his 18-hour work days.

"Let's talk about it when you get home," I suggested, knowing that the topic – if he really meant it- deserved more than the five minutes he had to give it. "But I did read that other sailing book."

"Was it good?"

"Well, it was very informative. I learned that if your boat flips over, you can swim inside the cabin, breathe from the air pocket and eat canned food. You might have to dive to get the can opener," I added, "but, hey, it's possible!"

Paul laughed and we said our goodbyes.

When the week was over, Paul flew home. He hadn't had time to ponder his outlandish suggestion of sailing around the world and I didn't want to give credence to his idea by having a serious discussion about it. Instead, we chose the nonthreatening approach of reading more sailing books. As long as we were just fantasizing about it, and not actually doing it, I welcomed the distraction of remote tropical islands and sunny anchorages in our otherwise gloomy lives.

As fate would have it, the annual Annapolis Boat Show was coming up. I called my dad who lived in Charleston, SC, to invite him to go with us. Twenty-five years ago, he had owned a small sailboat, which he had named after my sister and me. Even though he never owned another boat after KellySu, he still liked to walk around marinas and check out the yachts.

Dad was puzzled by my call; he knew I didn't like boats. I explained that Paul had gotten this crazy idea of sailing around the world, and while I didn't think we were actually going to do it, the idea of it seemed to help Paul through this tough time at work. I didn't mention our struggle to have a baby. Our repeated failures were too personal to share, even with family. Dad took this new information in stride and agreed to fly up for the show.

On the morning of the boat show, we collected Dad from the airport and drove directly to Annapolis. The day was gray, with a nippy wind and intermittent, frigid rain. Even the show's bright signal flags and colorful banners could not dispel the dreariness, but the excitement of actually seeing boats buoyed our spirits.

To board the boats, we had to take off our shoes, which made me regret the lace-up boots and worn-out socks I was wearing. But once on board, it was fun checking out the living spaces and kitchens. Thanks to my dad, and KellySu, my sister and I had learned the basic terms of a sailboat. I knew, for example, that the kitchen was called a galley. But it seemed pretentious to use these nautical terms because it might imply that I knew what I was talking about – which was far from true.

I was sitting on a comfortable couch inside a spacious sailboat. Unlike the numerous other boats we had seen, I actually liked this boat. Perhaps I could do this, I thought for the first time, perhaps I could live on a sailboat.

Dad sat down next to me.

"Wow, Dad, this is nice. I like the airiness and brightness of this boat."

"Well, this is not a boat you'd buy to sail around the world," he replied.

"What?" I asked, surprised by his comment. "Why not?"

"Because it is too big, too airy. In rough seas, things will inevitably get thrown about the boat and with so much air space in this cabin, things will really fly. And where are the lockers?" he said, frowning and looking around the cabin. "You need a boat that has plenty of lockers to store spare parts and provisions. You want a boat that feels tight, cozy. The tighter, the better," he said, standing up to investigate some instruments.

Deflated, I got up and made my way to the dock. Maybe I couldn't do this. Did I really want to consider rough seas and flying objects?

Toward the end of the show, we finally saw a boat that earned my dad's approval. It was a 42-foot Valiant and, with all of its varnished teak, it was beautiful. Paul gave me a quick smile to show that he, too, was impressed before he and my dad sat down to discuss the engine and sail configuration with the salesman. Mere feet away, I investigated the kitchen while they chatted.

All was going well until Paul asked the cost. It was $495,000. Paul sputtered, stood up and hastily said his goodbyes, making my dad grin at his speedy exit. I tried to hide my surprise, but seriously, this boat cost more than our house!

On the ride home, we all agreed that Paul and I would be in the market for a used boat, if we were ever to buy one.

"Are you serious about sailing around the world?" Dad asked. "Because when I had KellySu, I dreamed about it. In fact, I have some cruising books that you can borrow."

"Thanks, Ron. We are thinking about it." Paul said.

I added, "We like the idea of seeing those remote tropical islands, experiencing new cultures and meeting new people. It's just the sailing part that we're not sure about."

Paul corrected me, "That's the part *you're* not keen about; I want the challenge of man-against-the-sea."

I groaned.

Dad stopped us. "Regardless of why you might want to go sailing, you can't do it without experience. If you are serious, you should buy a small, forgiving boat, not one of the offshore boats we just saw. And then you should spend the next couple years sailing around the Chesapeake Bay before you contemplate foreign shores."

"But Ron, we read this book about a teenage girl who didn't know how to sail; she just set off with a bunch of books on the boat and learned as she went along," Paul pointed out.

I cringed in the backseat; I knew Dad would think that the girl – and Paul for even mentioning such an idea – was foolish.

Sure enough, Dad shook his head in disapproval and dismissed the notion. A real sailor wouldn't do that.

But we weren't real sailors.

As the weeks passed, Paul and I started to question our life and its purpose. Like most couples, we had assumed that we would have children, raise them, retire and spoil our grandchildren. But what if children were taken out of the equation? Because it looked as if we weren't going to have any.

Our fertility treatments were approaching the final step: in vitro fertilization. After the doctor referred to the procedure as "surgery," that was a step I was hesitant to take. After all, if there wasn't anything wrong with me, what *exactly* was surgery going to fix?

For Paul, it was a financial consideration. At over $10,000 a round, he thought IVF was like gambling on an expensive table at Vegas. The cards were still stacked against you and few people won, especially with a single hand. Any chance of success would require several rounds of IVF. That made it a very costly gamble without any guarantee that it would work. We were depressed enough without throwing away $30,000 too.

It seemed like there was never a winning hand at the high-stakes table of infertility. Losing the chance of having a baby was overwhelming. But the loss didn't stop there, as the ramifications of not having children sunk in. Our hopes and dreams of raising our baby were shattered, too. We wouldn't get to enjoy our baby's first steps, first soccer game, first love or first job. We wouldn't bake cookies, build a Lego spaceship or visit Mickey Mouse at Disneyland together. Lastly, the chaotic – but priceless – future of family get-togethers and family holidays, which would hopefully include grandchildren, was gone. We now faced a quiet, orderly and lonely future with just the two of us. And there wasn't anything we could do to change our future's course.

Powerless to control our future, we latched onto sailing like a life ring. The decision to sail around the world was one that we could make and we desperately needed to be in charge of our lives once again. Only I wanted to ditch the life ring – and climb ashore. With my seasickness, how could I possibly sail around the world?

Paul wasn't concerned as many of the books we had read dealt with this very problem. It seemed that after a couple of days at sea, most people got over their queasiness. Apparently the cure for seasickness was to stay on the boat. Silly me for thinking that getting off the boat was the solution!

With Thanksgiving quickly approaching, I thought it was time to address this issue. I needed to go sailing to see if I could manage my seasickness. If I couldn't, then sailing around the world was out.

Considering that we didn't know how to sail anything larger than our windsurfers, we couldn't charter a boat. But we could sign up for a five-day live-aboard sailing course, which had several advantages. First, we would learn the fundamentals of sailing. Second, it would placate my dad who was constantly reminding us that we didn't know how to sail. And finally, the course was held in the Florida Keys, and I figured we could use a little sunshine in our lives.

I enrolled us in the class, bought the school books online, and we studied them as instructed before the holiday weekend. Armed with scopolamine patches which were supposedly a better solution for seasickness than Dramamine, we flew down to Florida.

Besides Mark, the instructor, there were four students in the class: Paul and me and two women. Tina worked for the sailing school, as an office assistant, and needed to experience the course as part of her job. Tracy was a law student. Our days were spent scrambling on deck, learning the basics of sailing. Our evenings were spent sitting around the salon table, reviewing the course books and taking tests.

I wasn't queasy, but prolonged use of the patch made my throat scratchy and my head hurt. It felt as though I had a cold, which was bearable but less than ideal. So were our sleeping quarters.

Our cabin was at the back of the boat, and our bed had walls butting up against three of its four sides. It reminded me of a coffin and seemed every bit as claustrophobic. There was one tiny window above the bed which I kept open to remind myself that I wasn't dead and I wasn't on a boat waiting to cross the River Styx.

One day, as we were sailing along, Mark announced that we were going to practice our man-over-board skills.

"Man Overboard!" Mark yelled, pretending. "Now, what's the first thing you do?"

"Litter the water with anything that floats," I responded immediately. I had studied those course books.

"Right," said Mark, "that's what you would do. But for this exercise, we are not going to do that--"

It was too late.

Paul had already tossed two cushions and the life ring into the water.

Mark surveyed the water, glanced at Paul and said, "You get to go first. Bring the boat around."

Paul steered the boat while Mark handed me the boat hook to pull the cushions and life ring out of the water. Then the other girls took their turns practicing the man-over-board drill with imaginary floats. I was last.

As I timidly took the wheel, Paul kicked off his shoes, stripped off his shirt and, before anyone knew what was going on, jumped into the water.

"Damn it, Paul!" I shouted at him, stomping my foot. With half a mile of water between us and land, we were now facing a real man-over-board situation. But for the moment I was quite content to leave that man in the water.

"What do we do first?" asked Mark calmly.

"Throw him the life ring," I grumbled.

Tina tossed it out.

"Steer into the wind, then release the sails to slow the

boat down," Mark ordered.

I turned the boat while Tina and Tracy released the main and jib sheets, causing the sails to flap noisily in the wind. Only our forward momentum propelled the boat.

I steered toward Paul, who was grinning in the water and casually resting on the life ring. Seconds later, I couldn't see him. The bow of the boat obstructed my view of the water's surface. That wasn't a big deal when rescuing a boat cushion; who cared if I ran it over? But run over Paul?

In my foul mood, it was tempting.

"I can't see Paul," I snapped, craning my head. "What do I do?"

Mark joined me behind the wheel. "Steer more to starboard."

"But I'll run him over," I protested. That was where I had last seen him.

"No, you won't." Mark leaned over the side of the boat and, looking forward, said, "Perfect." He dropped a line into the water and said to Paul, "Grab this."

Mark led the line to the rear swim platform and Paul climbed aboard, still grinning from ear-to-ear.

"In all of the years I have been teaching, no one has ever jumped overboard before," Mark admitted, chuckling and tossing Paul a towel.

It was a classic Tigger stunt and I could just imagine my sister tilting her head and asking me, as she always did in these situations, "For life, Kel?"

Yes.

Lucky me.

I was married to him for life.

That is, if our marriage could survive a childless future. Many didn't.

No Regrets on Rosie

Philadelphia, December 2000

As we flew back to rainy Philadelphia, we weren't thinking about our marriage. Our doctor hadn't counseled us, or even warned us, of the havoc that infertility could have on a relationship. Common problems include the fear that one partner might leave the other to have children with a different mate; the stress of agreeing or disagreeing to gamble thousands of dollars on potentially fruitless IVF; and the sexual difficulties that commonly resulted from infertility.

Not being aware of these pitfalls didn't give us immunity from them. While we hadn't encountered the first two issues yet, sex had become a prescribed chore, noted on the calendar next to paying the bills and returning the library books. On the physician-assigned dates, we had to perform - whether we wanted to or not. Since romance and intimacy refused to appear "on demand," they were absent from these clinical sessions. Trying to relax was impossible; our future was dependant on the outcome. No pressure there.

Sex lost its appeal, but that was normal, right?

We knew two couples who couldn't have children. One couple divorced after their IVF attempts failed; the financial strain and emotional guilt were too much. The other couple threw themselves into their jobs during the day and into the bottle at night. But we didn't associate our plight with theirs, or with other infertile couples. We still had the vague hope that we might get pregnant. After all, nothing was wrong with us.

We resumed our usual routine of work, reading sailing books and discussing the meaning of life. If we couldn't have children to nurture, what was our purpose in life? Should we sail around the world?

We tried to stack the pros against the cons but struggled to weigh intangibles, such as quality of life and growth experiences, against the monetary worth of stock options and bonus checks. Invariably, our conversations went around and around, without any satisfactory conclusions. Deciding whether to sail around the world seemed as evasive as making a baby.

With Christmas upon us, Paul and I opted to enjoy a quiet holiday in Charleston. The weather was gray and rainy, but we defied it by taking long walks along the Battery and shopping on King Street. Most evenings we curled up in front of a crackling fire and chatted. On one such night, the subject of sailing came up again. Sipping red wine with our legs intertwined on the couch, we were having our usual circular conversation when it came to me: the definitive answer.

We had to do it. While we had been struggling to offset the negatives of sailing against the positives, neither of us had considered how we would feel if we *didn't* go – and that turned out to be the most compelling reason *to* go.

If we passed on this opportunity, our life would resume its usual, and still unsatisfying, course. How would we feel when we were older? I doubted that, in our golden years, we would be reminiscing over some promotion that Paul had earned, or some garden I had scouted. When we totaled up our lives' achievements, would any of these really matter?

"But what about my job?" Paul asked. "And all of my stock options?"

Yes, he had golden handcuffs, three pairs, to be exact. But they became golden in three, four and five years. Right now they were just handcuffs.

"I guess you'll have to walk away from those stock options," I said. "If we were concerned about money, or stock options, we wouldn't even be having this conversation. This is about trying to find some purpose for our lives. Who knows? Maybe a change in our lifestyle will help us conceive. Or maybe we will discover that we don't need children to feel fulfilled" -- Paul looked doubtful here, but I carried on -- "but at least we will have the time to reflect on it, and on what we want out of life."

"What will we do when we get back?" he asked. "I doubt I would get my current job back."

"Honey, we are both intelligent, hard-working people," I said. "I'm sure we could get jobs at McDonald's if we had to. Don't worry, we'll find jobs."

Then he turned the tables, and asked about my seasickness.

"If it is really bad or if we decide we don't like sailing, we'll quit, sell the boat and come back," I said. Oblivious to the underlying assumption I had just made – that Paul and I would agree when it was quitting time – I continued, "Even if we aborted the trip, we'll know that we gave it a shot. We won't have any regrets."

Thoughtfully, Paul swirled his wine. Then he looked at me, lifted his glass and toasted, "Here's to sailing around the world."

Perhaps we should have remedied our life crisis with a shiny red Porsche instead of a boat. Like infertility, a boat presents its own challenges for a couple. As the popular sailing saying goes, "Living on a boat can make or break a relationship." If we were trying to sabotage our marriage, we were on the right course.

Our plan to sail around the world started with selling our house, finding and buying a suitable boat, sailing it to Philadelphia and living on it. There were some marinas in downtown Philadelphia, along the Delaware River, and we would moor the boat there. Then we could keep our jobs, and during our spare time, learn her systems and fix her up. When we had vacation, we'd motor the boat down the river to the Chesapeake Bay and practice sailing.

January, February and March were hectic. In an effort to get the house ready to sell, we had to finish the basement first. Paul and I had constructed a multi-angled rock climbing wall in the basement – oh, the things I did for Tigger! – and we had started putting up the studs for an adjacent sitting area. But that was as far as we had gotten. As a result, we spent our free daytime hours completing the basement. At night, we surfed the web, looking for suitable, used boats. At the end of March, we found Cherokee Rose on-line. She was docked an hour south of Charleston, SC.

I phoned Dad to tell him we would be flying down to check her out; did he want to come along?

"If you think I am going to sail with you and Paul on your maiden voyage," he exploded, "you are sorely mistaken, young lady. I have forgotten more about sailing than you and Paul know about the subject. You are foolishly risking your lives!"

This outburst came from nowhere, and I was stunned because my dad seldom lost his cool. How could he possibly think I'd want him to sail with us on our maiden voyage?!

"Relax, Dad," I said reassuringly, "I don't want you to sail with us. It was bad enough learning how to drive with you."

Sweating in the heat of South Carolina's summer, on black vinyl seats in a car without air conditioning, my sister and I had endured Dad's military-style driving lessons. The experience was best forgotten; and certainly not one I wanted to relive on the boat.

"Well, you should have a seasoned sailor on board when you sail the boat to Philadelphia." He was calmer now.

"I'll take that under advisement, Dad."

After we hung up the phone, I realized that he was really worried about us.

Dad met us at the airport and drove us to Beaufort, S.C., where Cherokee Rose was moored. The owners, Bob and Barbara, had sailed her from San Diego to Beaufort by way of the Panama Canal. Their trip had taken three years. The boat had everything we thought we would need, including a reverse osmosis water maker, a water-cooled fridge/freezer; wind generator; solar panels; wind vane; automatic windlass; autopilot and a 48-horsepower diesel engine. The boat had lockers galore – and she felt airy compared with every other we boat we had seen. She even had a washing machine. I loved her.

Paul liked everything except the teak-covered decks, which were shedding hunks of black rubber caulk. Cherokee Rose's decks weren't the only thing that needed some tender loving care. Her hull was powdery white, instead of shiny; the plastic windows on the canvas dodger were etched from sea salt; her rolled-up sails needed stitch work; and all of her stainless steel was heavily speckled with rust.

We discussed the boat with Dad and decided to make an offer, contingent upon the results of the sea trial and survey, which was similar to a pre-purchase home inspection.

"You should ask Bob to sail the boat with you to Philadelphia as part of the deal," my dad suggested. "That way you can learn about the boat's systems, and gain some sailing experience."

"What a great idea," I said.

Bob was not enthusiastic when we presented the idea to him. In the end, he agreed to sail the boat with us from Beaufort to Charleston, a 60-mile journey along the Intracoastal Waterway that would take 10 to 12 hours.

We received the results of the boat survey and engine oil test. Our surveyor said that the oil in the engine was very clean – in fact, the cleanest he had seen – and didn't reveal any problems. Given that the engine, like the boat, was 20 years old, that was good news. Via phone and fax, we finalized our offer and signed the contract to buy Cherokee Rose.

On the home front, we completed the basement and a friend offered to buy our house. We now had one check on our list. The house was as good as sold.

In April, I flew to Charleston to sail Cherokee Rose with Bob and Barb from Beaufort to Charleston, where we would close the deal. Paul was in the midst of another software installation and would join me in Charleston. Dad dropped me off at the marina in Beaufort and I walked down the dock, noting that 42-foot Cherokee Rose was the largest boat in the small marina.

I was early and surprised Bob, who was tinkering with the engine. He said Barb would join us at lunch time and if I wanted, he would show me how to do an oil change.

Yippee.

Knowing that Paul would want me to explain the process, I pulled out my notebook and took copious notes. Barb brought lunch, dinner and breakfast supplies; we were going to anchor and spend the night along the way.

This stretch of the Intracoastal Way consists of narrow channels and rivers, so sailing – tacking back and forth – wasn't an option. We motored most of the way. When a turn in the river gave us a favorable wind direction that didn't require tacking, Bob pulled out the gib and briefly turned off the engine.

Without the engine's loud hum, I was amazed at how

quiet sailing was. It was peaceful on the water. There were puffy white clouds in the sky, and the sun's warm rays promised that summer would soon arrive. I actually enjoyed myself whenever I wasn't taking notes on how to run the refrigerator, how to read the amp meter, how to work the windlass, where to find the sea cocks and bilge pumps, how to flake the anchor chain. By the end of the day, my head was spinning.

Shortly before dusk, Bob took the wheel while Barb went forward to drop the anchor. I followed her, again taking notes. She looked back at Bob and made a hand gesture. Wordlessly, Bob signaled back.

"He just told me we are in 20 feet of water."

She dropped the anchor and let out some chain. She made a different hand signal and Bob reversed the engine.

"There. Now we've set the anchor. Let me give you some advice. When it comes to anchoring, learn how to communicate with Paul by hand signals. Everyone in the anchorage will watch you anchor and, if you don't use hand signals, they will listen to you shouting and cursing at each other. Besides, you can still curse with your hands," she added, laughing.

Anchoring the boat looked easy; I wasn't sure why anyone would have to curse – but that was just another mystery to add to a day full of mysteries.

That evening we ate spaghetti with Italian sausages that had been cooked on the small BBQ grill mounted on the back of the boat. We chatted about their trip. I learned that they had never sailed out of sight of land and that they had anchored every night. Who knew you could day-hop from San Diego to South Carolina?

"What about provisioning? How did you do that?" I asked, curious to talk to a real cruiser.

"I never understood all the fuss," Barb replied. "The night before we left San Diego, I went grocery shopping. That was it. You know, people eat everywhere. You can buy food anywhere."

Huh. Her experience had been unlike any I had read about and it was fascinating to hear another, different approach.

Bob, Barb and I arrived in Charleston without any problems, did the paperwork and voila! Paul and I now owned Cherokee Rose. Another check on our list. Dad told me an old saying: The two happiest days in the life of a sailor were the day he bought his boat and the day he sold it. True to the saying, Bob and Barb seemed as pleased as we were.

The next day, Paul and Bruce, our friend and experienced sailor, flew to Charleston to join me and to get Rosie, as we nicknamed the boat, ready for our maiden voyage to Philadelphia. Bruce had an exhaustive pre-departure checklist, which included mundane items like filling up the diesel tanks and topping up the batteries to bigger jobs like changing the oil, which was already done, and cleaning the bilge. His list kept us busy.

The evening before we left, Dad and Lynn invited the three of us over for our "last hot meal." After dinner, we sat with Dad and watched the Weather Channel to get the latest forecast. That's when we heard about the gale that was expected to hit the East Coast later in the week. We modified our plan accordingly. We would sail offshore for a couple of days before tucking into the Intracoastal Way for protection from the storm.

"If the storm lasts several days, we might only get as far north as Norfolk, Virginia," said Bruce.

The problem was simple math. The trip was 600 miles. If we sailed offshore, we could cover 100 miles a day, because we would sail day and night; after all, in the ocean there was nothing to hit. In the Intracoastal Way, we could sail only during daylight hours so that we could see and avoid the shoals, the land spits and any boat traffic. Instead of a six-day offshore trip, the Intracoastal Way could take twice as long. Both Paul and Bruce had taken just one week of vacation, so wherever we were next Sunday, that was the end of this trip.

As we said goodbye on the front porch, Dad shook Bruce's hand and impulsively hugged him. "Thank you for going with these two on their maiden voyage. I feel much better knowing that there is a real sailor on board."

Bruce looked embarrassed but chuckled at Dad's comment.

As Dad hugged me, he pressed a leather necklace with a pendant of St. Christopher – the patron saint of travelers – into my hand. "Your grandfather gave this to me when I had KellySu. Put it in the pocket of your foul-weather jacket," he suggested, adding, "That's where I kept it. I figured if I needed my foul-weather gear, that's probably when I needed St. Christopher's help."

Tears welled up in my eyes; despite his gruffness, my dad was a softie at heart. I hugged him. Then we headed back to Cherokee Rose for our last night of sleep before sailing to Philadelphia. As soon as we climbed aboard, I tucked the pendant in my jacket pocket for safe-keeping, unaware that I would soon need it.

Surviving Cape Fear

**Atlantic Ocean near
Cape Fear, NC, April 2001**

I gasped as icy sea water, whipped off a frothy wave by 40-knot winds, blasted me in the cockpit. I jammed one of my wet hands into my jacket pocket and unexpectedly felt the St. Christopher's pendant. I clenched it briefly, hoping for divine intervention or at least some sort of rescue plan.

The boat pitched as another 10-foot wave barreled out of the impenetrable darkness that enfolded us and smacked Rosie. I fell against the cockpit bench and reflexively sat down, grabbing the nearest hand rail.

Caught in a gale off Cape Fear, we'd found Mother Nature to be merciless. In addition to the overheated engine, the wind had ripped our staysail and mainsail. Sheets of rain had short-circuited our GPS. Paul was out of action, suffering from hypothermia due to the freezing, wet conditions.

And now Bruce had it too. He was shivering across from me in the cockpit.

Repeating my earlier plea, I yelled over the howling wind, "Bruce, please come below with me and get warm."

"No, someone had to stay in the cockpit, and keep watch," he replied, slurring some of his words.

Panic seized me, but I impatiently pushed it aside. Think, Kel.

In the midst of the shrieking wind, driving spray and battering waves, a moment of calm and clarity struck me. I needed Bruce. And he needed to get warmed up.

I leaned toward him and demanded, "Why does someone have to stay out here?" I recalled a book I had read by Lin Pardey. During a gale at sea, she and her husband had stayed inside their cabin. They had only gone on deck to adjust the sails and to scan the horizon for traffic and weather changes. "Are we near land?"

"No."

I looked forward at the sails. Except for a meter of the front sail, they were rolled up. On a boat Rosie's size, the sail resembled a handkerchief.

"It doesn't look like the sail needs any tending," I said.

"No, we're hove-to."

I nodded. That was a nautical expression that meant that the sails and rudder were set to basically stall the boat. From what I had read, it was a technique often used in storms.

"Okay, so we are not near land and we're hove-to. Why do you need to stay in the cockpit?"

"To see if there are any boats that might hit us."

"We have radar down below. We can see any approaching boats on that," I reasoned. I looked around us; only blackness loomed beyond the faint glow of our masthead light. "Besides that, what can you really see sitting here?" I paused and then cajoled him, "Please come below, Bruce."

"I guess I should get our position and check it on the chart," he said slowly. Shivering, he pulled our back-up GPS – a handheld unit that Paul had purchased years ago for camping - out of his coat pocket and pushed a couple of buttons. Then he held it out to get a better signal.

We both waited.

"Got it," he said.

With a final search of the non-existent horizon, Bruce reluctantly followed me down, closing the hatch doors behind him.

It was amazing how much quieter, and warmer, it was in the cabin. It actually seemed cozy down here. I snapped off my harness and jacket and then saw that Bruce was struggling to unclip his harness with his numb fingers. I unclipped him and helped him take off his heavy yellow coat before the pitching motion forced me to bolt to my sea bed. Lying down helped quell my nausea.

I heard Bruce sit down heavily at the navigation station's desk just behind my couch, flip on the radar and chart our position. Then the floorboards creaked as he

Kelly Watts 33

retreated to the bed in the quarter berth, located behind the navigation desk. I heard him shifting on the cushions, getting into his sleeping bag.

"Thanks for coming down," I said, speaking to the ceiling since he was out of sight. I fervently hoped he'd get warm.

"We need to check the horizon and chart our position every 10 minutes," Bruce said.

"There is no way I can plot our position." On this bucking boat, concentrating and writing on a piece of paper would be the end of me. I was sure of that.

"I'll chart it," Bruce said.

"Okay. Then I'll check the horizon and get our position."

With our tasks divided, I snatched the egg-timer off the desk behind me and set it for 10 minutes.

I lay back down and dozed.

Beep, beep, beep.

I awoke with a start, groped around for the egg-timer and turned it off. I grabbed the GPS off the desk, strapped on my harness, which doubled as a life-jacket, and tethered myself to the boat. I was not going to fall overboard while everyone else slept. Gripping onto the cockpit doors tightly so the wind wouldn't catch them, I gingerly opened them. Trying not to get wet, I extended my arm as far as I could, holding out the handheld GPS and waiting for a signal. After a minute or two, it had our position. Then I sprang into the cockpit, pivoted around and scanned the horizon for any possible danger. Nothing.

Back in the cabin I woke Bruce with a nudge and laid the GPS on his sleeping bag. I glanced at the radar as I lurched past it; there weren't any green blips, an indication of boat traffic, on its screen. I crawled back into my bed, reset the alarm for 10 minutes and listened as Bruce charted our position.

"Are we safe?" I asked, referring to our location relative to land, sunken ships and other submerged dangers which were noted on the chart.

"Yep."

The floorboards creaked as Bruce returned to his bed.

We repeated our choreographed routine 71 times that night, for 12 long hours.

Paul never budged.

In the morning, Paul poked his head out of his sleeping bag and said that he felt better.

At the sound of Paul's voice, Bruce got up to make some tea. Once they had sipped a warm cupful, and eaten cold soup straight from the can, Bruce informed us that we were now off the coast of Georgetown, South Carolina. While we hadn't sailed during the night, the wind and current had pushed us south.

I groaned. After three nights and nearly three days sailing, we were only 60 miles north of where we had started! In light of the boat's condition, it was unanimously decided that we should head into port. We altered our course to Georgetown.

The excitement of approaching land, sweet immobile land, combined with the boat's gentler motion, enticed me to abandon my couch and join the guys in the cockpit.

"Well, well, well," Bruce said, "she moves."

I smiled good-naturedly at his teasing.

Even though the skies were still overcast, it was surprisingly bright in the cockpit.

"Hey, what happened to the bimini?" I asked, looking up. Yesterday a canvas awning had covered the cockpit, providing protection from the sun and rain. Today there was none.

"The bimini's stainless steel frame became unbolted last night and was swinging wildly in the cockpit," Paul explained. "I had to cut it down before it knocked me or Bruce overboard."

It had been quite a night.

I looked eagerly forward, toward the tree-lined shore. A mile or two ahead of us, I spotted another sailboat with one of its sails up. "Hey, we weren't the only ones caught in the storm last night," I cried out, strangely pleased to know that we hadn't been alone. As we continued east toward the coast, and the submerged breakwater that protected the entrance to the Winyah Bay, we gained on the other boat.

"Wow, they are really heeled over," I exclaimed.

Something didn't seem right. Their front sail was flapping loosely in the wind.

I gasped when I saw it. There was a huge hole in the side of the boat's hull.

Paul grabbed the binoculars out and we silently passed them around. Then Bruce pulled out the VHF radio, one of the few things that still worked on the boat, and called the Coast Guard. They were aware of the boat; last night they had responded to its Mayday calls and rescued the crew.

With horror, I realized that these people had tried to dash to a safe harbor when the storm had hit – as I had so badly wanted to do. In their haste, they had hit the hazardous breakwater that lurked just under the water's surface.

That could have been us.

I looked at Bruce and gratefully said, "Thank you for making us go back out to sea. I'm sorry I gave you such a dirty look."

He chuckled and said, "I'm glad looks can't kill, 'cause otherwise I'd be dead."   Under his three-day old stubble, he blushed.

As we continued up the river to the marina, I was proud of myself. I had kept a clear head and pulled us through a dangerous situation. The next thought startled me as much as it excited me.   If this was as bad as sailing got – and my vast experience of three days said it had to be – then I could do this.

I could sail around the world.

And that just proved how naive I was.

Life with No Means

Philadelphia, May 2001

With Cherokee Rose in dire need of repairs, Paul and I faced a new problem. Our plan to live aboard the boat in Philadelphia and keep our jobs was no longer viable. Rosie wasn't going anywhere.

Once we docked the boat at the marina in Georgetown, I headed to the office to rent a boat slip and to phone my dad. I knew he'd be worried about us. As I walked down the dock, I was startled to see alligators frolicking in the water just three feet below me. Yikes! No swimming or falling overboard here.

Dad was pleased to hear my voice, dismayed to learn the condition of the boat and anxious to hear about our trip. Rather than explain over the phone, I invited him to join us for lunch.

That surprised him. "Where are you?"

"Georgetown, South Carolina," I said sheepishly.

With that, he chuckled and said, "Gee, I'd love to have lunch with you. Why don't I bring up some French bread, pâté, and wine?"

"That sounds great."

He said he'd be there in an hour. Then teasing, he added, "Remind me: how long did it take you to get there?"

"Hey," I protested, "Stop rubbing it in!" I couldn't help but smile. I was in a good mood. We had survived a gale.

Later that day, Paul and I formed a new plan. We would fly back to Philadelphia. I would complete the garden photo shoots I had already lined up and Paul would give his boss ample notice to find his replacement. At the beginning of July, we would quit our jobs. While we hadn't intended to give up our jobs this soon, quitting them had been part of the plan. We would just have to make do. Then we would drive to South Carolina and fix Rosie so that she was ready to sail around the world.

We rode back to Charleston with my dad, leaving the alligators, a massive "to-do" list and a forlorn Rosie to await our return.

With the sale of our house pending, I concentrated on finding a furnished apartment for us to rent until July and a long-term storage shed for our furniture and household belongings. We figured we'd be gone for two years.

At least, that was how long Jimmy Cornell said it would take to have a comfortable and safe circumnavigation. He had written a book suggesting possible cruising routes, based on the local weather at certain times of the year. His premise was simple. There was a better probability of having a safe, and more pleasant, trip when the weather was good and the wind direction favorable. Paul and I now wholeheartedly agreed with him.

As a freelance journalist, taking two years off wasn't a big deal. But it was a huge deal for Paul. We spent a week of evenings working on his resignation letter.

"How are you going to do it?" I asked. "Tell your boss first and then give him the letter?"

"Why don't I just leave the letter on his chair after he's gone home for the day?" Paul suggested hopefully.

"Coward!" I said, laughing but understanding how he felt.

It was scary to quit a safe job for an unknown future. I knew. I had done it years ago, when I switched careers from selling laboratory equipment to writing about food.

Where the world had seemed so limited when I was selling liquid chromatography instrumentation, it was now full of possibilities. This remembered sense of empowerment, of taking charge of my life and my happiness, helped me give Paul the confidence he needed to do the same.

He resigned. He gave his boss two months' notice, instead of the usual two-weeks, to find his replacement. His boss appreciated the extra time but not enough to unlock Paul's golden handcuffs and grant him the stock options he had earned. When Paul announced at a team meeting that he was resigning to sail around the world, everyone stood up and applauded. We weren't the only people who wanted to do something more exciting with our lives...we were just the only ones who did.

Before we lost Paul's health care benefits, I set up an appointment with our general physician, Dr. Smith. I told her about our sailing plans and asked her for some advice on our first aid kit. She did more than that.

As a sailor herself, she understood that when we were at sea, we would have to be ready to handle any medical emergency. She suggested that Paul and I come back on Friday – Paul's last day of work – at lunch time and she'd show us how to give each other injections and sew basic sutures. Then she rummaged through the catalogues on her bookcase and handed me one for emergency medical technicians; it contained a huge selection of first aid kits. She also told me to bring two oranges and two pigs' feet for Friday. As I walked out of her office, I couldn't help but wonder. Where does one buy pigs' feet?

Friday came fast. Paul parked his car next to mine and, smiling like the Cheshire Cat, walked with me into Dr. Smith's waiting room.

"How does it feel, this being your last day at work?" I asked.

"Good, but too much to do," he replied. "Let me see the trotters."

"The what?"

"You know, the pigs' trotters, the feet."

I laughed and pulled them out of the bag.

"Yuck," Paul said, shuddering.

They were pretty gross.

Once we were in Dr. Smith's office, she started with the oranges. "Giving an orange an injection is similar to giving a person one. Like an orange, a person's skin is tough to break but once you're past the surface, it is soft."

She handed us each a plastic syringe, equipped with a metal needle on the tip and full of water. It was our turn. I injected my orange, but Paul squirmed in his chair. He was terrified of needles and injections.

"Come on, Paul, it's just an orange," I said matter-of-factly.

Paul shuddered and explained how even his mum, who was a nurse in England and drew blood for the Royal Blood Bank, couldn't get near him with a needle. As a child, if the doctor required a sample of Paul's blood, his mum would draw his blood while he was asleep.

"In the morning I'd wake up with a bandage on my arm; that's how I knew she had done it." Paul concluded.

"But what if Kelly needed a shot while you were sailing?" Dr. Smith persisted.

"Yeah," I chimed in.

Paul positioned the needle, closed his eyes and pushed the syringe barrel, giving the orange its shot.

Appalled by his blind approach to administering injections, I was relieved that we weren't going through IVF. He would have to give me daily shots.

Dr. Smith then took the pigs' feet and gave them each a two-inch incision with her scalpel. She took a needle off her desk, threaded it and, using one of the trotters, showed us how to make basic stitches. It looked easy.

"There," she said, tying off her handiwork. "Now it's your turn."

The room was silent as Paul and I bent over our pigs' feet.

"Ugh," I complained. "This skin is so tough, it's hard to push the needle through it." I made a couple of stitches then peeked over to see how Paul was doing. "No fair!" I protested.

He had beautiful stitches, all the same size and uniformly spaced. My trotter was starting to resemble Frankenstein.

Dr. Smith frowned at my handiwork, saying, "Try to be neater."

To Paul she said, "Good job."

When we finished, mine still didn't look any better.

Paul chuckled, "I hope I don't need any stitches on the boat!" He glanced at his watch. "I've got to get back to work." And with that, he abandoned his orange, his trotter and me.

I showed Dr. Smith the first aid kit I had ordered from her catalogue as well as two lists of recommended medicine for cruising that I had found online. She agreed with some items, added some others to the list and pulled out her prescription pad.

On July 1st, we said goodbye to Philadelphia and life as we knew it. We loaded up our Ford Explorer and Honda Prelude with our three windsurf boards, four windsurf sails, two mountain bikes and our few remaining belongings -- items we figured we would need on the boat – and drove the 10 hours to Charleston. Curled up in his carrier cage, our cat Howie slept most of the way. Once we arrived, we left Howie and most of our stuff at my mom's house, before heading to Georgetown and Cherokee Rose.

I noted that the alligators were still there, as well as another predatory animal of sorts. Tommy – "but my friends call me Tom Cat," he told me with a wink -- was the best diesel engine mechanic in Georgetown. Calling Paul "son" with a thick southern drawl and examining our engine under the floorboards, he said he could fix it. He'd even show Paul what he was doing, so Paul could learn how to repair the engine himself. He said he'd return the next day, but not before pointing to his cheek and asking for a kiss. He was almost as old as my grandfather, so I shrugged at Paul and obliged. Only ole' Tom Cat turned his head at the last second, a sly move to land my kiss on his lips!

Every meeting with Tommy ended with a similar dance, and yet we continued to work with him because we learned so much. He taught us how to lift out the engine to access the transmission. He showed Paul how to pull apart and fix the transmission; and finally how to put it back together again. By sight, he could tell if he needed a 3/8th-inch wrench or a 5/16th-inch wrench, and he wasn't bothered that there were a couple of nuts and bolts left over when the engine was reinstalled. He knew his work was good, son.

There was one way to test the transmission repair: take Rosie for a ride. Early one morning, with a slack tide, we bravely pulled Cherokee Rose out of her slip and motored toward Winyah Bay and the Intracoastal Waterway. The sun was warm, the breeze felt good and Rosie was humming along nicely.

"Let's keep going," I suggested.

We could be in Charleston by late afternoon. Most of the marine stores and boat services were in Charleston, as well as my parents and Howie. And so we did. How exhilarating, being free to move on a whim!

Once in Charleston, Paul worked full-time on Rosie: ordering new sails for her; moving blocks and winches so the sails could be reefed from the cockpit; getting a new bimini and dodger with clear plastic windows that we could see through; installing an Inmarsat-C satellite e-mail system that delivered free weather reports; and cleaning, lubricating, and polishing just about everything else.

While Paul worked on the boat, I spent the next six weeks interviewing homeowners over the phone and writing manuscripts for the photo shoots I had done in Philly. We were so busy with manuscripts and boat work that we didn't have time to practice sailing; something my dad urged us to do every week. Every Sunday, Dad rode his bike to the marina and good-naturedly volunteered to help us.

One day in early October, Dad asked if we could take him and some of his friends out for a sail in Charleston Harbor; his old sailing buddies wanted to see the boat. No doubt Dad had told them that we didn't know how to sail, so I was sure they were coming to see "the show" as well as the boat. We agreed to take them.

They got a better show than they – or we - expected.

Beginners on Board

Charleston, SC, October 2001

Showtime arrived with bright skies and little wind as we prepared to leave the marina. On the dock, I checked the river's current with a test I had just invented. I plucked flower petals off a nearly dead flower arrangement, tossed them into the water, and watched them drift away. When they stopped drifting, it would be slack tide and we would pull Rosie out of her slip.

The current in the harbor, and in the two rivers that define the Charleston peninsula, runs up to 6 knots, which was Rosie's top motoring speed. That meant that if we pointed into a 6-knot current, we would stay in place with the engine running full speed ahead. If we ran with the current, we could do a heady 12 knots.

It also made the timing of getting out of our slip crucial. If we left at peak flow, depending on the direction, we would either be jammed against the dock, or worse, against the poor boats that were moored behind us. The safest time for us to enter or leave the slip was during slack tide, which lasted only a couple of minutes as the tide switched direction.

Dad and his sailing buddies guffawed and chortled as I continued to toss rose petals into the water. Clearly, I wasn't a real sailor. I ignored them while Paul readied the lines. When the petals stopped moving on the water, we threw off the lines, put Rosie into reverse and backed out of our slip without hitting any other boats.

Once in the harbor, we put up the sails and turned off the engine. All was going well until a US Coast Guard dinghy sped up to us and matched our pace.

"Who is the captain of this vessel?" demanded the man standing on the dinghy's bow with a bull-horn.

For law enforcement officials, the six black-clad men in the black dinghy looked sinister with their guns, crew-cut haircuts, dark sunglasses and grim faces.

"I am," Paul shouted.

"Permission to board your vessel," he asked, although it sounded more like a command. I could hear my dad and his friends sniggering like schoolboys. The show was getting better by the minute.

"How?" Paul shouted, clearly puzzled as we were both moving. "I need to drop the sails and anchor."

"No need. We'll match speed."

As the dinghy pulled alongside, Dad offered to sail the boat so we could deal with the Coast Guard officer who was stepping aboard.

"Do you have any firearms on board?" he immediately demanded while the Coast Guard dinghy stayed on our hip.

"No," Paul said, bewildered.

He waved to his men and the dinghy pulled away.

The Coast Guard officer introduced himself and said that this was a routine safety check. He explained what he needed to inspect and followed us into the cabin.

"Would you like a glass of iced tea? And some chocolate chip cookies?" I asked him. Behind the officer, I could see my dad in the cockpit rolling his eyes at my hospitality.

I continued, "I am so glad you came aboard. We are planning to sail around the world in a couple of months, so if you see anything we should do to improve our safety, we'd really like to know."

The officer smiled. He'd be glad to help us, and sure, he'd like a glass of iced tea.

Paul pulled out our boat documentation, life jackets, and safety gear as needed but kept quiet. In dealing with government people – such as US Immigration and highway patrolmen -- I did all the talking. Paul got impatient easily and tended to create more problems than he solved. I schmoozed.

We got one citation. Our boat documentation numbers were not prominently displayed in the cabin. Rather than write up a ticket, he gave us a warning. And, while Paul climbed up the steps to the cockpit, the officer slipped me his business card.

"This is my direct line. Call me if you have any more questions. I'd be happy to help you," he said, giving me a friendly smile before he disembarked.

The following week, we took Rosie out for another sail but it didn't go as smoothly as we hoped. We were taking her up to a boat yard to have her hauled out of the water. We needed to paint her keel to prevent algae and barnacle growth; we also planned to inspect and lubricate the underwater seacocks. After that, if we still had time, we wanted to paint her hull so she looked shiny and new. Given how much work we were going to do, we asked my sister's husband, Kevin, to help us. His work schedule was flexible and he was game.

It was mid-October, shortly after 5 a.m. and still dark, when Paul, Kevin and I guided Rosie out of our slip. As was quickly becoming our pattern, our schedule was dictated by the tide. While our marina was located on the Ashley River, the only boat yard that allowed boat owners to do their own work – just call us cheap and cheerful – was up the Wando River. We needed a boost from the incoming tide to get us to the boat yard.

We had just cleared the marina pilings and entered the Ashley River when Paul flipped on the autopilot.

He studied the autopilot control panel for a moment, leaned back to try to turn the wheel then suddenly reported, "We don't have control over the boat."

"What do you mean?"

"I mean the autopilot is steering and I can't control the autopilot." He pushed some buttons on the Robertson autopilot controller, but it continued to ignore his commands. A cryptic code was flashing on its screen.

"What does that mean?" I asked anxiously; Rosie was drifting closer to some yachts that were moored in the river. Without waiting for an answer, I brushed past the guys and raced down into the cabin, "I'll get the manual."

"There's no time for that. We need to put down the anchor."

Empty-handed, I scrambled back into the cockpit as Paul and Kevin ran forward on deck to the anchor locker.

I stepped behind the wheel. Dread filled me as Rosie drifted closer to the moored yachts. This was our first time anchoring. With the threat of hitting another boat, we had better be quick learners.

Paul let out the anchor, and then barked, "Put her in reverse so we can set the anchor."

I shoved the red handle into the upright position before sliding it back into reverse. The engine revved in neutral and jumped when put into reverse. Oops. I had forgotten to pull back the throttle. Fortunately there were no alarms for "dummy at the helm" and the boat seemed to forgive me.

"Neutral, Kel, put the boat in neutral. The anchor isn't setting. We are dragging."

Our shouting must have woken up the owner of the boat that Rosie seemed irresistibly drawn toward, because I noticed a man standing on her deck. He was attentively watching us but thankfully not yelling at us. We were doing enough of that for everyone.

Couldn't something go right on this boat?

I yanked the throttle back first and then shoved the boat into neutral. Paul ran back to the cockpit. I jumped into the cabin, grabbed the autopilot manual and quickly found the cryptic error code listed under troubleshooting. Paul pushed the buttons as I directed and voila! We had control of Rosie again. Paul turned the wheel to avoid the moored boat we were about to hit and motored 20 feet away. Once we got the anchor up, and were finally on our way, Kevin chuckled and asked, "Sail much?"

We motored down the Ashley River into the harbor and then started up the Cooper and Wando Rivers. The sun came out and the day became pleasant. I started checking the chart more often and updating our position. We were close to the boat yard but, from the river, we could see only marsh grass, and trees. Where was it?

As we searched the shoreline, it became obvious that we weren't moving very fast; the tide had switched.

Paul pulled out our hand-held GPS. Our speed over ground was 1 knot, and falling. That meant the current was 5 knots against us, and getting stronger.

"This is ridiculous," he said, "We are wasting diesel. Let's anchor."

"But the boat yard is just around the next bend," I said. I did not want another anchoring fiasco.

"You said that before this bend, and the bend before."

What he said was true.

Reluctantly, I agreed to anchor once we discussed how we were going to do it. No more dragging, thank you very much.

Paul let out the anchor and chain out while I tried to hold Rosie in the same relative position despite the strong current. Suddenly the boat bumped. Into what? I couldn't see anything as I frantically looked around. Paul hurried back to the cockpit.

"Look," he said, pointing to the depth indicator.

I had been so busy trying to keep Rosie lined up with a clump of trees on shore that I hadn't checked the instrument panel. We were in 6 feet of water. The keel of our boat extended 6 feet below the waterline. We had run aground with that bump and, with the tide rushing out, we couldn't get her off the bottom.

The water became shallower and shallower until mere inches remained. Without the water's support, 15-ton Rosie gently laid down on her side on the muddy bottom of the Cooper River. We were so heeled over that the lower side of Rosie was only a foot from the river bed; the upper side towered 10 feet above.

Inside, the cabin was a disaster. Cushions and books had fallen off the high salon couch and book shelf. Spare oil filters and miscellaneous parts had rolled across the floor as their cabinet door had swung open by sheer gravity. Mugs and plates had slid across the kitchen counter and tumbled into the sink that blocked their downward path. To make matters worse, the cabin stank of diesel. Fuel had dripped out of the observation port on top of one of the two 60-gallon tanks.

In the cockpit, it was impossible to sit on the benches. There was standing room only – and that was if you stood on the side of the lower bench. It was like being in an amusement park's fun house; except I failed to see the humor.

The guys were perched on the high side of Rosie's deck, with their legs thrown over the hull of the boat to keep from sliding down the diagonally-pitched deck. They were cracking jokes, laughing at our ridiculous predicament.

With the ease of someone who had once had a climbing wall in her basement, I climbed up to the high side of the boat and straddled the edge next to them. I arrived just in time to watch a passing fishing boat veer off its course in the channel to rubberneck at the sight of reclining Rosie.

What else could we do? We smiled and waved from our high perch, but inside, I felt like crying. The early start, the stupid autopilot, the dragging anchor, and now this heeled-over humiliation. What in the world were we doing? We didn't know the first thing about sailing.

My despair must have shown on my face because Kevin gave me a reassuring sideways hug. "It'll be okay," Paul said kindly before he climbed down to the kitchen and returned with three cold Coronas. We sipped our beer and settled down to wait for the incoming tide.

Six hours later, the tide finally came in and my spirits lifted as Rosie slowly floated and righted herself. We pulled in the anchor and set off. The boat yard was a mere 10 minutes away. Paul steered Rosie alongside the T-dock and two men caught our ropes and secured our lines.

Once the engine was turned off, one of the guys said, "What happened to you? We saw your mast coming toward us hours ago, and then your mast just disappeared."

Paul, Kevin and I looked at each other and started to laugh.

An hour later, Rosie was chocked and standing in the middle of the boat yard's sand blasting pit, also known as "the litter box."

The next day, we discovered how apt the name was, when dozens of stray, but evidently well-fed, cats came to do their business around our boat. We, too, had plenty of business to do and dived into our list of chores.

On one of our numerous trips to the marine store across town, we decided to swing by my mom's house and pick up Howie. We missed our cat; he made us feel like a family. We had been hesitant to bring him aboard when we were docked at the marina because he could have fallen into the river and either gotten swept away or eaten by Georgetown's alligators. But here, with Rosie on land, the cabin and deck were at least 10 feet off the ground, making it impossible for Howie to get down. Kevin was enthusiastic about the idea; he adored Howie.

Everyone loved Howie because he was one cool cat. Not only did he sit in his own chair at the table when we ate; he'd wait at the front door until we came home from work and he would come if you called his name. He was part of our family and Paul and I intended to take him on our trip.

My family had other thoughts. While they had resigned

themselves to the fact that Paul and I were going to sail around the world, they did not approve of us taking the cat.

"It's okay if y'all want to kill yourselves on that boat,' my Southern stepmom had drawled, "but y'all cannot take that cat. He can stay with your father and me."

Kevin and my sister had two cats, but they were willing to find a way to integrate Howie into their household. My mom, too, had volunteered to take Howie -- until he had recently peed on her couch.

Nearly 10 years old, Howie had never done this before. The poor guy. I assumed that this was his way of telling us that he wasn't happy. And after having to buy my mom a new couch, we weren't too happy, either. The boat yard provided an ideal opportunity to bring him aboard before he did any more damage at Mom's.

Work on the boat was progressing well until Howie disappeared. We discovered he was missing at dinnertime, when he wasn't standing and meowing next to his food bowl. The three of us combed the boat yard but to no avail. Once it was dark, we had to call off the search until the next day.

We spent two more days searching for the little purr-monster. On the third day, we expanded our search to include the neighborhoods surrounding the boat yard. Paul was walking down a neighborhood street, calling Howie's name, when he heard a familiar reply.

Meow. Then a frantic meow, meow, meow!

Howie was trapped under a house on stilts and its crawl-space was surrounded by a chain-link fence. Paul jumped over the garden fence, raced to the house and freed the cat. That night Howie had his fill of canned tuna fish and lots of cuddles.

We stayed in the boat yard for almost two weeks; our initial to-do list had grown once we inspected Rosie. We were exhausted but happy when we finished our jobs. Rosie was ready to splash back into the water, or so we thought.

With one of the boat yard workers on board the boat, the travel lift picked up Rosie and gently lowered her foot-by-foot into the water. "Pull her up!" shouted the man on board.

Standing next to the travel lift dock, Paul and I repeated the alarm.

The travel lift operator stopped her descent and abruptly hoisted her until she hung over the water.

The guy on board leaned over and said to Paul,

"Captain, you'd better get on board. You've got a leak – probably a seacock that's been left open."

Aaughh. I thought I had cleaned, lubricated and, most importantly, shut all of the seacocks.

Paul quickly stepped toward Rosie and then stopped. With her hanging from the straps of the travel lift, there was no way to get on board.

The guy on board understood the problem and yelled, "Lower her down so Cap'n can climb aboard."

"But isn't that going to flood the boat?" Paul asked as the travel lift sprang to life.

"Yep, so you'd better hurry."

Paul jumped on Rosie's decks as soon as they were within reach and bounded down the companionway steps, into the cabin. A couple of minutes later, he reappeared. His hair, glasses and face were wet, but he looked calm. That was a good sign.

"It was the speedo," he said.

The speedometer on Rosie consisted of two parts: the electronics, which were mounted in the cockpit, and the transducer, which was mounted underwater through Rosie's hull. We had removed the transducer when we were painting her bottom and had obviously forgotten to reinstall it.

That was the single mishap on our otherwise uneventful trip back to City Marina. Things were already looking up.

Two things changed once we returned to the marina. First, Howie stayed on board. We found a screened-in enclosure for the cockpit buried in one of the lockers and we tried it out. It was perfect. Howie had access to outdoors and we didn't fear for his safety.

The second change was less tangible. Our focus shifted from repairing the boat to getting ready to go. We consulted Jimmy Cornell's book and decided to sail to the British West Indies island of Tortuga. From there, we would cruise some of the Caribbean islands before heading through the Panama Canal. We would then island-hop our way across the Pacific, arriving in New Zealand in about a year.

But first we had to get to Tortuga. Sailing southeast, and into the wind, the trip would be difficult. But the reward would be a pleasant westward sail across the Carribean Sea. It was a good plan for an experienced crew.

Provisions, Preparations and the Harmonica

Charleston, November 2001

Before we departed, I had to buy a year's worth of groceries. After reading Lin Pardey's book, I wanted to provision the boat with enough staples and canned goods to last us until New Zealand where selection and prices were good. I figured we would buy fresh meat, fruit and veggies in the countries that we visited along the way.

As part of my preparations, I spent three hours studying the food items and aisles at Costco before I wrote my grocery list. The big "provisioning day" arrived and Dad was pleasantly surprised when I handed him and Paul their respective grocery lists. Everything was listed in order of the aisles, so it was as easy as walking and grabbing.

Two hours later, we pushed our eight brimming giant-sized shopping carts to check-out. An employee at Costco graciously opened up a closed checkout lane just for us. After we paid $3,500 for groceries, someone rang a bell, and kept ringing it as we self-consciously paraded our carts out the store. We were apparently Costco's big spender of the day.

Buying the food was easy; getting it to Cherokee Rose was another matter. In the Costco parking lot, people stared as we ripped off and threw away bulky, unnecessary food packaging. After 45 minutes of finagling, we packed every free inch in our Ford Explorer, including the recess in the spare tire compartment, and in Dad's Toyota Camry. With so much added weight, both vehicles resembled low-riders with their chassis inches from the ground. We folded ourselves into the two vehicles and drove back to the marina.

Rosie's slip was a healthy walk away from the parking lot, so the marina's dock master sent a man in a golf cart to help us unload.

Upon seeing the overloaded cars, he exclaimed, "Where are you going? Antarctica?!"

On the fifth and last golf cart trip, he let Paul drive. Big mistake. Paul took the corner next to Rosie's slip too fast and, in slow motion, I watched big boxes of snack-sized M&Ms, Almond Joy bars and Skittles cartwheel into the brown water of the Ashley River. Paul jammed on the brakes, threw himself down on the dock, and grabbed the soggy cardboard boxes before they sank.

With boxes of food stacked on our dock and piled high in our cockpit; and bags of candy scattered across Rosie's deck, drying in the sun, we were a sight to behold. Dad was given the more labor-intensive jobs, such as putting flour, sugar, rice, and grits into storage tubs; putting wine bottles into thick socks for cushioning; and consolidating items into plastic storage bags. Because there was no room to execute these tasks on the boat, Dad sat on a cardboard box on the dock and worked.

Paul and I stored canned goods and packets of food everywhere we could jam them: in all of the lockers, in the space under the bottom dresser drawer in our bedroom, under the settees in the living room, and even in the engine compartment below the floorboards. It was a huge job, and despite our best efforts to organize everything well, we still ended up shifting contents from one locker to another many times. At the end of the day, Rosie sat inches lower in the water, weighed down by a year's worth of food.

Paul brought home another bell-ringing purchase; but in my case, it was an alarm. He set the heavy cardboard box and the slim, black rectangular case that looked like a giant harmonica in the cockpit.

Pointing to the cardboard box, he said, "I got you a present."

Delighted, I eagerly opened it up. I stared at dozens of gray and fluorescent orange... hockey pucks? "What are these?"

"Clay pigeons."

"Paul," I asked sharply, turning to look at the slim black

case, "Did you buy a gun?"

"Yep, look, it's a 12-guage pump action shotgun." He opened the harmonica case and pulled it out. "Watch," he said excitedly, "You can even pump it like Sylvester Stallone, see?" He held the gun vertically, with the point up, and jerked the gun down abruptly, causing the barrel to slide down the gun.

"Paul! Put that thing away! I don't want a gun on board." I was upset. We had discussed this.

"Kel, I know you don't, but I consider it a tool. We don't have to take it out of the toolbox if we don't need it," he said. "But if we do, we have it."

"Honey, if pirates see that we are armed, the fight will escalate. And I doubt they'll be using shotguns."

"You're right. If pirates approach us with guns, we won't pull it out. But if they are a bunch of thugs with knives, I'd definitely pull it out and give them a warning shot."

Looking at the gun and clay pigeons, I sat down and contemplated the situation. Despite my wishes, he had already bought the shotgun and ammunition. The only thing I could hope was that we'd never need it.

"Why did you buy the clay pigeons?"

"We'll need to practice our aim."

"So, you're thinking clay pigeon shooting at 4 p.m. on the Promenade Deck?" I asked, remembering a cruise ship I had once taken that offered this sport.

"Yeah," Paul grinned at me. "It'll be fun when we're bored at sea."

I looked skeptically at our tiny forward deck - no room for a promenade – and sighed. "Well, you bought it. You get to stow it."

There was more to stow. We brought the personal belongings we had kept at my mom's house to Rosie, after weeding out the things we didn't need. With each successive move, from the house, to the temporary apartment, to my mom's house and finally to the boat, we had had the chance to reevaluate our belongings and eliminate items that didn't seem practical. Our two mountain bikes, three windsurfers and rock climbing gear made the "boat cut," but rollerblades, the ice cream machine and the blender didn't. Despite these efforts, we still had too much stuff to cram onto the boat.

I was moving some items onto Rosie when someone behind me said, "Nice boat. What is she?"

"It's a Tayana," I replied, turning to look at the couple

who were standing on the dock. "Do you have a boat here?"

"We have an Island Packet," responded the guy, pointing toward a boat anchored on the river. "We're out on a mooring."

Hearing our conversation, Paul poked his head out of the cabin.

Janet and Blaine introduced themselves and mentioned that they were on their way to the Bahamas, via Florida. Until now, we hadn't met anyone in the marina who was actually going anywhere. I told them we were headed to Tortuga.

Blaine asked when.

In a couple of weeks, maybe a month.

Janet smiled and looked at Blaine, "They are cruisers our age!" Then she invited us to join them for dinner the next night, after checking that we weren't afraid of dogs. They had two golden retrievers on board.

The dogs barked, greeting us as Blaine pulled the dinghy up to Charbonneau, their boat. Janet invited us down below, where we oohed and ahhed. Their boat was lovely and new. Janet handed us sun-downers, a rum punch that she had made, and within minutes we were chatting like old friends, comparing sailing plans, boats and pets. At the end of an enjoyable evening, Blaine dropped us off at Rosie.

As he parted, he said, "You should sail with us to the Bahamas. Then you'll gain some sailing experience before you make the windward trip to Tortuga."

"We'll think about it," I promised.

There were some advantages to this idea. For starters, it made me feel more comfortable. We had never done a passage by ourselves; it might be helpful to have someone experienced nearby if we ran into trouble. It also seemed safer to hug the eastern coastline, rather than cross part of the Atlantic Ocean. Lastly, one of our textbooks said that sailing into the wind requires some practice, and that the motion could be hard on the boat, and on the crew. Did we want to test ourselves like that? On our first passage alone?

Paul finally agreed.

We met with Janet and Blaine several more times and firmed up our course. We would sail with Charbonneau overnight from Charleston to St. Augustine, Florida. After a day or two there, we would sail down to Cape Canaveral and tuck into the Intracoastal Way. We would continue south to Vero Beach and then to Miami before crossing the Gulf

Stream to the Bahamas.

Just when everything was coming together, our smallest crew member threw us a curveball. Howie peed on the salon couch. Something was wrong with him.

I took him to the veterinarian the next day. The vet examined Howie and said that he probably had diabetes. He would have to spend the night at the clinic while the vet ran some blood tests and pulled a rotten tooth. Howie meowed frantically as I left the office, and I felt badly for my little buddy who had to face the dentist and doctor all in one visit. The next morning, it was confirmed. Howie was diabetic.

I explained that we were just getting ready to leave Charleston to sail around the world. How could we possibly take a diabetic cat with us? The vet calmed me down and explained that Howie's diabetes could be controlled with specially formulated cat food. Relieved, I took a purring Howie and an expensive bag of cat food home with me.

I measured out Howie's daily ration and calculated how many bags of cat food he would eat in a year. By tossing in some extra bags for good measure, several cases of specially-formulated wet food for variety, and 300 pounds of clumping kitty litter, I completed Howie's shopping list.

When I phoned the vet's office to place my order, I could imagine a bell ringing somewhere. I was, without a doubt, their day's big spender. Ordering the stuff was a cinch. Figuring out where to store it, once the food had been painstakingly vacuum-packed, was harder. Somehow, we crammed it all in. And, once again, Rosie sank a little lower in the water.

From releasing our mooring lines in Charleston to dropping our anchor in St. Augustine's, our first passage was hardly what I expected. Perhaps I had watched too many reruns of "The Love Boat," but I had envisioned confetti, streamers and lots of well-wishers when we finally cast off on the first leg of our circumnavigation. Instead the day came, and went, uneventfully. On the afternoon of December 1, 2001, we motored out of Charleston Harbor for the second time, this time in convoy with Charbonneau and heading south to Florida, and the world beyond.

As on our maiden voyage in April, there was no wind as we motored out of Charleston Harbor and into the Atlantic. While there weren't any waves on the ocean, there was a gentle swell that didn't rock the boat as much as rolled it, and

I felt ill before we even cleared the last harbor marker.

We had decided upon three-hour watches, but I couldn't even stomach the thought of sitting, never mind tending to the boat. Paul agreed to take the first watch. Before I retreated to my sea bed, I double-checked the harness that Paul was wearing.

Satisfied that it was securely tethered to the boat, I reminded him, "No peeing over the side of the boat."

It seemed that numerous men drowned every year after losing their balance and falling overboard while doing exactly this.

It was dark when Paul nudged me.

"Wake up, Kel. It's 10 o'clock. I let you sleep as long as I could, but now it's your watch."

I opened my eyes and stretched in the darkness that was eerily illuminated by a red light over the kitchen sink. Most of the lights on Cherokee Rose toggled between white and red bulbs. Red light helped maintain night vision.

I had hardly slept because the engine was so loud. While I had placed foam earplugs within reach of my bed, I hadn't used them for fear that I might miss some telltale noise that meant that the boat was sinking or that Paul needed help. Was I being paranoid? Probably. But now it was just the two us; Bruce wasn't here to bail us out.

"Where are we? Where is Charbonneau?"

"They are a couple of miles ahead of us. We are off the coast of St Catherine's Island, Georgia."

Reluctantly, I climbed out of the sleeping bag so Paul could climb in.

"Oh, this feels good," he said, lying down. "Wake me if you need me."

I walked to the companionway, put on my coat and harness, and tethered myself to the boat before climbing into the cockpit. The ocean was still flat and the coastline on our right was dotted with clusters and sprinkles of lights. The moon was bright and its beam followed us as we trailed behind Charbonneau.

For months, I had imagined this moment: being on watch all by myself. But I had never expected it to be so...boring. I didn't want to turn on any lights and risk losing my night vision; I didn't want to play music in case I woke Paul or missed some ominous boat sound. I still felt queasy, so reading a book with Paul's headlight was out of the question.

There was nothing to do and three hours to do it in.

Howie must have sensed my restlessness because he poked his head of out the cabin, meowed and jumped into the cockpit. He made a complete circle next to me before plopping down against my leg and looking at me expectantly. I rubbed his head and his ears and was rewarded with a multi-decibel lengthy purr. The poor cat. He, too, suffered from seasickness.

Our uneventful passage of three days and two nights ended tensely. Around 4 p.m. on December 4th, the entrance to the St. Augustine Inlet finally appeared. We turned off the autopilot as we altered course for our approach. I volunteered to take the wheel, hoping that steering the boat might make me feel better. It did in a car.

Paul climbed up the companionway steps and announced that there was a sandbar five feet underwater that blocked the entrance to the inlet. Rosie's keel extended six feet down.

"Charbonneau said that we need to catch a wave and surf Rosie over the sandbar."

"What?" I exclaimed, "How am I supposed to surf 15-ton Rosie over anything? I can't even see the sandbar."

Paul searched the water ahead of us and consulted the chart several times before pointing at a standing wave that marked the sandbar's position.

"Yeah, well, I still don't know how I am going to surf ole' Rosie," I grumbled. Sleeping in three-hour snatches did not agree with me; neither did the threat of running aground. As we neared the standing wave, I started giddily singing one of the Beach Boys' songs; Paul joined in.

Rosie caught a wave and before I knew it, we had surfed over the sandbar. Well, I assumed we did because we didn't go bump.

The shoreline of St. Augustine surprised me with its quaint, low, Spanish-style stucco buildings and walls. The anchorage – our first one – was not so quaint. It was packed with sailboats, some on mooring balls and some anchored. Paul and I discussed our anchoring strategy and we quickly agreed on our hand signals. Somehow, we got lucky with our first attempt. After Charbonneau anchored, they took us to shore in their dinghy. We walked into town for some Christmas shopping and an early dinner.

Nothing prepared us for our first night at anchor. The

wind picked up and blew 20 knots in a direction that opposed the strong outgoing tide. This made the water choppy and the boats behave in erratic ways. Some boats were being pushed around by the wind. Others were being directed by the current. Rosie responded to both so she zipped around, testing the limits of her anchor chain like a frolicking puppy on a leash.

When we had arrived, the anchorage was like a packed parking lot, with all the boats parallel-parked. Now that parking lot was chaotic with boats randomly zipping around. We used to be a safe distance from our neighbors; now we could shake hands with one of them.

After watching Rosie's and this other boat's behavior for half an hour, Paul concluded that we wouldn't collide and went to bed. I didn't feel so confident. I brought my sleeping bag and pillow into the cockpit and tried to sleep with one eye open. By 2 a.m., after having been on passage for two nights and now on solo watch in the anchorage, I was too tired to care. If we hit another boat, I would hear it just as well from the comfort of my bed. I went down below and collapsed next to Paul.

After two nights of playing "bumper-boats" in St. Augustine, we were more than ready to leave the following lunchtime for Cape Canaveral and the inland Intracoastal Waterway. Another boat joined our little southbound convoy. This was their first offshore passage. And, in a pattern that was getting remarkably familiar, I was seasick before we had even cleared the sandbar at the inlet entrance.

I dozed on and off, while passing squalls kept Paul busy taking in and letting out the sails. Around 11 p.m., Paul plopped down on the couch next to me. It was my watch – and just in time. He felt queasy.

"You should put a scopolamine patch on," I said, touching mine to make sure it was still behind my ear.

"I did," he said and then he showed me his wrists. "I am also wearing the electronic band on this wrist, and on the other, the acupressure band. Plus I popped a Bonine."

I had bought every possible remedy for seasickness before we left, but who would have thought to try them all simultaneously? Only Paul.

Around 2:30 p.m., after a 20-hour journey, we dropped the hook off Cocoa Beach, Florida. Within minutes of arriving, one of the boats in the anchorage invited us to a cruisers' potluck dinner on the beach at 5 p.m. How novel, being invited to a party by people you didn't know!

When it was time to go, I climbed into the cockpit with my plate of bruschetta topped with red pepper tapenade. Paul was trying to launch our inflatable dinghy. While sailing, the deflated dinghy was stored upside down, on the forward deck. Within a minute, it was obvious that he needed help so I put down my plate and pitched in. Flipping the dinghy over, pumping it up, hoisting and lowering it into the water, as well as attaching the outboard motor, turned out to be a 30-minute aerobic workout for both of us. Our shirts clung to our bodies with perspiration as we motored ashore. So much for the glamour of living aboard a yacht.

It was a strange evening. The inherent frugalness of a potluck dinner was countered by preppy, well-dressed sailors who passed out embossed boat cards. I leaned over Paul's shoulder to see the first card of many we were given. It listed the boat name along with the names and address of the crew: a nautical social calling card. We quickly discovered that couples were often referred to by their boat's name, as if they and the boat were a team, instead of by their first names. Last names were never used. Instead of talking about work or jobs, everyone talked about boat problems and where they were headed. It seemed no one was going farther than the Intracoastal Way or the Bahamas – except us.

For the first time, we felt like cruisers. We rented a car in Cocoa Beach and drove to Disney World for the day; Paul had never been there. Another day, we surfed behind the wake of our dinghy, using our small windsurf board. We barbecued on a deserted islet in the river one night and even saw the local production of "Annie Get Your Gun."

The little girl who had starred as Annie had been so convincing, Paul had gotten teary-eyed during the show.

Walking back to the boat, Paul said, "If we had a daughter, I wonder if she'd be able to sing like that."

A wave of sadness washed over me; I didn't know what to say. Would we ever have a daughter, or a son? Our past experience pointed to a childless future yet the fact remained: Nothing was wrong with us. Now that we were finally cruising, and had taken a break from our fertility treatments, maybe we would get pregnant. I still held a glimmer of hope and that was the blessing – and the curse - of being an "unexplained" infertility.

Was it false hope?

If so, there was no point in sharing it with Paul. He had been through enough; we both had. Instead I took his hand and kindly replied, "Well, if we did, she would probably sing beautifully with you as her dad."

Paul had played the trombone for years and had a good ear for music; I didn't.

We walked silently hand-in-hand until the anchorage came into view. At the sight of the boats, our conversation resumed on the safer topic of Rosie.

We were to have lots of discussions about Rosie the next day, and unfortunately, in the months ahead. The next day we motored down a narrow section of the Intracoastal Way toward Vero Beach. Suddenly, the engine alarm blared, causing both of us to dash to the instrument panel to see what was wrong. The oil pressure had dropped. We needed to turn the engine off. But we couldn't because the dredged-out channel of deep water was too narrow for sailing. We had to motor. I studied the chart to see if there was any place nearby to anchor, but the surrounding water was too shallow for Rosie's 6-foot keel. And we couldn't anchor in the channel because we would block boat traffic. Paul grabbed the radio and called Charbonneau, informing them of our situation.

Blaine suggested that they tow us and, seeing no other alternatives, we agreed. For nearly four hours, over 18 miles, we hitched a ride. Aside from nearly decapitating a reckless speedboat captain with our tow line, we arrived without any problems at the Vero Beach Municipal marina.

What should we do with the engine? I wanted to get rid of it. Throw it away. Perhaps the engine was too old, perhaps it was a lemon, but whatever it was, it didn't work. Paul was more analytical. It didn't work because something was broken. Fix the broken part and the engine will work.

We got the name of a reliable diesel mechanic and called him. A new engine would cost roughly $20,000 – yikes! – or he could repair our existing engine in four to five weeks. It was mid-December and we didn't want to wait that long. The mechanic suggested that Paul perform a series of troubleshooting tests. Once Paul had the results, he could call the mechanic for advice on how to proceed.

Paul was dismayed to find diesel in our crank case. The mechanic told Paul to pull apart the engine, remove the faulty injector pump and ship it for repair. He gave Paul the address of a shop that specialized in these repairs; it wasn't something either the mechanic or Paul could repair.

Paul removed the floorboards over the engine to expose it. I knelt on what remained of the kitchen floor while Paul knelt on the adjacent salon floor. We were both leaning over the engine, peering at it. His face was just inches away from mine. "Do you know how to take apart the engine?" I asked him. It looked complex.

He smiled and said, "Taking the engine apart is easy. Putting it back together isn't." He leaned back, grabbed a wrench and starting loosening a nut.

"What are you doing?" I asked, alarmed.

"Taking it apart."

I couldn't just let that go. I offered to bag and label the parts so that Paul would know where they went, once he started rebuilding the engine.

"Don't bother. I'll figure it out. It's like the Meccano building set I had as a kid. It's logical."

I groaned; everything was logical to him.

"Besides, Tomcat just ripped it apart," he replied, referring to our cheeky mechanic in Georgetown.

"Yeah, but you're not him," I retorted.

Paul rocked forward on his arms and kissed my lips.

"Am I Tomcat now?" he asked mischievously.

I laughed, got up and grabbed some plastic bags and a permanent pen.

Paul proceeded to take apart the engine and didn't comment as I bagged nuts, bolts, washers, and all sorts of items I didn't recognize. After 15 minutes, I was frustrated. I didn't know the names of the parts, much less the name of where they came from. How should I label the bags? Widget 1 attaches to whatchamacallit A? Now that was helpful. Finally I brought out an empty plastic kitty litter tub and told Paul to dump everything in the bucket. I was done. Paul smiled sweetly and asked for a cup of tea.

Because we had to wait for the injector pump to be serviced and shipped back to us, we worked on our endless "to-do" list. I removed the rust from all of the stainless steel pieces on deck; cleaned and lubed the nine winches and scrubbed mildew off the cabin's ceiling. Paul installed roller furling for our staysail and had our sails re-cut to give us better sail shape, and performance, while sailing.

Three weeks later, we left with Charbonneau. We were

going to sail to Miami before crossing the Gulf Stream for the Bahamas. Minutes into our trip, not even a mile from the marina, the engine alarm blared - again! Frustrated, we said goodbye to our friends and limped back to the marina.

We were anxious to get the engine repaired as quickly as possible so that we could catch up with Charbonneau. Within minutes of tying up Rosie, Paul was on the phone with the mechanic. I consoled myself with the fact that he was gaining valuable engine repair experience. It might be useful to have a diesel mechanic onboard if a problem arose at sea. Given the engine's track record, that seemed likely.

A week before Valentine's Day, we left Vero Beach with our fingers crossed. While we had originally planned to sail offshore to Miami, we prudently decided to motor down the Intracoastal Way to test the engine. I'd like to say that it purred but the sound level was closer to a roar. However no red lights flashed; no alarms blared. The engine was noisy but good.

Because we had lost so much time in Vero Beach, we imprudently decided to take a short-cut. We would sail to the Bahamas from West Palm Beach instead of Miami, which was further south. We anchored in Hobe Sound and waited for a favorable weather forecast. We turned on the single sideband radio (SSB) and listened to other cruisers calling the legendary "Herb" for high seas weather advice. Unlike the VHF radio, which worked only within line-of-sight and therefore short distances, the SSB transmitted and received over great distances. That was useful, because Herb lived and worked in Ontario, Canada.

Considered a guru by many sailors, Herb was experienced at studying meteorology and interpreting the weather. Relying on several sources of weather data, he recommended good weather windows based on an individual boat's current location and planned route. Before I could hail him on the radio, another boat in our vicinity asked him when they should set to sail for the Bahamas. He forecasted that tomorrow would have good weather for crossing the Gulf Stream, so Paul and I readied the boat, and ourselves.

This was our first offshore passage alone. No Bruce. No Charbonneau. My stomach was upset and I hardly slept that night, knowing that soon we would face the Gulf Stream, whose waves had been likened to gray elephants. In spite of my dread, the sun rose the next morning and we motored to the pass that led to the ocean.

As we entered the narrow pass with our main sail up and engine going full speed ahead, a bizarre thing happened. We didn't move. We spent an hour trying to go the length of a swimming pool, with power boats and fishing boats blowing their horns for us to get out of the way. I only heard their horns; with Rosie's wild see-saw motion, I was too busy leaning over the side of the boat. Paul, too, felt ill.

With minor encouragement on my part, he turned Rosie around and we retreated to the anchorage. Bummed that I was sick before we even left the Intracoastal way, I didn't appreciate one sailor's comment that seasickness was just a mental state. Maybe I was mental. After all, what was I thinking, trying to sail around the world when I couldn't even get out of Florida?

In chatting with other sailors, we learned that it was nearly impossible to get out of the pass when the current opposed the wind, which is what we had encountered. We tuned into the SSB daily, and, a week later, Herb gave another positive weather window to the Bahamas.

Having learned from our previous attempt, we left at 8:15 a.m. on February 24, 2002, with favorable wind and current conditions in the pass. But would the so-called gray elephants of the Gulf Stream be equally favorable?

Woman Behind-the-Wheel in the Bahamas

West Palm Beach, FL, February 2002

Any elation at heading to our first international port-of-call was erased by stormy skies and 30- knot headwinds. With our engine on, and two sails out, we pounded into the waves on a southeasterly track. Our first solo passage was a tricky one.

We had to cross the strong north-flowing Gulf Stream that ran up the eastern seaboard. The current averaged 3 knots and peaked at about 5 knots; any boat crossing the Gulf Stream had to account for this. If we aimed east, for example, the current would push us northeast. To reach the Berry Islands, where Charbonneau was anchored, we had to go east *and* south, against the current. That's why many cruisers bound for the Bahamas didn't take our "shortcut." Leaving from West Palm Beach meant battling the current whereas the current gave boats leaving from Miami, which was seventy miles farther south, a helpful boost.

We adjusted our course by aiming Rosie farther south than we needed to go, hoping to counteract the northerly current while still make some southeasterly progress. Selflessly, Charbonneau offered to check in with us hourly, over the SSB, and track our position.

The motion was brutal. With each wave, Rosie rode up its steep face just to fall off its back, slamming into the trough between the waves with a boat-and-bone-jarring shudder. Then the next wave lifted her up and the process repeated.

Leaving Paul to manage everything, I crashed on my couch, fastened its newly installed lee cloth to keep me from rolling out of bed, and wished I were dead. With each shattering bang I expected the boat to crack apart. Sleep was impossible. Instead, I watched an oil painting that hung in the salon swing with Rosie's motion, scratching a deep, arc-shaped groove into the teak wall. Eventually it fell off its nail. As Rosie mounted a wave, the painting slid across the floor by my bed.

I grabbed it and awkwardly slid it into the food locker next to me. Several cans of soup were rolling around in the locker; their bangs hardly noticeable over the sound of the ocean rushing by the hull and the beating that Rosie was taking.

It was dark when Paul nudged me and silently proceeded to take off his harness, and coat. It was my watch. I groaned and got up.

"I've reefed the sails, so you shouldn't have to do anything with them," he said. "Wake me when it's time to call Charbonneau." With that he climbed over the lee cloth and slipped into my warm sleeping bag. I lurched to the companionway, tethered myself to the boat, and climbed into the cockpit.

The night was starless. Faint moonlight penetrated the thick clouds above us, casting a Halloween-like glow over the dismal night. Standing at the companionway, I searched the horizon. Battleship gray waves charged at Rosie head-on, creating a refrain of whoosh, splash, bang, shudder, pause and repeat.

The conditions had been like this for hours, so although I was frightened by the thrashing we were taking, I could only deduce that all was well. I sat down and Howie meowed, surprising me. He had hidden himself in the little nook that held the VHF radio, and I envied him his safe haven. I'd climb in that little cubbyhole if I could too. The hour passed anxiously and then it was time to check in with Charbonneau.

I noted our position on the GPS and jotted it down in our ship's log along with the time. Then I woke Paul who plotted our position on the chart.

"Kel, are you sure this is our position?" Paul sounded alarmed. "At this rate, we are going to miss the Bahamas."

"What do you mean? We'll still hit Grand Bahama Island, north of the Berrys, right?"

"No, I mean we are going to miss all of the Bahamas. The current is pushing us north. The wind is pushing us north. We're fighting just to go east, never mind going south." Paul sighed.

If we missed the Bahamas, the vast, empty Atlantic Ocean awaited us. I double-checked our position on the GPS. It was correct.

Paul called Charbonneau.

"Ahoy, On-the-Nose-Cherokee-Rose," responded Blaine.

Paul smiled fleetingly at our new nickname and then relayed our position and current conditions.

After a static-filled moment, Blaine commented, "You haven't made any southerly progress in this last hour."

"I know. We might not make it to the Berry Islands."

Just hearing Paul admit possible defeat made me sick to my stomach. What will we do? I didn't want to be stranded at sea.

"Hmm, well, you are in the middle of the Gulf Stream where the current is the strongest. Hopefully you'll be able to correct your course when you get through it."

Blaine was right.

We finally sailed out of the Gulf Stream. After making some southward progress, we entered the North West Providence Channel, which divided the northern Bahamian islands from the central islands. Gradually the waves got smaller, Rosie's motion got smoother, and the wind eased off our nose. We even saw three cruise ships, sparkling like diamond tiaras, on the horizon. For awhile, the world was a friendlier place.

In the morning, around 9 a.m., we altered our southeasterly course to due south to approach the Berry Islands, and Charbonneau. The light wind was on our beam, and I convinced Paul to turn on the engine to increase our speed. I wanted to be there. Now.

A gust hit and Rosie heeled over 15 degrees with all of our sails up. Suddenly, the engine alarm blared. We both leapt up to see what the problem was. Red bars lit up the engine's temperature gauge. Paul turned off the engine and joined me below. Lifting the floor boards over the engine, we both examined it.

"I'm mystified," said Paul. "I installed that bigger heat exchanger when we were in Vero..." His voice trailed off as he contemplated this new problem. Paul finally topped up the coolant reservoir, which was half-full, and we hoped the solution was that simple.

We arrived at White Cay at 3:30 p.m. without further incident. Spotting Charbonneau at anchor, we chugged over to them – the engine's temperature was back to green bars – and anchored. Paul and I hugged each other. We made it!

I wanted to jump in the turquoise water but Paul thought I was nuts. It was cold.

"I don't care," I said, "we've sailed to a tropical island! We are in the Bahamas." I quickly put on my bathing suit.

Seeing that I was serious, Paul stripped down to his shorts.

I grabbed the swim ladder and mounted it, recalling a chilling story I had read,

A couple had been becalmed on an ocean passage. Without any wind, the heat apparently had been insufferable, and they had jumped in the ocean to cool off. When the Coast Guard found the unmanned boat, they discovered fingernail scratch marks covering its side. It seemed this couple had forgotten to put down their swim ladder and had been unable to climb, or claw, their way aboard.

Paul and I held hands and jumped in the water while Blaine and Janet laughed from the deck of their boat. Janet fixed us dinner and we toasted Rosie, the completion of our first serious solo passage and our arrival in Paradise. As we crawled into bed, the wind started to increase and suddenly Paradise faded.

For two nights, the wind averaged 40 knots with gusts up to 50 knots. There was very little protection in White Cay, so we bounced around, slept with our lee cloths up as if we were on passage, and checked the anchor hourly.

We were worried that the anchor chain would gouge a hole in Rosie. As gusts of wind pushed and released Rosie, the chain reacted in a similar fashion, jerking and snapping violently whenever it became taut, then relaxing. Paul rigged a snubber, basically a shock absorber, by attaching some rope to the slack anchor chain with a large stainless steel gated hook. By morning, the hook's gate was ripped away from the hook; the forces were that strong.

I felt gypped. I knew the sailing part wasn't going to be fun, but I had assumed, once we dropped the hook, that our daily life would consist of beautiful anchorages, swimming in the sun, drinking fruit cocktails and meeting new people. I hadn't counted on anchor watches, rough weather, and being cooped up on the boat. I certainly hadn't expected a near collision.

We were anchored behind Charbonneau, adjacent to a small, 30-foot high, rocky islet. Paul and I were on deck, checking the snubber, when we heard a prop plane. We searched the sky but couldn't see it. The roar of its engine got louder and then deafening; still there was no visible sign of the plane. Suddenly it appeared, zipping over the top of our neighboring islet. It was flying so low, it was barely skimming over the islet's scrub and bushes.

I saw the pilot's surprised expression as he came face-to-face with the top of our mast, which loomed 64 feet above sea level. He pulled the plane up sharply and narrowly missed our mast before zooming off, disappearing over the next islet as quickly as he had appeared.

Paul and I were stunned. It took a moment for our brains to register what we had just seen. In unison we exclaimed, "He almost crashed into us!"

"Did you see how close he was to hitting our mast?! He could've dismasted us," I cried indignantly. "What was he doing, flying that low?"

Paul thought the pilot was trying to avoid radar detection. As a student at the University of Sheffield in England, Paul had joined the Royal Air Force. He had logged hundreds of hours of flying, including 18 solo hours, before his poor eyesight ruined his chances of becoming a fighter pilot.

We didn't know how right Paul was.

Drug-running, by small airplanes and go-fast speed boats, is an on-going problem in the Bahamas due to its close proximity to Florida. I read that the most notorious drug running operation occurred from 1978 to 1982 when Columbian smugglers used the islands as a trans-shipment point for cocaine headed to America. One of the cartel kingpins bought a substantial amount of property on Norman Cay and used the island, and its runway, as his personal base of operations. He apparently tried to "revolutionize" drug smuggling by using small planes to transport large quantities, instead of smuggling smaller amounts in suitcases on commercial flights. Thankfully, the low flying airplane that nearly collided into our mast was our only glimpse into this dark world.

After the storm finally passed, our world turned bright and sunny. On Monday morning, we up-anchored and raced Charbonneau to Chubb Cay. It was exhilarating to sail in calm waters with a pleasant breeze and, miraculously, I wasn't seasick. It didn't hurt that we won the race which put a huge smile on Paul's face.

As we entered the channel leading to the marina, Paul suggested that I dock the boat. I hesitated. What if I messed up?

"You should learn how to drive her. Just remember that she doesn't drive like a car. When you turn the steering wheel, she pivots from the middle of the boat."

I must have look a little confused because he added, "Don't worry; I'll be here to help you."

I took the wheel while Paul called the marina on the VHF radio and was given directions to our slip. It sounded simple: straight in and a right turn into our slip. I put the engine in neutral once we entered the marina and let Rosie's momentum carry us forward while slowing us down. There were no brakes on a boat.

Our speed decreased to a nice crawl, which caused Paul to complain, "Come on, Kel; give her some gas!"

I didn't want to. If I hit something, I wanted it to be a love tap not a smack.

"But, Kel, you've gotta have some speed to keep steerage. You need water running past the rudder to be able to steer."

With that, he leaned around me, put the boat into gear and pushed the throttle forward. As soon as Paul released the gears, I defiantly put the boat back into neutral. Paul didn't say anything, apparently satisfied with our speed.

When we neared our slip, Paul said, "Put her in reverse to slow her down."

I gave Rosie a burst of reverse then put her back into neutral.

"Good."

I started to turn the wheel to point Rosie's nose toward our slip, which was ahead of us.

"No," Paul said, "Keep her straight."

I straightened the wheel.

"Remember, she pivots, she doesn't turn. She needs to be almost abreast of the slip before you turn the wheel hard to the right. Okay, now!"

I spun the wheel, and realized we were going too fast; mere feet separated Rosie's nose from the marina pier. I looked down at the gears, threw Rosie into reverse and bang! We rammed the pier with vengeance. I double-checked the gear and throttle. Oh no, I had accidently put the engine into forward gear! I slid the engine into neutral. Paul, who had raced forward to fend off the boat, ran back to the cockpit, shoved me aside and reversed Rosie away from the dock.

Once we were tied up, he demanded, "What happened? You almost wiped out the dock boy!"

Before I could respond, the uniformed dock boy who was loitering nearby added disgustedly, "Women drivers."

"Hey," I protested. I had done a good job until I had accidentally gotten the gear shift and the throttle mixed up.

Once it was ascertained that neither Rosie, nor the dock, were irreparably damaged – although I was sure my confidence had been – Paul came over and put his arm around me. "You just need a little practice," he said.

After clearing Customs and Immigration, who apparently weren't bothered by the presence of Howie or our harmonica (aka the shotgun), we topped up our diesel and fresh water tanks and set off to Nassau. The sky was bright blue, there was almost no wind and the sea was flat except for a barely perceptible swell. As we motored, Paul cast his fishing line.

Zzzing! The line streamed out of his reel.

"Kel, I got a fish," Paul shouted excitedly. "Put the boat in neutral. Oh, and grab the fish hook and the spray bottle of alcohol."

I complied while Paul continued to reel in his fish. It looked like hard work.

Once the fish was visible underwater, Paul told me to follow him with the hook and bottle. We walked along the side deck of the boat, Paul still working his reel. Then he told me to open the gate.

The perimeter of our boat was enclosed by lifelines, basically a hip-high plastic-coated wire fence, to prevent anyone from falling overboard. On each side of the boat, there was a gate that allowed people to step on and off the boat, without having to climb over the lifeline.

"I'm going to swing the fish through the gate. Whatever it is, it's too heavy to lift over the lifeline!"

After another couple of minutes of struggling, Paul got

the hook through the fish's gills. The four-foot turquoise fish with yellow spots wriggled madly, suspended over the water.

On the count of three, Paul swung the fish on board where the fish plopped, flopped and wrestled on our deck. Paul sprayed alcohol liberally in the fish's gills to humanely kill it.

After a moment, the fish was still. I breathed a sigh of relief. The fish was so big and strong, I had been afraid that it was going to knock Paul overboard.

"Okay," Paul rubbed his hands together enthusiastically, "We're having sushi tonight!" He squatted down to look at it more closely. Suddenly the fish sprang to life, pounding its tail and banging its head in a frenzy. Paul fell back on his bottom and scooted out of the way. Just as suddenly the fish stopped.

"Is it dead?" I asked.

Paul didn't know so we decided to wait a couple more minutes. In the meantime, he called Charbonneau to see if they knew what type of fish he had caught.

It was a mahi-mahi and it was mine to fillet. Prior to becoming a food journalist, I had attended the Cordon Bleu cooking school in Paris. There we had practiced filleting fish daily so I was reasonably good at it. Of course, those fish were nine inches long and neatly arranged on the kitchen counter. I squatted next to the four-foot fish with our puny-by-comparison knife and started to fillet it with Paul as my attentive student.

When I finished, the deck was a bloody mess of fish bones, guts and mystery bits. Seagulls circled and cawed overhead. Howie meowed incessantly. Once the carnage had been rinsed away by copious amounts of sea water, peace prevailed again on Cherokee Rose.

We anchored north of Nassau and Paradise Island, off Salt Cay. Charbonneau came over for dinner that included sashimi and grilled mahi-mahi. We admired the lights of the city as evening settled in.

"That's Atlantis," said Janet. "According to my guide book, it has a water park, casino, disco and a huge aquarium. And a marina. I read that if you stay in the marina, you can use all of the facilities. But the marina charges two dollars a foot for a slip."

With Rosie's 42-feet, that would be $84 a night, very expensive for a slip but cheap for a resort stay. I looked at

Paul.

"When was the last time we had a vacation?"

Paul, Blaine and Janet all exchanged looks. "Kel, this is vacation," Paul chided me.

"Are you kidding me? We have worked non-stop for the past year: finishing the basement, selling the house, moving, fixing up Rosie, repairing the engine three times, and writing all of those manuscripts." I silently added our fertility treatments to my list. The subject was still too personal to share. No doubt about it. The past year had been hard. "Honey, I am due."

The next day, we tied up our boats in Atlantis' marina, having agreed to stay for one night. Among the 200-plus-foot mega yachts with their gleaming hulls, swimming pools on deck and smartly, uniformed crew members, Charbonneau and Cherokee Rose looked like poor, distant relatives that no one wanted to know. Maybe that was why our slips were the farthest away from the resort and tucked out of sight. One mega yacht was moored two slips away from us in the hinterland. According to the dock boy, Bruce Willis was on board.

With a famous actor as a neighbor, who were we to complain about our location? We immediately set off to explore the resort and enjoy its amenities. That night I decided that a one-day vacation wasn't enough. I wanted more. Paul didn't want to spend the money – after all, we were unemployed – but he, too, was enjoying the break.

Charbonneau was eager to cruise the Exuma Cays, and left the next day for Rose Island and beyond. We agreed to catch up with them at one of the cays in the Exumas, a 95 nautical-mile chain of islands that lies south of Nassau.

For three days, Paul and I plunged down the steep slides at the water park, and enjoyed reading the newspaper and ordering room service which were delivered to the boat. Then we, too, departed for Rose Island via Nassau's busy harbor. In mere minutes, my relaxed demeanor vanished.

As soon as we entered the harbor, we turned into the wind and raised our main sail. Then Paul headed down below, leaving me behind the wheel. Cruise ships, ferry boats, tour boats, day sailboats, fishing boats and skiffs buzzed around the harbor randomly, and I vainly tried to remember who had right-of-way on the water. The rules were complicated.

As I checked the water around us, I saw a double-decker

tour boat speeding up behind us on a collision course. I scanned the power boat, searching its decks and finally spotting the cockpit. No one was there!

"Paul, help!" I shouted. "There's a tour boat that going to hit us!"

Paul leapt into the cockpit, saw the speeding boat and grabbed the air horn from Howie's nook.

Bleeep! Bleep!

The tour boat was 25 yards away – the length of a swimming pool – and nearly upon us. It was going to ram us!

"Paul, let's alter course."

"No, we have right-of-way. We're under sail."

"Who cares about right-of-way?" I retorted. "I want to live!"

Suddenly a dread-locked man appeared in the upper cockpit of the tour boat.

He glared at us, veered off course to narrowly miss our boat and shouted down to us with his heavy Bahamian accent, "Put a man behind the wheel!"

I couldn't believe it! An obscenity was about to roll off my tongue when I noticed that two levels of people were staring at me, including a young pig-tailed girl sitting with her parents.

"At least I am behind the wheel!" I shouted indignantly. "Maybe you should watch where you are going." And lest anyone on the tour boat think that I – a woman – was in the wrong, I screamed, "We have right-of-way."

The tour boat zoomed away, leaving us to bounce around in its wake.

My legs were shaking, I was so mad. "Put a man behind the wheel..." I muttered.

"What a moron," Paul said, putting his arm around me. "You did good."

I shrugged off his arm. "No, Paul. Nearly colliding with another boat is not good. We should have altered course."

"But we had right-of-way..."

I shook my hands in frustration and went down below. Men!

When I had calmed down, I realized that I was mad at myself. I hadn't altered course because the sail had been up and I hadn't known how it would respond to a change in direction. My lack of sailing knowledge had made me ineffective in a dangerous situation. One thing was clear. I needed to learn how to sail.

    We arrived at Rose Island, dropped the hook and planned our next passage to Allan's Cay, our first stop in the Exumas. This was a treacherous trip because the dreaded Yellow Bank lay between us and our destination, some 30 nautical miles away.

Chickentown

Bahamas, March 2002

The Yellow Bank was hazardous for several reasons. It was strewn with coral heads, some which were mere feet below the surface of the water. In addition, at low tide, the average depth of water across the Yellow Bank was 6 feet, which was the depth of Rosie's keel. Lastly, if the wind was southeasterly and greater than 20 knots, there were steep, nasty waves. The key to successfully crossing the Yellow Bank was to go with favorable winds, at high tide and with the sun directly overhead so we could do "eye-ball" navigation, i.e. read the depth of the water by its color and steer around the coral heads. The whole thing made me nervous.

"Hey, honey, here's a route that avoids the Yellow Bank," I said enthusiastically, pointing to a chart in our guide book. "We dogleg around the Yellow Bank by sailing south of it, between the Yellow and White Banks, then sailing a more easterly path to Allan's Cay."

Paul leaned over and looked at the chart. "How much longer is that trip?"

"About 5 miles."

That would add another hour to our trip, Paul pointed out.

"I know, but I'd rather take an extra hour than hit a coral head and sink the boat."

"We won't hit a coral head," Paul said. "But if it makes you happier to go around the Yellow Bank, then okay. We'll go that way."

We got the boat ready and went to bed early, just to be awakened by strong winds in the morning. The Yellow Bank would have to wait another day as we waited for better weather.

The following morning was still. We up-anchored, and as planned, Paul stayed on the bow to look ahead of Rosie for any lurking coral heads. If he spotted any, he'd signal me to steer around them. As we motored out of the anchorage, some new friends waved good-bye to us from their boat. Paul and I both waved back, and in that brief moment, we plowed into a sizeable coral head. Rosie jerked to a stop until her 15 tons of forward momentum mowed over the top of the coral head. It retaliated by scraping the length of Rosie's hull with a back-tingling s-c-r-a-t-c-h as Rosie resumed her forward, albeit slower, motion.

Paul raced back to the cockpit and jumped into the cabin, ripping up our floorboards and searching for any leaks. A tense moment passed as we waited for seawater to burst through some unseen hole or crack in Rosie's hull. Nothing. We were fine.

It wasn't the smoothest start to a day that threatened many such coral-head encounters, but at least we didn't hit any more. It turned out that the coral heads were easy to spot: big gray-and-black blobs under the surface of the water. We agreed it would be okay to cross the Yellow Bank, and save ourselves that extra hour.

That's when we discovered the real threat of the Yellow Bank. It wasn't the coral heads; it was the lack of water.

Everyone we had met in the Bahamas, as well as our cruising guides, talked about the importance of eye-ball navigation not only for spotting coral but also for ascertaining water depth. Climb the mast for the best view of the water. Wear polarized sunglasses that allow you see past the sun's reflection and into the water. Travel when the sun is high in the sky. These were some of the tips we had received, and I just knew that eye-ball navigation was going to be tough to learn.

Before we left Rose Island, I had studied our guidebook's photographs of water that depicted different depths. Dark blue, for example, was ocean deep, whereas a whitish tan was very shallow, perhaps a foot or less. Gauging big changes in water depth was easy; what was difficult was looking for minor color gradations.

Standing in the cockpit, gazing forward at the pale green sea that surrounded us, I tried to distinguish the difference between the 10-foot pale green and 5-foot pale green. The former was fine. The latter meant we would be aground.

While I struggled to predict the depth of the water that lay ahead, the depth sounder merrily flashed our present depth on the instrument console: 10 feet, 10 feet, 9 feet, 8 feet, 7 feet, 6 feet, 5 feet...

"Paul, we're in five feet of water," I shouted to Paul, who was still on the bow, looking out for coral heads. Just as I said this, the depth sounder flashed 6 feet, 7 feet, 6 feet...and so it went, for five anxious hours.

By the time we reached Allen's Cay, I was frazzled and weary of shallow water. Unlike the other boats in the anchorage, we shunned the pale green water off Allen's Cay's beach and anchored in 25 feet of comfortable, mid-green water. Once the anchor was set, we popped open two cold beers and toasted the end of a long day.

That night, we crawled into bed and fell asleep, listening to the waves gently lapping Rosie's bow.

Grunt, grunt.

I snapped my eyes opened, wondering what woke me. It was dark. Through the open hatch over our bed, I could see stars twinkling.

Grunt, grunt.

"Paul wake up. I think there's an animal on the boat!"

"What?" Paul asked groggily.

Grunt, grunt.

Now he was awake too.

I got up, grabbed the flashlight out of the nav station desk and tried to pinpoint the location of the noise.

"Over here," Paul said, stealing the flashlight from me and lifting up one of the seat cushions in the salon to reveal the interior of one of our lockers. He beamed the light around the locker. Nothing but canned goods.

Grunt, grunt.

The sound was behind us now. We checked another locker and another. Nothing. It was bewildering. After twenty futile minutes of ransacking the boat, Paul went back to bed and I reluctantly followed him. We later learned that aptly-named grunt fish had been swimming around our boat. Who knew fish could be noisy?!

The next morning we motored to shore and were shocked to find a pack of huge native iguanas charging toward us across the beach. What did they want? Food, as evidenced by the leftover bits of cabbage, apple and carrot that littered the sand. But we didn't bring any! We sidestepped all but one of the iguanas on this tiny islet. The largest one, and presumably the leader, would not be denied. He doggedly pursued us.

Thankfully, a red speedboat careened through the anchorage and dumped a group of Nassau tourists onto the beach. Their tour guide opened a plastic grocery bag brimming with cut melon and everyone started handing out pieces. Once the iguanas, and their leader, were otherwise distracted, Paul and I hastily retreated.

As we dinghied back to Rosie, we passed two men and a woman who were fishing from their dinghy. One of the men was struggling to reel in a fish. Paul put our outboard into neutral and we glided closer.

"What have you got?" Paul asked.

"Don't know," the man responded, straining to pull his rod back. "But it's a big one."

We all silently watched the water where the line entered it, waiting to catch a glimpse of the fighting fish.

"Hey, there it is," said the woman excitedly.

Sure enough, just under the surface of the water was a gray 4-foot barracuda. As quick as lightening, another gray form appeared from the deep and, without pausing, bit the barracuda on the line. And then it was gone with a powerful swish of its tail.

"Did you see that?" The man protested, snapping the remnant of his fish into their dinghy. "That was a shark. The scavenger of the sea. And the third one we've seen this morning."

That was how we met Rich and Sue on Free Spirit. They were retired, and cruising the balmy Bahamas to escape the winter months. Sue invited us for sundowners on their boat that evening and we gladly accepted.

As we motored away, Paul pointed to a patch of calm water that was protected by Allen's Cay and two partially submerged boulders. He suggested we go snorkeling there.

"No way! I'm not snorkeling with sharks," I exclaimed. Was he nuts?!

The next week passed quickly as we had fun fishing and, with much persuasion required on my behalf, snorkeling with our new friends on Free Spirit, as well as another boat, Peaceful Times. There was just one snafu: the fridge/freezer. It was fully stocked, but we had noticed that it didn't seem as cold as before. Then, one afternoon, it hissed and died.

I immediately put Paul and me on a high protein, frozen food diet. Paul and Rich vainly tried to troubleshoot and fix the compressor with the help of a reference book written by Nigel Calder. Without the proper tools and coolant gas, however, there was little they could do. We had no other option. We had to sail back to Nassau.

After braving the Yellow Bank again, we arrived at the Nassau Harbour Club Marina. The dock master agreed to let me store our remaining frozen goods in one of his freezers. Then we set off on foot to locate a marine refrigeration repair shop. The only shop we found was dingy, and sparsely filled. Neither the store, nor the laid-back shopkeeper who assured us that her best repairman would visit us the following day, instilled us with confidence.

The next morning a tall dread-locked man wearing a knitted Rastafarian beret with yellow, green and red stripes appeared at our boat. He was empty-handed. Paul and I glanced at each other. I shrugged. Maybe he left his tools in his car? The repairman sat down next to the compressor and deftly released whatever refrigerant – Freon? HFC-134a? – our system had into the air. Besides being illegal in the United States, releasing the gas without knowing the problem didn't bode well. After a painful 50 minutes of watching him do nothing, I paid the man $80 and firmly ushered him off the boat.

"He was clueless," Paul complained angrily. "Why did you pay him?"

"To get rid of him," I retorted.

We were quiet for a moment.

"What are we going to do?" I asked, my voice kinder upon seeing the frustration written all over Paul's face. "We could find another refrigeration shop."

Paul shook his head. "No. I can fix it if I have the proper tools. Besides, it might break again in the future."

Fixing a freezer seemed difficult and, for a moment, I questioned whether Paul could do it. Then I recalled the 16-foot silk curtains that Paul had sewn for our living room years ago, the rock climbing wall he had built, and the engine repairs he had performed on Rosie. If anyone could fix our freezer, I figured Paul could.

We bought the necessary tools, including an evacuation pump, and spent the next week in a pattern that would become standard throughout our journey. I read aloud the step-by-step instructions from Nigel Calder's book while Paul troubleshot the system. Turns out the compressor was broken. We ordered a new one.

Someone said that the definition of cruising was "fixing your boat in exotic locations." No kidding. While the Bahamas may be exotic, we had seen little of it because we were fixing the boat. Again.

I was bummed, but Paul sank into a depressing funk that neither he, nor my attempts at humor, could shake.

It was time to call the cavalry.

I phoned Mavis, Paul's retired mum, in England and explained that her son was very depressed, that we were in the midst of yet another boat repair and would she please come out and cheer him up? Two days later, she arrived in Nassau. As the Brits would say, Mavis is a little "bitty," standing 5 feet 2 inches tall, but her cheerful enthusiasm and practical, matter-of-fact approach to life, elevated her stature.

The boat instantly became a brighter place once she stepped on board. Without any prodding, she became Paul's assistant, passing tools and brewing endless cups of tea; she hung up our wet laundry. After dinner, she did the dishes.

She was standing at the sink in the galley, running the water and soaping up a dinner plate when I joined her. Out of habit, I turned off the water.

I explained that it was okay to freely run the water because we were in a marina where we could refill our fresh water tanks. Once we left the marina, though, we would be on water rationing. Our tanks held only 200 gallons. I told her how we shower. Just get wet then turn off the water, shampoo and lather before having a quick rinse. The same method applied to brushing our teeth.

Then I drained the sink she had filled with soapy water, and demonstrated how I did the dishes with a fraction of the water she had used. I pointed to a white spray hose mounted next to the sink, and added, "If something needs to be soaked, use this tap. It's saltwater from the ocean and there is plenty of it."

"Oh, Kelly, you and Paul have to think of everything on a boat, don't you?"

Paul, who was listening to our conversation, and I both nodded. There was a lot to think about on a boat.

Like how many tea bags we had when Mavis asked for the tenth time that day, "Would anyone like a cup of tea?"

And Paul happily accepted - for the tenth time that day.

I checked my provisions inventory list: 1100 tea bags. Whew! My British mother-in-law could stay a little longer.

When the compressor arrived, Paul and Mavis installed it while I went grocery shopping to replenish our meat, cheese, fruit and vegetable supply. That night, we invited Herb, from Peaceful Times, over for dinner. He had surprised us by docking in a nearby slip, having returned to Nassau to moor his boat before catching a flight home.

"Hey, do you think we could set Herb up with your mom? I asked Paul while Mavis was taking out the garbage.

"No way!" Paul exclaimed.

"Why not? Your mom is outgoing and fun; she'd be the perfect compliment for Herb's quieter nature--"

Paul nudged me; Mavis had returned.

Dinner in the cockpit was pleasant. Herb was charming and it was obvious that he was enjoying Mavis' conversation and funny stories. And he wasn't the only man to display an interest in Paul's mum.

Two days later, we crossed the Yellow Bank for the third time, once again practicing our eye-ball navigation. Mavis was impressed. We anchored at Allen's Cay again, so that we could take Mavis to see the iguanas – with a bag of food! - and give her a taste of the cruising life.

Mavis and I were chatting in the cockpit, soaking up the tropical sun, when a sailboat motored close to our boat. A tan, older man, wearing a skimpy bathing suit and jaunty captain's hat, was behind the wheel; he was appraising Mavis. Propped against the side of his mast was a large, crude plywood sign that read, "Female companion wanted to cruise Bahamas." Under the sign was his phone number.

Mavis and I burst out laughing. I leaned through the companionway hatch and told Paul to come look. The man brought his boat around and circled ours for the second time, making us laugh even harder.

I teasingly asked Mavis if she wanted to go.

Ever British, she regained her composure and haughtily

said, "Certainly he is joking."

I didn't think so; the man had actually taken the time to paint a sign.

Paul blurted, "And he wants you, mum! Go on, go for it."

I suddenly realized this was my best dishwasher we were talking about. I waved at the old guy and shouted, "Sorry, she's staying with us!"

He smiled, giving us an exaggerated shrug, as if to say, "It was worth a try." Then he motored out of the anchorage, still searching for a willing female.

Paul and Mavis decided to pursue their own game. Paul baited a fishing pole and showed Mavis how to cast it. Zing! She immediately had a fish, and with some gleeful shrieks, managed to reel it into the cockpit.

Grunt, grunt.

The fish wiggled so much on the line, it seemed to be doing the Mexican Hat dance.

"Oh, Paul, help!" cried Mavis.

Paul grinned at his mum, and started to lean over to take the fish off the line when Howie suddenly pounced on it. Like a pendulum, the fish swung away from the cat only to swing back and hit him on the nose. Startled, Howie meowed and recoiled at this sudden turn of events. Retreating a safe distance away, he crouched down, his tail twitching and his eyes following the fish's every move.

Paul laughed. "Don't worry, little buddy, we'll catch you a fish too."

And sure enough, Mavis did.

It was decision time with regard to Mavis' travel plans. We could sail north, back to Nassau so Mavis could catch her flight home. Or we could change her airline ticket and cruise the Exumas with her by heading south.

"Living on a boat makes or breaks a relationship" is an often-quoted expression among cruisers. We had discovered that living in Rosie's confined space did require a high degree of compatibility, and a lot of compromise. Paul and I did pretty well, but I had wondered how my mother-in-law and I would manage. As a precaution, I had only booked Mavis for a short one-week stay. But I needn't have been concerned. Mavis was a great playmate, snorkeling and swimming with us. Whenever there were chores to be done, she pitched in; and through it all, she kept a sense of humor.

We headed south, and Mavis stayed.

The wind was blowing 20 to 25 knots, fifty-degrees off our port side, and we flew, passing six other sailboats as we sailed to Waderick Wells.

Go, Rosie, Go!

Even Mavis got into the spirit. "Paul," she said. "Our speed's dropped to 6.2 knots. Adjust the sails!"

And Paul would tweak them accordingly.

One of the sailboats we passed, a cat-ketch called Acclaim, had taken a photo of Rosie under sail and hailed us over the VHF radio. They, too, were headed to Waderick Wells and invited us to their boat for sundowners that evening.

For the next couple of weeks, we cruised with Alida and John on Acclaim. At their recommendation, we stopped in Staniel Cay to visit Thunderball Cave, which was featured in the 1964 James Bond movie, Thunderball. "Majestic" was the word they used to describe it.

"If we visit Thunderball Cave at high tide, when its entrance is submerged, we will have to swim underwater to enter the cave," Paul informed Mavis and me, "or we can go at low tide, when we would just have to duck our heads and snorkel in."

Mavis and I voted for low, and slack, tide as there was also a strong tidal current running through the cave.

At the appropriate time, we dinghied to the cave's islet, anchored and slid into the pale green water. We found the cave's large entrance easily and snorkelled into its dark recess.

The cave formed a high vaulted dome, lit by shafts of sunlight from holes between the rocks above. On the water, the sunlight created a pattern of glowing sapphire patches against an indigo background. Schools of fish darted through the luminous water, only to vanish in the surrounding dark areas. There must have been hundreds of fish in this cave and we were awed by their beauty, the dazzling shafts of sunlight and the cool, dark calm that seemed to permeate the cave.

The calm was broken by Paul, who announced that he was going to jump into the water though the big hole that loomed some twenty-five feet above us.

"Paul, no!" I exclaimed, "The water's not deep enough for that drop. You could break a leg, or kill yourself." Rocks and boulders littered the edge of the cave

"Don't be daft, Paul," Mavis said matter-of-factly.

Paul dove under the water, probably to escape us, and swam out of the cave.

Exasperated, I looked at his mum, "He's giving me gray hair!"

"I know, Kelly. Why do you think I'm so glad that he married you?" She smiled, "Now he's your problem."

Thanks a lot.

We looked up when Paul's head and shoulders blocked some of the sunlight streaming into the cave as he peered down the hole.

"It's a long way down from here," Paul said, laughing nervously.

"Paul, don't do it," I pleaded.

Whoosh! And there he was, falling, splashing, grinning.

Yes, Suzanne, I was married to him for life.

On April 13th, after two weeks of island-hopping in the Exumas with Acclaim, we sailed into Georgetown Harbor. Georgetown, sometimes referred to as Chickentown, was the unofficial cruising capital of the Bahamas. Over 300 sailboats crowded the anchorage. Every day there were planned activities for anyone who wanted to join in: volleyball on the beach, games of horseshoes, potluck dinners. It was also the final southbound destination for many yachts, before they sailed back to Florida and the States.

On our first morning in Georgetown, we tuned into the cruiser "net" on the VHF radio. Besides announcing the day's activities and the weather forecast, boats that had just arrived were encouraged to introduce themselves, their crew and their next port-of-call. Three boats did and, after each introduction, the radio crackled with calls from other boats who shared similar cruising plans.

Then Paul got on the radio. "This is Cherokee Rose. I'm Paul, my wife is Kelly and we are headed to Panama. If anyone is sailing there, please get back to us."

We waited eagerly, expecting the radio to crackle with calls as it had for the others. There was nothing but unnerving silence.

I chuckled anxiously, "I wonder what that means?"

"Maybe it's too dangerous to sail to Panama," ventured Mavis.

"No, it means that we've arrived in Chickentown," Paul

replied, "and true to Georgetown's nickname, no one ventures beyond here."

"Except us," I pointed out.

"Hear, hear!" said Paul.

"Oh dear," sighed Mavis.

I cried when we said good-bye to Mavis at the Georgetown airport; I had enjoyed her three-week visit so much that I had invited her to sail with us to Panama. She had hastily declined, no doubt concerned that we were the only boat out of hundreds that was headed there. It *was* disconcerting but I shrugged it off. Paul and I had too much to do to worry about what others were doing. We repaired minor breaks and topped up our diesel, propane and grocery supplies.

Alida from Acclaim and I were provisioning at the grocery store when a local Bahamian man rushed in. The Bahamians were starting their Annual "Family Islands Regatta," and one of the boats needed extra crew. Would we and our husbands help them?

Ten minutes later, John and Paul joined us. We rushed over to the dock where the traditionally designed Bahamian sailboat Sea Star was moored. The crew, clad in canary yellow T-shirts, was busy preparing the boat for the race. Ron, Sea Star's captain, greeted us and tossed us four T-shirts: our uniform. We were now part of the 14-man crew.

But was our crew proficient at sailing? We were about to find out.

We anchored at the start line, next to the dozen other anchored boats in the race. A horn sounded, and two men on the bow of our boat started to pull in the anchor by hand. Simultaneously, two men hoisted the tremendous sail. The mast was 60 feet tall and the boom extended beyond the stern of the 28-foot boat, creating a huge sail area.

The sail team was faster than the anchor team and before anyone could react, the boat jumped forward as the wind filled the sail. The forward motion dug the anchor deeper into the seabed; we couldn't hoist it. I looked around; we were the last boat on the starting line. Ron pulled a knife out of his shorts and slashed the anchor rope, leaving the anchor on the seabed. We were off!

As the gust hit the sail, the boat tipped steeply over and

my shoes lost their grip. I slipped down the deck and would have fallen into the ocean except there were too many people in the way.

"Ride the pry! Ride the pry!" Ron shouted.

There was a shuffle as three wood planks on deck were slid eight feet over the high edge of the boat. The Bahamians confidently scrambled on the planks that were suspended over the water, and sat down.

"Come on," one of the men impatiently said to me, patting the pry in front of him.

I crawled out on the pry, and tried not to look at the turquoise water rushing underneath me. I sat down gratefully and then two more men sat down in front of me. I was snugly sandwiched between five men. I searched for the other woman on board among the yellow shirts and found Alida, similarly situated, two planks away. Paul was seated on the stern of the boat, working the mainsheet and trying his best to understand the captain, whose Bahamian-accented English resembled a foreign language.

As we rounded the first buoy, we bumped into another boat – oops! – and tacked. The boom swung around quickly, but rather than being above head height, as on Rosie, this boom was level with my knees. I threw myself down on the deck to avoid being knocked off my feet, just to land on a pry that a bunch of men were trying to slide to the other side of the boat.

"Ride the pry! Ride the pry!" Ron shouted.

I clumsily got out of the way and obediently scrambled on the nearest plank. Two more turns and the race was over. We finished second-to-last.

But there was more.

The regatta consisted of a series of races, and each start for Sea Star was worse than the one before. On one start, the anchor rope got tangled up with the main halyard – the rope that pulls the sail up to the top of the mast – when a neighboring boat bumped into us. In the confusion, someone must have tied the anchor rope to the halyard. Once the sail was hoisted, Sea Star was now anchored from the top of the mast!

If our starts were bad, so were our finishes. We were routinely second-to-last. On the positive side, no one lost any fingers while sliding the pry or fell overboard, as had happened on other boats. And we didn't capsize or sink the boat, as three others had. We had an exhilarating, if chaotic, day.

Fun aside, we had some serious sailing ahead of us. While our first passage across the Gulf Stream was approximately 100 miles, it was nearly 1,000 miles, or 10 days' worth of sailing, to Panama from Georgetown. Our unexpected refrigeration repair and leisurely cruise down the Exumas had eaten the time we had set aside for cruising the Caribbean. While we didn't have a set-in-stone schedule, we were determined to follow the favorable weather windows that Jimmy Cornell outlined in his book. According to him, this time of year was good for sailing to Panama, as the hurricane season had not yet started, the winter trade winds should have lessened by now and tropical storms were less frequent.

We sailed out of Georgetown at 2:30 p.m. on April 29, 2002 with light winds and flat seas. The expression, "the calm before the storm," didn't cross our minds, just as it hadn't on our maiden voyage. We motored along, with just the mainsail up, at 5 knots. Because the sea was tranquil, I made a large pasta salad, ran a load of laundry and sent Dad a satellite e-mail, letting him know that we were now en route to Panama.

We debated stopping some 200 miles away, at Matthew Town on Great Inagua Island. But once we got going, we didn't want to stop.

Panama, here we come!

No Emergency Exit

Caribbean Sea, May 2002

We headed south through the Windward Passage, a channel of water that separates Cuba and Haiti, before passing east of Jamaica. Then we entered the Caribbean Sea for a southwest approach to Colon, the Atlantic portal to the Panama Canal.

As we plodded along our course, the waves grew from small, to medium, to large and then became super-sized. The wind had also steadily increased and we found ourselves in 20-foot tall breaking waves with 40 knots of apparent wind from behind us. We reduced sail and were running with just our triple-reefed main sail.

It was mid-day, halfway to Panama, and I was on watch. With my harness on and securely tethered to the boat, I sat transfixed in the cockpit. I couldn't tear my eyes away from the spectacle behind us. Gaining on us. Overtaking us.

An enormous, two-story wall of translucent teal-blue water chased us. Only six feet behind, the gigantic wall of water was so close; I was tempted to stick my hand in it. Towering over us and threatening to crash down upon Rosie, and me, the giant wave was frothing and foaming on top. Just as the wave started to break, and my heart skipped a beat or two, the bottom part of the wave lifted us – miraculously! – up.

At the top of the wave, Rosie paused for an instant. I caught a glimpse of the stormy gray sky above us and, stretching as far as I could see, endless rows of translucent walls below us. And then the pause was over. As the wave rolled out from underneath us, 15-ton Rosie surfed down the 20-foot wave at an incredible 15 knots, rounding up slightly at the bottom of the wave as the autopilot fought to keep our careening boat on course.

I glanced over my shoulder. Another two-story wall of water was encroaching on us; its cap already curling then breaking, its white water plummeting toward us. I clutched the steering wheel's mount and held my breath, praying for Rosie to be lifted up. No luck.

The wave crashed over the boat, in one second dousing me and filling the cockpit with several feet of tepid water. Salt water rushed down the companionway steps, drenching the kitchen and quarter berth.

Rosie was now on top of the wave and I burst into tears, scared of the infinite waves surrounding us, threatening to sink us. Awaken by water pouring into the cabin, Paul appeared at the companionway hatch, then Rosie careened down the wave. In the brief pause at the bottom of the wave – while the next wave was gathering up its strength – Paul leapt into the cockpit and, concerned, put his arm around me.

I sobbed into his chest, "Where is the emergency exit? I want to get off this ride!"

Paul hugged me. "There isn't one. Hurry," he said, prying my white-knuckled hands off the steering post, "Let's get you down below before the next wave. You'll feel better once you're out of those wet clothes."

"No, I won't," I wailed. "I want off!"

But there was no way off Rosie, who teetered on being out-of-control, and no way to get out of the heavy weather conditions that tested our survival. We were stuck on this nightmare roller coaster ride, with each powerful wave prodding and pushing15-ton Rosie as if she were a flimsy surfboard. We closed up the companionway hatch to prevent any other waves from barreling into the cabin and kept watch from inside, monitoring the radar and poking our heads outside every 10 minutes.

The cabin was stifling in the near-equatorial heat, but due to the conditions, we were unwilling to open any hatches. My body was clammy with perspiration, my head ached and my throat was sore from the new seasickness medicine that Paul and I had taken. I even had occasional heart palpitations, but whether that was due to the medicine or the stress of not-being-sailors-in-scary-seas was unclear.

To add further worry to our trip, we were following a straight line from the Windward Passage to Panama. So was every cargo- and container- ship, it seemed.

"To the big ship at approximately 15 degrees 25 minutes North, 76 degrees 34 minutes West, this is sailing vessel Cherokee Rose at nearly the same coordinates. Do you copy?" Paul asked, speaking into the VHF radio.

We waited anxiously for a reply.

On our radar screen, the green blip that represented the ship was on a collision course with us. They were several miles away and closing fast.

We had read, and heard, horror stories about ships running over or dismasting sailboats that they hadn't seen. Like us, they were steering their vessel with an autopilot, so there was no guarantee that anyone was even looking out of their window. And, with us bobbing up and down in 20-foot waves, we were probably just a tiny flashing blip on their radar screen, if we registered at all.

There was no response.

Paul pulled the wood slats out of the companionway, waited until Rosie reached the top of the wave, climbed into the cockpit and searched for the ship. It was still on a collision course.

"Can we sail out of its way?" I asked him when he came below.

"No," said Paul. "It's too risky in these strong winds; we might accidentally jibe."

Accidental jibes occur when the wind unexpectedly catches the mainsail on its backside and slams it, and the boom, across the cockpit. The stress of a 40-knot slam on the boat's rig is tremendous and can seriously damage the boat. If the boom hit either one of us, we'd be dead.

"To the big ship at approximately 15 degrees 25 minutes North, 76 degrees 34 minutes West, this is sailing vessel Cherokee Rose at the same coordinates. We are on a collision course. Repeat: We are on a collision course." Paul said again.

No response. A minute passed.

"There! Look at the radar screen!" The green blip had changed directions. The ship had heard us, and altered course.

And so our passage went, getting pooped by the

occasional wave, side-slapped by rogue waves and making frequent "big ship, big ship, this is little boat" calls.

One evening, a car-carrier ship – the biggest of the bunch – returned my call.

"This is pretty rough weather for a sailboat," the ship's captain said with a charming Spanish accent, "Where are you headed?"

I laughed, overwhelmingly pleased to hear another person's voice resonate in our cabin. "Yes, it is rough. We're headed to Panama. Where are you going?"

"To Georgia."

I asked him if it was for business or pleasure.

"A bit of both, actually. I am going to unload these cars and then visit some family that lives there."

We chatted for another minute, agreeing that his ship would pass on our left - his port side to our port side - and then signed off. It was the first time I had laughed, or smiled, in days. There was someone else out here. We were not alone.

As we drew closer and closer to Panama, the waves subsided and the ships multiplied. Our radar screen was covered with "bogeys" and yet we were no longer afraid of ships. After nine days at sea, we dropped our hook behind five other yachts anchored in the Atlantic-side port of Colon.

Before Paul had even uncorked the celebratory bottle of wine I had earmarked for this occasion, I blurted, "Let's sell the boat and go back to Philadelphia. I hate sailing. We're lucky to be alive!"

Paul took a moment to formulate his response, "We've given up everything to do this trip. I'm not ready to quit yet."

We sipped our wine in silence.

I realized that I had fooled myself several times since we started this journey. When we decided to go sailing, I assumed that Paul and I would agree when it was time to quit. After all, we had agreed when to stop our fertility treatments and when to quit our jobs. We had been in sync so often, I just figured we would naturally agree. Wrong.

I also thought that the expression "living on a boat makes or breaks a relationship" simply referred to the challenge of living in close quarters. Now I knew differently. Being on a boat, and dealing with Mother Nature, challenged a couple's tolerance – and compatibility – in an area that was normally not tested: danger. Now that we were safely anchored, I faced a delayed "fight or flight" dilemma to our ordeal, only Paul chose the first while I wanted to flee.

Surviving the gale off Cape Fear during our maiden voyage, I had wrongly concluded that sailing and the weather couldn't get any worse. The twenty-foot, breaking waves en route to Panama had dwarfed that storm, proving that the weather could get much worse.

What was I going to do?

Realizing how naïve I had been didn't change the fact that Paul and I currently disagreed. He wanted to stay; I wanted to go. But go where? From a practical standpoint, I analyzed my predicament. We didn't have a house. We didn't have cars. We didn't have jobs. If I left, I wouldn't have Paul.

Life without Paul? I couldn't imagine it; he was my best friend, my soul mate, my honey. But stay on the boat? No way.

And yet, what option did I have?

Paul wisely suggested that we continue this conversation after a good night's sleep, and because neither of us had slept much during our roller coaster ride, it sounded like a reasonable idea. Besides, I was too depressed to talk.

After Paul cleared Customs and Immigration the next morning, we dinghied to the boat anchored directly in front of us. Besides ours, it was the only boat with an American flag flying from its stern. Anne and Oreon welcomed us aboard "Scott Free," and introduced us to their two children, Samantha and Michael, 9 and 12 years old. Seasoned sailors, they had taken time off work, and pulled the kids out of school, to sail around the world. Paul and Oreon started to discuss the procedure for transiting the canal while I sought Anne's opinion.

Skirting my problem, I asked Anne if sailing was always terrible. Three passages said that it was: our maiden voyage, crossing the Gulf Stream and our trip to Panama. If we continued to sail around the world, was I going to be terrified and have heart palpitations the entire time?

Anne comforted me by saying that most sailors never faced the gigantic breaking waves and frightening conditions that we had. Most passages were not as bad as ours. Without any sugar-coating, she gave me a glimmer of hope. Sailing might get better.

Returning to Philadelphia where nothing awaited me, except the likelihood of losing my husband, was a dim prospect. If sailing improved, then my problems were solved.

Paul and I wouldn't have to reconcile our different thresholds for danger, or agree upon a quitting time. There would be nothing to fight or flee from. Hope, however faint, seemed like a preferable alternative to leaving Paul. With my fingers crossed for pleasant weather, I stayed on board.

As a consolation prize, or perhaps like a carrot dangling in front of a donkey, I promised myself a Tahitian black pearl necklace when we finally reached French Polynesia. A carrot wasn't going to cut it.

Transiting the Panama Canal Twice

Panama, May 2002

Our time in Colon was consumed by two tasks: provisioning the boat for crossing the Pacific and getting ready to transit the Panama Canal. On our first shopping venture, a taxi driver accosted us as soon as we had taken our first step off the Panama Canal Yacht Club's property. He warned us that Colon was dangerous and insisted that we take a taxi to get around. Paul and I were unconvinced. When Miguel informed us that the taxi ride only cost a dollar, we relented.

As Miguel drove us through town, we passed mainly vacant buildings with broken windows and graffiti on the walls. Hookers and drug dealers stood in the doorways of these forlorn buildings, some trying to hustle the scant pedestrians, others just staring with glazed eyes and whipped expressions. After that, we called on him for all of our subsequent shopping trips.

With so many ships transiting the canal, provisions were cheap and plentiful. We purchased bottles of quality rum for US$4 each, filled up Miguel's trunk with bulk fruit and vegetables for less than US$40, bought 12 cases of American and Panamanian beer for practically nothing and replenished our canned goods supply.

While shopping was easy with Miguel's help, preparing to transit the canal proved to be more difficult. The requirements to transit the canal are strict. Every yacht going through the canal needs four 100-foot long lines, and four people to handle these lines. That is in addition to the captain of the boat, and the Canal-appointed Captain who accompanies each yacht.

The boat must maintain a speed of 6 knots to transit the 50 miles in one day. If the boat goes too slow, then the Canal-appointed Captain will leave the boat and its crew at Gatun Lake for the night; Gatun Lake is sandwiched between the Atlantic- and Pacific- based locks. Before departing, the Canal-appointed Captain promises to return and complete the transit the following day. But sometimes the Canal-appointed Captain doesn't return for days, or so we heard.

We felt reasonably confident that Rosie could maintain 6 knots, as long as the engine behaved, so we figured we'd finish the transit within a day. We had the necessary 100-foot ropes but we needed three volunteers to handle them. Where would we find crew?

Most cruisers typically volunteered to line-handle on a friend's yacht before taking their own boat through the canal so they could see what the day entailed. Paul and I volunteered to help Scott Free. They were going through the canal two days ahead of our transit date. In return, Oreon would help us with our transit.

Now we needed only two line-handlers. We were told that there were clusters of backpackers and university students that hung out at the Panama Canal Yacht Club's bar; perhaps two of them might volunteer?

Paul and I were preparing to dinghy ashore on our recruitment mission when there was a loud knock on the side of the boat. A man with a gray bird's nest of a beard was standing in his dinghy, outside our boat.

"My transit is tomorrow morning and I can't find anyone to help me line-handle," Jim explained after he introduced himself. "That's my boat, Coogee, over there," he added, tossing his head over his shoulder toward a tired boat, which had laundry hanging from its lifelines.

"Did you check at the Yacht Club?" I asked.

"Yes. But everyone is transiting tomorrow or the day after, so no one has time. Could you help me out?"

Paul and I glanced at each other. We didn't want to volunteer on two boats, but we felt obliged. So many cruisers had helped us along the way.

"Okay," Paul said.

Jim smiled at us, visibly relieved. "I'll pick you up

tomorrow morning at 3:45 a.m. The Canal Captain is due to arrive at 4 a.m. to take us through the canal."

He motored off to knock on the side of another anchored yacht while we headed ashore to look for volunteers for our transit. When we arrived at the bar, we saw Scott Free and told them that we were crewing on Coogee the following day.

"That'll be interesting," said Oreon, chuckling. "I was at the marina's repair shop this morning and Jim was trying to find a used propeller to buy. He just installed a new engine on his boat, but didn't know that the new engine requires a left-handed propeller. He has only a right-handed prop."

"Oh, no," Paul groaned.

Oreon grinned.

"Could he use his existing prop if he can't find a new one?" I asked, not pleased with their expressions and not understanding the problem.

"He could." Paul explained, "But if he did, he'd have to put the boat in forward gear to go in reverse and he'd have to be in reverse gear to go forward."

"Oh, man!" I exclaimed, "It'd be too easy to make a mistake!" How could I forget throwing Rosie accidentally into forward gear when I had wanted reverse? At least that had happened in a small Bahamian marina, and not in the busy Panama Canal.

"I'm not concerned about the wrong propeller," said Paul. "I'm worried that he hasn't tested his new engine yet. How do we know that he'll be able to maintain 6 knots? I don't want to spend the night on his boat in Gatun Lake."

I hadn't thought about that. I didn't want to go anymore. Could we get out of it?

"That would probably be smart," Oreon said.

"I don't know," Paul said. "His transit is tomorrow morning. I don't think we can leave him in a lurch like that."

I nodded unhappily. Paul was right.

That evening, Jim called us on the radio. His transit had been rescheduled, and was now a day before Scott Free's. We told him the timing was too close.

"But it's no problem getting back to Colon from Balboa," Jim protested. There's a bus that runs every evening. You'll get back with time to help your friends the next day."

Paul bluntly explained that we thought Jim's transit might take longer than a day because his new engine was still untested; who knew what problems might arise? Grudgingly, Jim removed our names from his crew list.

On the day of their transit, Oreon met us at 3:30 a.m. at the Yacht Club's dinghy dock. He ferried us to Scott Free, where we joined his family, and another cruising couple. Anne had fresh fruit, muffins, and yogurt spread out on the table along with an ample supply of coffee and tea. We sat down in their spacious cabin and I admired their boat.

It was a new 53-foot, center cockpit Hallburg-Rassy. The large U-shaped galley was adjacent to the living room, and I was more than a little envious when I spotted a dishwasher tucked under one of the counters. How many amps and how many gallons of water did that cost to run? Then I remembered that they had a diesel generator on board, so the power to operate the appliance and make enough fresh water to run it wasn't an issue. Imagine that.

The Canal captain arrived and Scott Free effortlessly passed through the first three locks, rising 85 feet to Gatun Lake. Gatun Lake was one of the largest man-made lakes in the world, having been formed when the Chagres River was dammed. As we motored 24 miles across the island-studded lake, we saw monkeys swinging in the trees and alligators basking in the sun.

Ropes, suspended over the water and tied between trees on adjacent islands, connected the islands together like a giant daisy chain. The Canal Captain explained that when the valley had been flooded, the hill tops had been transformed into the islands that we now saw. The monkeys, who had once been able to roam the valley, had been stranded on these little islands. The ropes allowed the monkeys to swing from island to island.

By noon, we were approaching Gaillard Cut at the far end of Gatun Lake. Paul and I were sitting on Scott Free's deck, trying to spot alligators in the water, when we motored by an anchored Coogee. We were surprised to see the boat.

The crew was overjoyed to see us.

Two young, shirtless men frantically waved at us while Jim yelled, "Telephone the Canal Captain. We started our transit yesterday and he promised to come back for us today but he still hasn't shown!"

Oreon put Scott Free into neutral while our Canal Captain made the necessary call on his mobile phone. Oreon shouted, "The Canal Captain is coming this afternoon!"

"When?"

Oreon shrugged, "He didn't say. If we don't see you tonight in Balboa, I'll call again."

Everyone on Coogee stood on deck, and silently watched our departure as we continued our transit. Paul and I glanced at each other and our relieved expressions mirrored each other's.

With their 145-horsepower engine, Scott Free made great time. In fact, we had two hours to wait before we could go through the last three locks. The Canal Captain directed us to tie up to a moored tugboat in Gaillard Cut.

The day had become hot and sticky, so Oreon flipped on their central air conditioning – how civilized – and we devoured a gourmet lunch that Anne had prepared. Afterward, we watched a movie while munching on popcorn and homemade chocolate chip cookies. Scott Free had set a high standard for transiting and there was no way poor Rosie could compete with her 48-horsepower engine and basic features.

After we cleared the Pedro Miguel locks, Scott Free entered the Miraflores locks. Lo and behold! there was Coogee. They must have motored past us while we were enjoying the movie. They were directed to raft up on Scott Free's port side while another yacht rafted up on our starboard side.

One of the young guys on Coogee leaned over the tire fenders that separated our boats and asked me, "Have you got something to drink? We ran out of water yesterday."

"Of course! What would you like?"

"Do you have a Coke?"

I smiled and said, "I'll get you one."

When I went below, I told Anne that there had been a water shortage on Coogee, and within minutes, she was passing out bottles of cold water and drinks to their appreciative crew.

When we returned to Rosie, the green light was illuminated on our satellite e-mail system, indicating we had a message. My sister Suzanne had checked out the Panama Canal webcams in anticipation of Rosie's transit and just happened to see Paul and me on board Scott Free!

Our own transit wasn't nearly as stress-free, as we now had to run the show. At least we had ample crew. We found three willing backpackers at the bar. While we needed just two people, the three friends came as a package deal. We were out of time so we agreed.

Because of our pre-dawn departure, they ate dinner and spent the night on board, as did Oreon and his son, Michael. Oreon and Michael had ridden the bus back to Colon from Balboa. Early the next morning, the Canal Captain showed up with his trainee. Cherokee Rose looked like a floating clown car with nine people, including us, and our cat milling about her small decks.

We arrived at the first locks while it was still dark. Being the only boat to transit at this hour, we nudged Rosie into the center of the lock. Towering above us, the Canal line handlers on shore tossed us their monkey balls, which are small hunks of lead, wrapped in rope, and attached to a thin line which they held. We dutifully tied one end of our four beefy lines, two at the bow and two at the stern, to their monkey balls. We cleated the other end of our lines to our boat. Then the Canal line handlers pulled up their monkey balls and secured our thick lines to their cleats on shore. We were now fastened to shore – or so we thought.

The lock gates closed and water rushed in, filling the chamber until it held 101,000 cubic meters or approximately 27 million gallons of water; the process took eight quick minutes. As Rosie started to rise with the torrent of water, the Canal Captain trainee ordered us to take in the slack on our four lines. Paul pulled in the starboard stern line.

It fell in the water! It wasn't attached to land; nor was Michael's line on the starboard bow. Rosie, held merely by her port lines, was shoved diagonally across the lock by the surging water. Her weight, and the tremendous force of water against her keel, was held by two small cleats that were bolted onto a bit of fiberglass. It was only a matter of moments before the cleats would be ripped off and Rosie would be smashed against the lock doors.

The Canal Captain barked at the men on the starboard shore, who hastily tossed us their monkey balls for another round of "let's-tie-up-the-boat." Paul then winched Rosie back to the center of the lock. After that predawn shot of adrenaline, who needed a cup of coffee?

On the Pacific-side locks, the Canal Captain suggested that we tie Rosie to the lock's sidewall and let out her lines as the water drained from the lock. .Paul and Oreon would handle the lines on the wall, releasing them at the same rate that Rosie was sinking. Too much slack would cause Rosie to sit diagonally across the lock again; too little slack and Rosie would be hung against the wall by her lines.

That left me to drive the boat and parallel park Rosie against the wall. The Canal Captain trainee sat next to me, ordering me when to give Rosie more throttle or when to ease off. It became apparent that he didn't know how to handle Rosie as well as I did, and I discreetly ignored his commands. Despite the strong current, I eased Rosie against the wall and close – but not too close – to the lock doors. I was proud of myself.

Then a container ship entered the lock behind us. Up close, and it *was* close, the gray ship was gigantic. Despite being led into the lock by railroad cars, the ship approached quickly. If the ship didn't stop in time, Rosie would be crushed.

"Show some leg, Kel," Paul said, "Make sure that ship's captain sees us!"

I leaned over the stern pulpit and craned my head to look for the ship's bridge towering above us. Behind the bridge's glass window, I saw the Captain and several men solemnly watching their ship's progress. One man looked down and I waved, giving him an ear-to-ear smile. He waved back. Despite the lack of leg display, the ship slowed down and stopped meters behind Rosie.

It was nearly 5 p.m. when we motored under the Bridge of Americas, a suspension bridge that unites North America with South America, and took a mooring ball at the Balboa Yacht Club. Paul put a cooler of beer on deck and, popping one open, toasted, "Here's to the Pacific!" Oreon and Michael stayed briefly before Paul dinghied them back to nearby Scott Free. The backpackers stayed until the last beer was finished.

I smiled as I drifted to sleep that night. We were now in the "peaceful" ocean as Magellan had described and named it. Since I had my fingers crossed for better weather, and better sailing, the name boded well. Unfortunately, the ocean didn't live up to its name.

Storms, Pirates and the Galapagos Islands

Panama, May 2002

If Colon was the city ghetto, Balboa was its rich suburb, with manicured lawns, wide streets and tree-lined sidewalks. The next morning, with Paul grumbling that our rollerblades should have made the boat cut, we went for a walk. We hadn't exercised since leaving the Bahamas and it felt good to walk farther than the 42 feet our boat allowed.

Along the way, we met an experienced cruising couple, Rupert and Judy from the sailboat Kayaha. They were gathering ripe mangoes that had fallen to the ground – all of the trees that lined the road were mango trees – and we didn't need any persuasion as we joined them, filling our own bag. There were hundreds on the ground; and even more in the trees. And to think that I had paid a dollar per mango at our Philadelphia grocery store!

We moved Rosie from her mooring ball at the Balboa Yacht Club to the adjacent and free anchorage off Flamenco Island. There were two catches with this anchorage. It was not protected from the west or the south, and it was tough getting ashore. There wasn't a beach per se, just a huge retaining wall of boulders and a narrow, steep road that served as a boat ramp. Because the tide rose and fell 8 feet, we had to drag our dinghy, and its 15-horsepower outboard engine, forty or fifty feet up this steep road, which gave us another chance to exercise.

One afternoon, the wind started to pick up from the

southwest; a storm was brewing. By 5 p.m., the water in our little anchorage was highly agitated. Five-foot-tall white caps crashed against the retaining wall, and the resulting ebb collided with the oncoming flow of waves as they rolled toward the rocks. If Rosie's anchor were to drag, she – and we – would be dashed into pieces against the boulders. We called Kayaha on the radio to see what they thought of the weather. They were going to move around Flamenco Island and anchor on its lee, or protected, side. We decided to follow them.

Scott Free was going to stay. Oreon and Michael had taken a taxi that morning to Panama City for boat parts, and Anne and her daughter, Samantha, were going to wait until the guys returned before moving the boat.

Paul went forward to hoist the anchor while I motored the boat into the waves to create some slack in the anchor chain for him. Every time the boat dove into a trough, the waves crashed over the bow and Paul. Then pop! her bow sprung up the next wave, making the chain taut and difficult for Paul to up-anchor. Up, down, up, down, Rosie went. Once the anchor was finally secured, we waved to Anne who had been watching us from Scott Free's cockpit and motored around the island. We anchored near Kayaha.

The conditions were significantly better on this side of the island even though the weather was worsening. We called Anne frequently on the radio, checking to see if she and Samantha were okay and if the guys had returned.

When the taxi dropped Oreon and Michael off at the anchorage, Oreon called Anne on his hand-held radio and asked to be picked up. Paul and I, snug on Rosie, eavesdropped on their conversation. Anne explained that the waves were pounding the rock retaining wall; how could she get ashore in these conditions?

Oreon suggested that Anne dinghy to a nearby restaurant that had a beach landing. He and Michael, and another cruiser who needed a ride to his boat, would meet her there. Anne dinghied to the beach, but the conditions forced her to return alone.

Six-foot waves battered the beach. Even if Anne somehow managed to surf the dinghy to shore without capsizing it – and that was a big "if" -- there was no way the three of them would be able to get the dinghy through those same crashing waves in order to return to the boat. In addition, it was too dangerous for Anne to take Samantha with her in the dinghy – and too dangerous to leave her daughter alone on the boat, especially if they couldn't get back to Scott Free.

Oreon and Michael were stranded on shore. They left to find a hotel for the night.

The other cruiser, the man who had hoped to ride with Oreon and Michael, did not give up. Every five or ten minutes, he called on the radio and pleaded for someone to give him a ride to his boat. As the night progressed, his relentless calls annoyed Paul.

"Can't he see that no one is going to help him?!" Paul said, exasperated, "It is too dangerous."

I felt uneasy about the growing panic I heard in his voice.

At 1 a.m., Anne called us; she, too, had panic in her voice, "We're dragging anchor! I am going to up-anchor and come over to your side."

"Okay. We'll be standing by. Call us when you're on your way," Paul said.

"Break, break. This is Kahaya. We're standing by too. Call if you need help," said Judy.

"Roger that," said Anne. The radio went silent.

I looked at Paul and demanded, "How is she going to single-handedly lift the anchor and drive the boat at the same time? One mistake and Scott Free will be crushed against those rocks. There has to be some way of helping her."

Paul shook his head. "There's nothing we can do from here. She'll figure something out."

I paced to and fro in our salon, anxious to hear Anne's voice again. It had been rough weather when we had moved. Now we had stronger winds, lightning and rain.

"Cherokee Rose, this is Scott Free."

Paul grabbed the transmitter before I could, "Hey, Scott Free, how are you doing?"

"I am motoring around the island but I can't see Rosie or Kahaya."

"We have our mast head light on, but I'll flip on our spreader lights too."

Rupert chimed in and said they'd do the same.

Putting myself in Anne's place, I asked Paul if she might need some help anchoring.

Paul pushed the button on the transmitter, and offered his help.

"That would great," Anne said with relief, "Then you can lead me into the anchorage. It is so dark out here, I can't see a thing."

I hugged Paul then watched him disappear into the stormy darkness. Minutes later, he re-emerged on the bow of Scott Free, our dinghy tied to her hip. I was elated to see Scott Free, and awed by Anne's bravery and competence.

We collapsed into bed that night to awaken the next morning with tragic news. The man who had been desperately trying to get back to his boat had been found dead. He had drowned with a rope tied around his naked body, presumably trying to swim out to his boat.

On May 29th, we left Panama for the Galapagos. Rather than sail a direct route, we were going to sail south along the Ecuador coastline. We would give Malpelo Island a wide berth, as pirates had been reported in the vicinity, and then "catch" the South Equatorial current heading west to the Galapagos Islands. It was a 900-mile trip and we figured it would take nine to 10 days.

Historically, there were two entry ports to the Galapagos: Academy Bay and Wreck Bay. Having consulted our cruising guides, we knew that neither port came highly recommended; years of inflated diesel prices and bribe-demanding officials had taken its toll.

A new entry port had just opened up, Puerto Villamil on the island of Isabela, so we elected to go there, as did Kayaha. Scott Free was meeting Oreon's niece at Academy Bay, but we hoped to catch up with them somewhere in the Galapagos or farther along in the Marquesa Islands.

Once again, we were On-the-Nose-Cherokee-Rose as the winds worked against us. It was dusk, halfway into our passage, and my watch. I was grimly sitting in the cockpit, surrounded by a turbulent, gray ocean and an equally turbulent, gray sky. I was monitoring a ship that was quickly overtaking us and had been looking behind us so intently that I had failed to notice what was happening in front of us.

As Rosie crested a wave, I happened to glance forward. Nestled among the waves was an aluminum dinghy with four hefty men in it. The shock of finding a boat 50 yards away was immediately replaced by deep misgivings. We were in an area noted for pirates; these men were in an open-air, unseaworthy dinghy over 150 miles from shore; and they were motoring directly toward us.

I leapt up and shouted to my sleeping husband in the cabin, "Grab the gun!"

I punched off the autopilot, scrambled behind the wheel and started the engine. Checking the sails and easing us off the wind, I gunned Rosie at full-throttle diagonally away from the men, the best I could do given our sails and wind direction.

Wide-eyed, Paul bounded up the steps with the gun in his hands.

"Prepare to tack," I barked, nodding toward the men in front of us.

Paul dropped the gun on the cockpit bench and released the main and jib sheets as I spun the steering wheel, making a hard right turn. Paul rapidly winched in the main sheet while I yanked the jib across Rosie's deck. It was our fastest tack ever.

Paul and I looked back at the men. They had altered course and were still pursuing us. I checked our speed: 7 knots. That was good for Rosie, but I could sprint faster than that. It wouldn't take long for those men to catch us. Paul briefly disappeared below.

He returned. "I turned off our masthead light and flipped on the radar. Let's travel in stealth-mode. We might be able to lose them in the dark."

It was getting hard to see them, in part because night was falling and in part because the waves obscured their low-profile boat. After an hour of traveling in stealth-mode, vainly searching the darkness and constantly checking our radar screen, we concluded that we had lost them. We never learned who they were or what they were after.

The next night, the radar screen had more fun for us. It was covered with large green patches, areas of rain, except for a narrow strip of black in the middle. That was where Rosie was: still dry in the black area but sandwiched between green converging rain clouds and thunderstorms. The night was so dark, it was impossible to see the rain or the waves except when lightning flashed.

I had put two wood slats in the companionway hatch, in anticipation of rain, and discovered that this was a good spot to sit. With a cushion on top of the slats for comfort, I could sit in the companionway hatch, scan the horizon around us and easily see the radar screen on the nav station desk below. In addition, I was protected from the wind and rain by the dodger.

The sole problem with my new perch was that I didn't want to see the horizon around us. The streaks of lightning frightened me, as did the fact that we had a 64-foot metal mast looming above us. It was the tallest point for miles around, and begged for a lightning strike.

If a boat is struck by lightning, the electrical surge often blows out the metal through-hull fittings, leaving underwater holes in the hull which subsequently cause it to sink. While we had a life raft on board, there was no guarantee that it would inflate when released.

All in all, it was best to avoid the lightning. I studied the radar screen. Ahead of us and slightly to the right was that narrow strip of rain-free and hopefully lightning-free black.

Two clicks to the right should do it, I thought.

I adjusted Bob, the nickname we had given our Robertson autopilot, accordingly. Bob's control panel was adjacent to the companionway hatch and easily accessed from my new perch. I checked the radar screen. We needed another click to the right. I adjusted Bob. The green rain patch on the right had shifted toward us. I gave Bob two clicks to the left. Then another two. I checked the radar.

I had invented my own video game, with the radar screen in front of me and the steering controls next to me. The object of the game was simple: Keep Rosie dry. And I was hooked. I was so intent on the game that I forgot to wake Paul for his watch.

When he woke up at 3 a.m., an hour after his watch was supposed to begin, he found me with my eyes glued to the radar screen and my fingers on Bob's controls.

"Come on, Kel," Paul cajoled, "lay down and get some sleep."

"No, no. You won't do as good of a job as me," I complained. "You'll get Rosie wet." I pointed to the predominantly green radar screen and comprehension crossed Paul's face.

He laughed, "Is that a challenge?"

"I better wake up and find a dry boat," I grumbled, feeling I had reached an advanced level in my video game and had to relinquish it to a beginner.

"Don't worry. She'll be dry," Paul reassured me, as I reluctantly climbed over the lee cloth into my bed.

The storms passed, the wind died and the sun came out.

So did a big, black military helicopter. We were still running parallel to the coast of Ecuador, about 150 miles offshore, and I was startled to see another sign of human life. Upon spotting us, the helicopter descended until it was about 120 yards above the water and circled us.

"Paul, there's a helicopter circling us," I said loudly, hoping to awaken my napping husband.

"What?" Paul mumbled.

"There's a helicopter above us."

"Oh," Paul said, rolling over and going back to sleep.

I suddenly felt vulnerable. We were alone in the middle of the ocean. Why was this helicopter circling us a second time? Were those guns mounted on its sides? I leaned out of the bimini's protective cover and waved to the ominous helicopter, hoping the pilot wouldn't harm us.

It wasn't comforting to later learn that nearly 70% of the cocaine brought into America that year was transported along the Mexico/Central American corridor, including the area we were sailing in. The US Customs and Border Protection and the US Coast Guard used helicopters in this area to monitor, track and seize drugs.

Perhaps my bright smile and Rosie's walking pace – smugglers preferred "go-fast" powerboats – reassured the pilot because the helicopter flew away.

Our speed soon became a crawl when the alternator died and we were forced to turn off the engine. Because the alternator charges our battery bank, which supplies electricity onboard, we also turned off any unnecessary electrical devices. Before we flipped off the satellite e-mail system, I sent a short e-mail to Dad letting him know our situation.

"I wonder what Nigel Calder suggests?" I said, referring to the author of what had rapidly become our most-used book on the boat. I pulled out the book and looked up alternators in the index. Paul and I resumed our usual roles, me reading aloud the diagnostic and repair steps while Paul did the work. A couple of puzzling hours passed then we stopped for dinner.

After we ate, we sat together in the cockpit, marveling at the carpet of glittery green diamonds that Rosie was leaving in her wake, caused by the phosphorescence of the Humboldt Current. Other than the star-studded canopy above us, that was the only trickle of illumination to be had on this moonless, velvety night. Due to our power shortage, there were no lights on Rosie. Without the engine on, and without a whisper of wind, profound silence surrounded us.

Chuff!

I jumped out of my seat in fright. Someone? something? had just loudly exhaled next to me.

What was that? Paul and I asked each other, looking down at the water.

Chuff! Chuff!

We were surrounded by a school of dolphins that had noiselessly snuck up on us and our barely-moving boat. We had seen plenty of dolphins while on passage. They liked to swim, jump and frolic alongside sailing Rosie as if they were racing an old friend. They had always been *in action* – until tonight. Now, over a dozen of them were wallowing and lounging next to their pal Rosie. We leaned over the side of the boat and admired them. A couple of minutes later, they swam away slowly, leaving fleeting, sparkly tails of phosphorescence behind them.

The next day we tried to fix the alternator again. Hours later, Paul decided it would be easier to just install our spare one. He'd repair the broken one another day, if it could be fixed.

The wind continued to be light, and our pace remained an unbearably slow 4 knots, but we crossed the equator and reached the Galapagos Islands at last. We motored into the tiny anchorage off Puerto Villamil and dropped our hook next to Kahaya, which had arrived, disgustingly, days ahead of us.

As we covered the mainsail, young sea lions frolicked around our boat. They sped by, twisting like cork screws, chasing and diving after each other. Older, larger sea lions slept on the low stern decks of anchored fishing boats. A sea turtle poked his head out of the water and looked at us before ducking under the clear water. On a nearby volcanic rock, a marine iguana sunbathed. We had definitely arrived in a special place.

Paul went to Puerto Villamil to clear Customs and Immigration while I tidied the boat. Except this time I had help as Howie proudly came down below and plopped a dead, stinky, flying fish at my feet.

Purr-purr, he said, looking up at me expectantly.

"Good boy," I exclaimed, scooping him up and rubbing his head. He purred and licked my face before I put him down and threw the dead fish overboard. Another minute passed and plop! Howie dropped another flying fish at my feet.

"Good boy," I said, laughing and petting his back.

He was so happy, his purrs became interspersed with squeaks.

Paul arrived in time to see – and smell – the third flying fish Howie found.

We joined Howie on deck to search for this marine version of road kill, not to take away Howie's fun but to spare ourselves the stench. We flicked nine more overboard, lifting up the canvas covers for the spare diesel cans on deck as well as checking under our windsurf boards tied near the bow. We thought that we had found all of them. Over the next couple of days, Howie proved us wrong by bringing three more to our attention.

Isabela Island consisted of six gently sloping volcanoes, five of which were active. One day, with Kahaya and a French boat, we took a horseback riding and hiking expedition to the top of the world's second largest volcano crater. The hardened black lava flows, and the complete lack of vegetation – save for a couple of hearty ferns clinging to the interior of a steaming lava hole – had me feeling like an astronaut, exploring some faraway planet.

On the way down the mountain, we rode in the back of a topless jeep, leaving the arid lava fields for the dark, shaded and humid mid-levels, which were full of orange, grapefruit and guava orchards. Back in Puerto Villamil, we encountered hundreds of pink flamingos fishing in an inland lake and visited the Giant Tortoise Breeding Center, where we saw several different types of tortoises.

Sleepy Puerto Villamil, with a scant population of 2000, came alive on Sunday when the weekly supply boat arrived and anchored near the pier. A hundred eager villagers crowded the shore around the pier to watch the supply boat unload. We watched the spectacle from Rosie's cockpit. Cows were shooed off the boat to swim ashore, herded by a man in a wood dinghy; bags of concrete mix, flour, and clothing were brought ashore on flat-bottomed boats. Even a car was precariously unloaded on a nearby beach.

Sunday evening was the best time to shop, after shopkeepers unpacked their new wares. We joined the villagers walking into town. While we didn't need a cow, concrete or clothing, I did get 40 passion fruit for $2, 40 oranges for $4 and 20 croissant-like rolls for $2 at a local bakery. I was preparing for our upcoming passage. Paul was also getting Rosie ready. He went into town to inquire about buying diesel and was told, no problem, a boat would come out to ours. Sure enough, an old man drove one of the flat-bottom boats out to Rosie; on deck was a large drum of diesel. No gas spigot, no pump.

Because neither of us spoke Spanish, I watched Paul playing charades, trying to ask the old man how the diesel was going to get from his drum into our tanks. The man showed us. He stuck a long hose into the drum and the other end into his mouth. Before we could protest, he sucked the air out of the line, thrusting the purged hose into our tank and spitting diesel out of his mouth. Horrified, I rushed to get the man a glass of water to rinse his mouth out.

That evening, all of the cruisers got together on Kahaya for sundowners. We sipped our Panamanian beer, and chatted about our upcoming 20- to 30-day passage; everyone was sailing to the Marquesa Islands. The closest island group in French Polynesia, they were located 3,000 miles west, and slightly south, of the Galapagos Islands. It would be the longest passage of our circumnavigation.

Paul admitted, "The worst thing about passages is not being able to sleep with my wife."

I blushed at the unexpected compliment while the others chuckled.

"What do you mean?" asked David. He was German and sailing with his girlfriend on one of the other boats in the anchorage. "We sleep together every night."

Puzzled, I asked him how they did that.

"Well, we both climb into the same bed…"

"No," I said impatiently. "How do you do that and keep watch?"

"We set the radar alarm," David said matter-of-factly. "If any boat comes within 12 miles of us, the alarm goes off and I get up."

"No one is awake on your boat when you are sailing?" I asked, still trying to comprehend this novel, if dangerous, concept. What if he slept through the radar alarm?

"How irresponsible of you," Judy said. "But thanks for telling us. Those of us who keep watch will now know to avoid your boat."

I had been thinking the same thing but hadn't dared to say it. I was inexperienced, but Rupert and Judy had already sailed around the world two times. They were veterans. They knew better.

David scowled, and his girlfriend's smile faded; the warm camaraderie was over. Within minutes, they made their excuses and left.

"I think we'll let them get a head-start to the Marquesas," Paul said.

Our conversation shifted to one of its islands, Hiva Oa, and to Atuona Bay, which was our next port-of-call. When Rupert had been a teenager, he had lived on Hiva Oa with a local family for several years. He was excited to see his adoptive parents and siblings.

"You know, if the locals find out that you can't have children, don't be surprised if they give you one of theirs."

"What?" Paul said, perking up. "They'd give us one of their kids?"

"Yes. Adoption is very common in the Pacific. If you," Rupert nodded toward me, "were Marquesan and couldn't get pregnant, and your sister had several children, she'd give you one of hers. She would always be the child's mother, but you would, too."

I sat back, stunned by the generosity of the Marquesan people and the simple truth that a child could have two mothers. This was the first time I had thought about adoption, and while the cultural difference was interesting, it didn't have any bearing on us. After all, we still might get pregnant. In fact, my friend Diane thought that a stress-free life, living on the boat, was just what Paul and I needed to conceive a baby. Of course, I wouldn't exactly call our new life stress-free.

Paul eagerly said, "Who do we ask? What do we say?"

Rupert and Judy chuckled, not realizing how serious my honey was.

I inwardly winced at the hope I saw on Paul's face. Did he really believe that someone was going to give us a baby?

Land Ho! after Twenty-two Days at Sea

Pacific Ocean, June 2002

We left the Galapagos for the Marquesas at 10 a.m. on June 19th, escorted briefly by three sharks. Once we were out of the vicinity of the Galapagos, sunny skies and puffy, regularly-spaced, trade wind clouds replaced the gray weather. The wind was a consistent but light 8 knots, and we were going 3 knots, the speed of someone walking. Our snail's pace was killing Paul and even I was frustrated. It would take a long time to walk 3,000 miles.

The wind conditions were perfect for our spinnaker and Paul wanted to use it. Rupert had shown us how to set the huge sail in the Galapagos but I was scared. With its enormous surface area, a strong gust of wind could capsize the boat.

I sighed and wished we had bigger fuel tanks. Rosie carried 200 gallons of diesel but used roughly a gallon an hour to go 5 miles. That meant we had enough diesel for 1,000 miles, a fraction of this journey. There was no way around it: we had to sail.

"Okay," I relented, "but you have to sit with me on my watch until I get used to the spinnaker."

"Deal," Paul said, smiling broadly and bouncing into the cabin to get the spinnaker out of its locker. Apparently, Tigger was back.

After clumsily hoisting the cheerful sail, we sat in the cockpit and admired it. All of that billowing blue-and-white fabric, swishing a foot this way or a foot that way, reminded me of lady's ball gown as she danced. Rosie certainly liked it, as her speed crept up to a constant 4.5 knots. Dancing to the Marquesas was better than walking any day. And my fear was unfounded. The trade wind was so constant we left the ball gown up for eight days and nights.

Night time was amazing. There were thousands of stars, and they covered the sky from horizon to horizon. On several occasions, I saw a ship's light appear on the horizon, causing me to flip on the radar to track its course. But there was nothing ahead of us. The bright light that had miraculously appeared was a rising star.

As the night progressed, I watched the dome of stars rotate around us...okay, I know that the earth is rotating, and not the stars, but it sure didn't look like it. And I was surprised to see that the Milky Way actually existed outside of planetariums. The white, fuzzy band divided the night sky and inspired me to search for our pocket guide to the stars.

Paul and I started a new nighttime watch game of finding some obscure constellation and challenging the other to locate it. The challenge was even greater, considering that our pocket guide covered just the northern hemisphere and we were several degrees south of the equator.

During the day, and to Howie's delight, Paul amused himself by trolling for fish, catching tuna and mahi-mahi. To my delight, Paul filleted them, vacuum-packed them and froze them. For the first time on passage, I felt well enough to cook something more than my usual one-bland-passage-meal-a-day. I made sushi rolls and tacos; I even baked Paul a lopsided birthday cake.

Five days after Paul's birthday, the replacement alternator died. We now had two broken alternators.

"Do you think you can fix one of them?" I asked, trying to weigh the gravity of our situation. With a limited supply of diesel, we tried to run the engine only when the wind was light and when our battery bank needed to be charged. The engine's alternator provided us with the majority of our electrical power which was stored in 8 gel golf-cart batteries.

"I don't know. I guess we'll find out. In the meantime, we need to turn off all power," Paul said, adding, "Including Bob."

We had been through power shortages before, but we had never turned off Bob, our autopilot. "But we're only halfway there," I protested. What a nightmare, I thought, being tied to the steering wheel, day and night. Depending on our speed, we might be at sea for another 10 – 20 days – a long time to hand-steer.

Paul said he'd try to get the wind vane to work.

The previous owner had installed this stainless steel contraption on the back of the boat. It consisted of ropes, pulleys, a rudder and a plastic paddle that somehow steered the boat relative to the wind direction.

I was encouraged. If it worked, we wouldn't have to hand-steer. I sent Dad, and Scott Free, a satellite e-mail with an update before we turned off everything that required electricity.

I steered the boat for three hours while Paul tweaked the wind vane. He started to explain how it worked, but even the boredom of being at sea didn't make the topic interesting. After I gladly relinquished the boat's steering to the wind vane, it was time to address the broken alternators.

"What's the rush?" Paul asked me, yawning.

He had a point. A couple of hours, even a couple of days, wouldn't hurt. We weren't using any power; the wind was propelling and steering us.

"Okay," I agreed, "but let's not wait too long. We have only 50 gallons of water left, and I don't want everything in the freezer to thaw."

Over the next couple of days, the wind decreased, and so did our daily mileage. For the past two weeks, we had averaged a good 140 miles a day. But we were now almost becalmed, and our speed was hovering just below 3 knots. The depressing prospect of a 70-mile day motivated us to resolve the alternator issue.

Shortly after dinner, we got down to business. Paul put on his rock-climbing head-light; I grabbed a flashlight and Nigel. Whether the author of the boat-repair bible liked it or not, Paul and I were now on a first-name basis with him. Heck, he was an honorary crew member.

First, we performed a series of diagnostic tests to confirm that our lack of battery charging was from the alternator – and not from a loose drive belt or from a faulty circuit. The alternator was, indeed, at fault. Then Paul soldered pieces of wire to a light bulb as a diagnostic tool and we stepped through the next series of tests.

Because these tests were so involved, it made sense to

pull out the other alternator and troubleshoot it as well. In the end, Paul determined that alternator 1 had no power output, probably due to bad diodes, while alternator 2 had bad bearings and might be overheating.

It was almost midnight when we convened in the cockpit to discuss our options, if we even had any. Nigel had concluded that both alternators required professional servicing, which was obviously impossible given our mid-ocean location.

Lost in thought, I gazed at our speedometer: 2.6 knots. "Aaauggh! It'll be Christmas by the time we reach the Marquesas."

"Let's turn the engine on."

"Can we run it with a broken alternator?" I asked.

"Yeah, we just won't charge our batteries."

"Let's go!" I said, eagerly. I wanted to reach the Marquesas by Bastille Day on July 14th.

Paul wanted to know why.

"There's a big party."

It turned out we had a party – a power party – on Cherokee Rose an hour later. For no apparent reason, alternator 1 started working again. We were bewildered, but thrilled. After we charged the battery bank, we made water, ran the freezer, and even did a load of laundry. Best yet, Paul and I took a shower, our second in 20 days.

Two days later, Paul exclaimed, "Land ho!"

I jumped out of bed and sprinted up the companionway steps. It was dusk, the seas had risen and it was drizzling. In the distance, the tall, dark mountains of Hiva Oa rose dramatically 1000 meters above the sea, their peaks shrouded in clouds. The sight of them heralded the end of our 3000-mile passage.

I hugged Paul and we jumped, and danced, around the cockpit. We had done it! But we weren't done.

After days without wind, fate played an evil trick, giving us too much wind as we approached Hiva Oa. At our current speed, we'd arrive at the Atuona anchorage in Baie Tahuku during the night. Despite being sea-weary, neither of us wanted to anchor in the dark, in a harbor we didn't know. We reduced our sails to just a triple-reefed main; and I went back to bed.

The sky was still gray in the morning as we entered the tiny bay at Atuona. Paul tossed out our anchor in the murky brown water, officially ending our passage on July 12th after 22 days and 22 hours at sea. Regardless of the early hour, we celebrated with a couple of beers and a bag of chips before taking a nap.

We woke up three hours later. After being on watch for nearly 23 days, our bodies no longer knew how to sleep for more than three hours at a time. How frustrating!

Paul inflated the dinghy to go into town to clear Customs and Immigration. While I was supposed to stay on board, as part of our quarantine, I just couldn't resist the temptation of land. We motored ashore and walked up a little road. Spotting a man in a – was that a Land Rover? – I asked him for directions to Immigration.

The French man graciously took us to the Police Station, le gendarmie, which was more than a mile away from our anchorage. En route, he explained that he was a French egg farmer. I guessed the Marquesans must eat a lot of eggs, given the man's expensive vehicle.

Paul cleared us into the country while I waited outdoors, admiring the small, primitive village that was densely shaded by breadfruit, star fruit, and mango trees. Under a towering tree and looking very out of place, was a shiny, red telephone booth. When Paul returned, we got money from the portable automatic bank machine, bought a phone card and called home.

On the walk back to the anchorage, I picked up a star fruit that had fallen to the ground. A hefty Polynesian man, carrying a baby in his arms, stepped out of the doorless doorway of one of homes, sauntered over and offered, "I give you bag of star fruit for your sunglasses."

Surprised, I touched my expensive, polarized Maui Jim sunglasses, and laughed, "No, thank you. I need my sunglasses on the boat."

Paul jokingly countered, "But we'll take the baby."

"Paul-," I protested, glaring at my honey. I turned to the man, who thankfully looked confused, and quickly improvised, "He said, 'maybe.' "

The man's face brightened. "Okay, two dollars for bag of star fruit?"

I nudged Paul, who pulled out his wallet and paid the man. I grabbed the bag of fruit and swiftly pulled Paul away.

Once we were out of earshot, I demanded, "What was that? You cannot ask a stranger for his baby, even if you are joking!"

"Yeah, but how will he know that we want one, if we don't ask? You heard what Rupert said."

The yearning in his voice softened me. "Yes, I did," I replied, giving his hand a gentle squeeze. "But, honey, you can't troll for a baby."

Paul laughed at my fishing analogy and, putting his arm around my shoulder, pulled me close. "No?" he asked teasingly.

"No," I said, giving him a sideways cuddle as we started walking back to the anchorage.

My heart ached for Paul, for me, and for our plight. Our sailing adventure had done nothing to diminish his – or my - desire for children, and thus far, "relaxing" on the boat hadn't improved our fertility. I felt frustrated – and helpless. We had quit our jobs a year ago to work on the boat and begin our circumnavigation. I had hoped that a break from our jobs and fertility treatments would somehow benefit us. Maybe we would become pregnant. Or maybe we would decide that life was okay without children. But I was wrong. Nothing had changed. And I couldn't figure out how to escape this predicament.

Paul's answer – to troll for a baby - had saddened me by its desperation. My poor husband! If only I could give him what he wanted. But his action had also shocked me. It seemed scandalous, somehow immoral, to ask a stranger for their baby. We were in a foreign country, and we didn't know the customs; what if someone thought he was trying to buy a baby?! We could be thrown in jail. Just how far was Paul willing to go to get one? And how far was I willing to go along with him?

I was relieved when we hopped into the dinghy and headed home. Sailing challenged us, but at least it was a fair fight. We had a chance of winning. The same could not be said about having children. As we dinghied back to Rosie, we noticed two new boats in the anchorage; both flying the Union Jack A blonde-haired woman, roughly the same age as us, waved from the bow of one of them. That made us slow down.

When we had first met Charbonneau, I hadn't understood why Janet and Blaine were so excited to meet cruisers their own age. But as we continued to sail, Paul and I noticed that most cruisers were retired couples, typically in their 60s. While we shared the sailing and cruising experience with them – a significant commonality – we were only out here for a short while. One day, we would return to land, jobs, house payments, and maybe kids, as I was just reminded. It was gratifying to talk with others who shared similar uncertain futures.

We pulled up alongside their boat, and introduced ourselves to Carole and her husband, Alex, on Solent Venture. They, and the other boat, had just arrived from the Galapagos. To celebrate their arrival, I invited them for dinner.

I should have turned them away, and the hangover that was destined to follow, when they showed up with five bottles of wine and a bottle each of rum and Coca-Cola. After a roast chicken dinner, we sprawled out around the table, swapping stories about our travels, passages and previous jobs, laughing and drinking into the wee hours of the morning.

With wicked headaches, Paul and I pulled out our mountain bikes the next day and set off to visit Paul Gauguin's grave. Paul Gauguin (1848-1903) was a famous French post-Impressionist painter who had moved to Tahiti, where he had painted portraits of beautiful Polynesian women and island life.

My French art history teachers had neglected to mention – but our local guide, with a twinkle in his eye, explained – that Gauguin had liked young girls. That penchant had gotten him kicked out of Tahiti and he had been exiled to Hiva Oa, where his reputation had preceded him.

After a year of good behavior, the village chief had allowed Gauguin to build a house. In an effort to protect their young women, the Catholic Church had placed a two-mile ban around Gauguin's house. Despite this stringent measure, Gauguin had fallen in love with one of the girls. Wooing the girl's parents with the lavish gift of a sewing machine, her parents had allowed Gauguin to marry their daughter.

Paul was sympathetic to Gauguin's plight. The Polynesian girls were gorgeous, with their straight black hair, caramel-colored skin and friendly smiles. They were downright seductive when they danced, as we soon discovered during the Heiva celebration. Heiva, a Tahitian word derived from hei (to assemble) and va (community places), is the French Polynesian observance of Bastille Day, France's national holiday.

On the morning of the Heiva, we banged on Scott Free's boat – they had arrived sometime during the night – and invited them to come into town with us. No cajoling was necessary. With the strain of sailing, homeschooling and being cooped up on the boat since the Galapagos Islands, both parents and kids practically leapt ashore.

While we didn't know the location of the celebration, it was easy to deduce. We simply followed the crowds of brightly-clad locals walking down the main dirt road. The people weren't the only ones festively dressed. Humble fences and buildings were beautifully covered with woven palm fronds and adorned with variegated foliage, ferns, wild ginger, birds-of-paradise and red-, purple-, and orange-colored leaves.

Our unknowing guides led us to a beach-front building constructed from a hodge-podge of corrugated aluminum, woven mats, latticed plywood, and palm fronds. Outdoors, men were roasting whole pigs over open fires while inside the women dished up shredded pork; grilled slices of French bread; breadfruit cooked in coconut milk; boiled taro and strips of dried, smoked banana. At another table, men were serving free Heineken beer, which immediately drew Paul's and Oreon's attention.

The food was also free and we were given paper plates that sagged from the weight of it. The pork was delicious. The breadfruit and banana strips were surprising. I expected the breadfruit to taste sweet, after being simmered in coconut milk, but it wasn't. Fresh coconut milk, made by grating, soaking and straining raw coconut meat in water, isn't especially sweet. The breadfruit tasted as bland as a starchy potato, but with a denser texture. Together, the ingredients made a ho-hum dish. The semi-dried bananas, with their chewy texture and sweet but smoky flavor, were delicious.

After everyone ate, the dirt floor was cleared and a dozen young women appeared, wearing black bikini tops, short black sarongs and shell leis. Around their hips and ankles were garlands made out of yellow leaves or calico-colored feathers.

"What are those for?" I whispered to Paul as they got into position.

Before he could respond, the music started and the girls swayed their hips, faster and faster with the music, their garlands accentuating their every move.

"Ahh," I said.

The girls smiled while they danced, their hips gyrating

quickly while their arms and hands gracefully moved, telling a story. A couple of Polynesian men joined the next dance, their bent arms flapping and their bowed knees opening and closing in time with the women's fast footwork. The men resembled dancing roosters and the contrast between the tantalizing, graceful women and their male counterparts made me smile.

I glanced at Paul to see what he thought of their dancing. Following his gaze toward the prettiest dancer, I doubted that he was even aware of the male dancers. My honey was mesmerized. His jaw was slack and his eyes were locked on her hips as she twirled in place.

I elbowed Paul's stomach.

He gave me a sheepish grin and whispered, "I can see why Gauguin got into trouble here!"

The next day, we took the bikes ashore to buy food – and ended up bartering for most of it. We rode into the little town and found three small shops. One sold – quelle surprise! – French bread, French butter and French cheeses, including Gruyere and camembert. The shelves were also stocked with pâté and cassoulet, along with canned corned beef. I eagerly picked up a wedge of camembert cheese. It was outrageously expensive, and while I was still tempted, Paul was not. He led me into the next store where I purchased, for significantly less money, two small heads of locally grown bok choy and a bundle of those tasty dried bananas.

Disappointed that there wasn't any other fresh produce offered, we decided to explore the island on our bikes. We followed a winding road that turned out to be someone's long driveway. As soon as we realized our mistake, we started to turn around. An old man, who had been weeding a random patch of ground next to the carport, beckoned us to follow him. So we did. Leading us through a thicket of shrubs and tree branches, he pointed at a small red hut. A young man greeted us, and I asked if we could tour his garden. After scouting gardens in Philadelphia for national magazines, this was a rare chance to see a truly tropical garden. Paul's expression was less keen.

The young man, who was pleased to practice his English, took us around his enormous unstructured garden, which was packed with little treasures: patches of blooming wild ginger; orchids and vanilla beans nestled in tree branches; and fresh herbs in scattered clay pots. That was in addition to a field of banana, papaya, orange and pamplemousse – a type of grapefruit – trees.

When we ooohed and aaahed over the fresh fruit, he smiled and offered to sell us some, in exchange for money or music CDs. He preferred music - country and techno were his favorites – to money. We returned later that day and gave him one of our old country CDs in exchange for two large crates of fruit.

We would learn that bartering, rather than buying, was the preferred form of payment on these remote islands. What good was money if the store didn't have the item you wanted to buy? The islands' small basic-supply shops offered few, if any, luxury items. When a shop carried sunglasses or music, the prices were steep and the selection small. I saw a single-disk album, the only music CD in the shop, with a $40 price tag! We were glad that we had our entire music collection of 200+ CDs onboard, especially since we no longer listened to all of them.

Paul and I enjoyed bartering with this young man and talking to the locals in French. The people were friendly and our conversations made the place memorable. With dismay, we realized how much we had missed in Panama and in the Galapagos by not speaking Spanish.

There were two negatives about Hiva Oa that we wouldn't miss. First, we didn't want to swim in the murky brown water of Atuona Bay. That became less of a negative when we learned that the anchorage was teeming with sharks. Run-off from the fertile mountains deposited nutrients in the water, which attracted little fish. They, in turn, attracted bigger fish and their dorsal-finned brothers.

The second negative started inconspicuously when I discovered a wasp in our cabin. Then there were two. Within a couple of days, we had a swarm of wasps, buzzing inside the cabin and above deck. Even Howie protested at their presence, swatting them away from his face with his paw.

Paul and I were clueless. Where were they coming from? And why were they on our boat? We never figured out the second answer but, when Paul found a dead wasp under our floor boards, he figured out the first. They had made a nest in our mast, which had openings above deck and below our floorboards.

The next question was how to get rid of them. Jiggling the sail lines inside the mast might break the nest, and scatter the wasps. But scattering them wasn't good enough; they might come back. It was time to set sail.

We had read about a beautiful anchorage on Tahuata, a neighboring island in the Marquesas and a short two hour sail away, with good snorkeling and a soft sand beach. We left Atuona with our new Dutch friends, Barbara and Rene, on Sueño and our simple sail quickly became a race between the two boats. The wasps did not like sailing and quickly abandoned ship.

We dropped our anchor in Hanamoenoa Bay. Unlike the dramatic cloud-kissing mountains of Hiva Oa, Tahuata is covered with steep ridges and valleys, radiating out of the island's central mountains which are half as high as those of Hiva Oa. But the water was crystal clear, and our anchorage was pretty. The bay's palm-tree lined beach was nestled between grassy, scrub-dotted hills.

"Want to swim ashore?" Paul asked.

I looked at the enticing beach ahead of us. It looked less than a quarter of mile away. Sure.

Once our bathing suits were on, we climbed into our dinghy and put on our masks, snorkels and fins

"Ready?" Paul asked me.

I nodded.

"Let's go!" He rolled over backward into the water, and splashed playfully around the dinghy. Afraid of sharks, I carefully slid in, put my head underwater and quickly spun around, searching for predators. I could see nothing but blue water, sand and coral.

My sister and I had been competitive swimmers for 12 years. We had competed in the Junior Olympics and we swam on our high school swim team as well as on the Hong Kong Island swim team when we had lived there. In my mid-20s, I had competed in a Bud-light triathlon, swimming past two waves of contestants that had started before my wave. By most people's standards, I was a good swimmer. The threat of sharks made me an even better swimmer, and before Paul had gotten halfway to shore, I was sitting on the beach, swatting away pesky flies and biting gnats.

When we got back to the boat, I called Scott Free on the radio and told them how beautiful and deserted the anchorage was and that they should sail over. The next day, Scott Free anchored next to us, as well as five other boats who must have listened in. Over the next couple of days, we and our friends on Scott Free and Sueño hiked the hills; dinghied to a nearby village, where I thankfully convinced Paul that getting a tattoo at the local thatched-roof studio might not be a good idea; and had a bonfire on the beach. We also discussed our next destination.

Dubbed the "Low or Dangerous Archipelago," the atolls of the Tuamotus were our next stop in French Polynesia. Unlike the mountainous Marquesas, only one of the 76 atolls in the Tuamotu Archipelago is raised. The rest are only as tall as their coconut trees, making them very difficult to spot from sea. Shipwrecks adorn these low-lying atolls.

The northern atolls of Manihi, Ahe, Takaroa and Rangiroa were en route to Tahiti, which was why many yachts stopped there. Oreon persuaded us, and Sueño, that we should sail farther south, to one of the less-visited atolls.

"Let's go to Katiu," I suggested, opening our copy of "Charlie's Charts of Polynesia.". "After we visit Katiu," I continued, "we can hop over to Tahanea and stage for our passage to Tahiti."

Rene took my book and started flipping through it.
"Why Katiu?" asked Oreon.
I grinned. "Because it has a black pearl farm."
Rene chuckled. "Hey, man, she's serious about pearl farms. She's highlighted every atoll that has one!" With that, he flashed a couple of pages, highlighted in fluorescent pink, making everyone laugh.

I blushed. Rene was right. I wanted my carrot, my black pearl necklace. It was my consolation prize for staying on the boat in Panama instead of fleeing to Philadelphia like I had so badly wanted to do. Buying pearls from a farm at hopefully a discount was one of the benefits of cruising, and I felt I had earned it.

Katiu it was.

Buddy-boating to Black Pearls

Marquesa Islands, August 2002

The day before we left for Katiu, Scott Free changed their itinerary. Oreon's niece needed to fly home, and Rangiroa was the nearest atoll with an airport. We agreed to meet Scott Free in Tahiti, after we visited Katiu and Tahanea as planned.

Later, Rene asked us if we wanted to "buddy-boat."

"What does that mean?" Paul asked. This was a new term.

"That means we sail together. Then, if one of us has a problem, the other boat is around to help."

Paul and I looked at each other, puzzled. Weren't we sailing to the same place at the same time? Wasn't that the same as buddy boating?

Barbara saw our confusion because she quickly explained how, on one of their previous passages, Rene had been knocked unconscious. She had been left to sail the boat and tend to Rene by herself. Ever since then, they preferred to sail with another boat.

Okay.

We soon discovered that buddy-boating inherently meant buddy-up-anchoring, buddy-motoring if the winds died, and buddy-slow-down if one of us got too far ahead. It was also buddy-look-at-the-narrow-pass when we arrived outside of Katiu five days later.

Sueño had beaten us to the pass that leads into Katiu's

protected lagoon and the suggested anchorage. Over the radio, Rene told us he was worried about the standing wave outside the entrance to the narrow pass; he also wasn't sure if the water was deep enough for our boats.

When we arrived, Paul and I assessed the situation. We had surfed Rosie into St. Augustine over a similar standing wave. And having crossed the Yellow Bank in the Bahamas three times, our trained eyes said that the light blue water was deep enough for our boats. Since when had we become the experienced sailors?!

We led the way. I steered the boat, constantly checking our instruments for the water depth and our speed. Paul stood on the bow, navigating us around coral heads. Sueño followed. As we drew near the standing wave, our speed dropped drastically; there was a strong current opposing us. Sueño had not yet encountered the current, so they rapidly gained on us.

I pushed the throttle forward, giving Rosie a boost, while Paul ran to the stern in case he needed to fend off Sueño. They were three yards away, two yards away...then they hit the opposing current while Rosie broke through the invisible barrier. There was no time for relief as Rosie suddenly accelerated. I hastily put her into neutral. I didn't want to race into the narrow pass, or into the coral reef at the end of the pass. As we neared the reef, we saw that it blocked the entrance to the lagoon and the so-called anchorage. The chart was wrong! Now what?

On our left was a small wood pier; on our right was a concrete wharf with six kids watching us. Paul took the wheel and spun Rosie around, making a tricky u-turn given the current and the fact that we were now sharing this narrow pass with Sueño.

On land, the kids beckoned to the wharf, shouting in French that we should tie up alongside it. We didn't see any adults to consult, nor did we see any other option. I quickly dug out our rubber fenders from the cockpit locker and tied them to our port side before Paul parked Rosie against the wharf, side-swiping a coral head in the process. Sueño rafted up to our starboard side.

To celebrate, I pulled out some cold Panamanian beer, smoked salmon, cream cheese and French bread. While the four of us ate in our cockpit, kids started to appear from nowhere. Within 15 minutes, more than 30 were swimming around our boats, hanging from our mooring lines and showing off. We had arrived in Peter Pan's Never Never Land, where it seemed that only children lived. Other than the pearl farmers, the oldest person we met during our five-day stay was 16 years old.

Her name was Florentina and she didn't need any pixie dust to show us the magic of her faraway island. One day she took us snorkeling in the lagoon where gigantic coral topiaries reached for the sky, growing in a lawn of lily-white sand and surrounded by crystalline, turquoise water. Angelfish and clownfish flitted by. It was a spectacular sculpture garden, and I was weightlessly gliding through it.

Another day, Florentina took us a couple of miles across the lagoon to an islet for a picnic. There, her brother and cousins chased and speared parrotfish in the larger tidal pools with such ease that Paul and Rene decided to try their hand. While they had limited success spearing the fish, their performance caused limitless laughter from their native teachers.

In the meantime, we women built an indigenous grill. First, we gathered discarded coconut husks on the beach and heaped them into a pile. Florentina lit the pile into a small fire. Then we scooped up bags of golf-ball-sized coral pieces from the beach. We blanketed the fire with them, taking care to leave a small breathing hole. We cleaned the fish, using coral to scrape off the scales, and placed them on the coral mound to cook.

One of the boys climbed a coconut tree to retrieve the island's version of "7-Up." Indeed, the juice from young green coconuts is slightly effervescent and sweet. Lunch was served on large breadfruit leaves. For the picnic, we had brought cans of Pringle's potato chips and Marquesan pamplemousse; both treats were devoured by our hosts within minutes.

Over lunch, the kids practiced their English while we grilled them with questions about the boarding school they attended on another island, about Katiu and their lives at home. I also inquired about black pearls. Florentina's face lit up and she offered to show us how pearls were farmed. Her family had a small pearl farm, near our moored boats, and she took us there after lunch.

Like all Tahitian pearl farmers, her family grew the black oysters that would ultimately produce black pearls. To harvest naturally-growing black oysters for pearls was against the law. She waded into the lagoon, and pulled up a rope that was suspended by a buoy. A string of black oyster shells appeared; she untied one of them. We followed her to a crude outdoor table that stood in the shade of a coconut tree. On the table, I was surprised to see stainless steel medical tools and equally surprised when Florentina skillfully used them.

She demonstrated grafting. Using forceps to hold the oyster shell open, she made a small slit in the oyster's gonad. Then she inserted a small piece of oyster tissue, called a graft, and a 6mm glass bead into the gonad. If the procedure was successful, she explained, the graft would act as an irritant, causing the oyster to produce mother-of-pearl material. This would coat the bead, which would form the nucleus of the pearl.

We learned that it took roughly a year and a half to form a 1.5 mm layer of mother-of-pearl around the nucleus; larger pearls took twice as long to form. Florentina proudly told us that most of the Tahitian black pearls were produced in the Tuamotus. In our cruising guide, I had read that the majority of Katiu's 250 inhabitants were occupied with pearl farming, and, judging from Florentina's smooth surgery on this oyster, I believed it.

Paul asked if her family had any pearls they'd like to sell and Florentina shook her head. Their farm was too small. But she must have told someone about our interest because late that afternoon, three young men knocked on our boat, asking if we wanted some black pearls.

"Yes, do you have any to sell?" Paul said, leaning over the lifeline to better talk to them on the wharf.

I eagerly sat down in the cockpit while the men spoke.

The young man shook his head, and explained, "Not to sell, but to trade."

Money had little value here; we hadn't seen any stores on the atoll. The men wanted whiskey.

We had only rum.

They conferred among themselves before agreeing.

"Climb aboard," Paul invited them.

They sat down in the cockpit and marveled at Rosie's instruments. One of them put his hands on the wheel, stood up and pretended he was driving, making the others laugh.

"Can we see the pearls?" Paul asked.

One man opened his hand to reveal a dozen round and baroque pearls, in a rainbow of silvery colors. We traded a $4 bottle of rum for his treasure. Then the man sitting next to him revealed five larger pearls, all round with varying colors; a couple of spheres had slight nicks, but two looked flawless. His handful cost us two bottles of rum.

After they left, we spread the pearls out on our bed's white coverlet and examined them. They were beautiful, but their irregular shapes and sizes would not form the pearl necklace I coveted.

I needn't have worried.

The next morning, another man knocked on our boat and offered to take us, and Sueño, to his pearl farm. We climbed into his fishing boat, and he motored us to the north side of the lagoon where two thatched huts, on stilts, stood in the vivid turquoise water. He pulled alongside one of the huts.

A robust Polynesian woman warmly greeted us; she was wearing an equally robust pearl necklace whose pearls were the size of candy jawbreakers. Passing three men who were efficiently scrubbing algae off oyster shells, she led us to a table inside the hut and invited us to sit down. Then she brought out three gallon-sized plastic bags, full of pearls and sorted by color: dark, nearly black, pearls; silvery colored pearls; and almost white pearls.

"Which color you like?" she asked.

I didn't know. They were all beautiful.

"You should wear this color," she said, pushing the silver bag toward me and Barbara. "It look nice against your skin. On brown skin, dark good. On your skin, silver good."

She had a point.

I didn't think a black necklace would look pretty on me: too gothic. And the silvery colors were so gorgeous.

"Okay," I agreed.

She dumped the entire bag of pearls on a pale pink towel that covered the table. The pearls shone in silvery shades of pink, purple, blue, green, and yellow. Without thinking, I rolled my hands over the top of them, as if they were marbles.

Suddenly worried, Paul asked how much they were.

"You pick them first and then I tell you how much."

"Come on, Paul," I said, "help me. They are all so pretty, it is hard to choose!"

And it was. But we managed to select enough to form my necklace, my reward for staying on board in Panama. Paul paid in American dollars, which was the woman's preference and we left. I felt positively elated, and so did Paul. At $15 per pearl, he liked getting a good deal.

The largest pearl in my cheerfully growing collection came as a surprise. The Katiu Kids, as we now called them, were doing their usual: swinging on our mooring lines and splashing around the boats. I was sitting in the cockpit when a buzzed-cut boy with a bright smile asked if he could borrow my mask and snorkel. I hesitated. It was my only set and I didn't want to lose it. Part of exploring the South Pacific happened underwater.

"Okay, but I am giving it to you and *only* you," I stressed in French. "You are now responsible for it."

"Okay," he said, beaming. I leaned over the stern pulpit and gently tossed my snorkeling gear to him. He excitedly put on my mask and popped the snorkel in his mouth. Through the clear water, he dove 15 feet to the coral carpet under our boat.

When he surfaced, he said, "Here, this is for you."

I leaned over and took his extended gift with amazement. He had found a peacock green pearl, flawless and huge, at 14 mm.

Now I was the one beaming, "Merci!"

At night, a smaller subset of the Katiu Kids gathered on the wharf to sing and dance. Florentina played her guitar while her brother played the ukulele. Everyone took turns dancing for us, becoming especially animated whenever I pulled out our camera. When I asked the kids to pose for a photo, they eagerly complied, giving me huge smiles and Hawaiian "hang-ten" gestures.

As we watched these children dance with such ease, I was reminded of the Marquesas. While the Marquesas, with their towering mountains, waterfalls and fertile land, seemed radically different from this flat, sandy atoll, these two island groups were united by their music, dance and friendly spirit.

After five days of non-stop field trips and energetic Katiu Kids, we needed a break. It was time to head to neighboring Tahanea for some rest and recovery. Uninhabited Tahanea was appealing for two reasons. It ignited our imagination, stepping foot onto a deserted island and exploring it like Magellan might have done hundreds of years ago. And because there were no people, we could finally relax. Being guests in a foreign country all the time was exhausting.

Before we left Katiu, I printed out triplicate copies of

the photos I had taken on our color printer, glad that I had stocked up on photo paper before we left the States. I gave the photos to the children, knowing that these might be the first photos of themselves that they had ever seen. Florentina presented us with shell leis, which she and her friends had made for us. While the Katiu Kids were still sleeping, we eased our boats out of the pass early the next morning.

The easy 35-mile sail to Tahanea became worrisome when Paul reported that his arm felt numb. He had punctured his arm on a rusty chain-linked fence in Katiu. While I had sprayed his wound with an antiseptic, and put antibiotic cream on it, it appeared that his wound was infected, and that the infection was spreading.

Anne, on Scott Free, was a nurse, so I sent them a satellite e-mail to arrange a single sideband radio date. Over the radio, Anne asked me what antibiotics we had on board; I read her our list of prescriptions.

"How did you get all of those prescriptions?" she exclaimed. "I was in charge of the nurses at one of Boston's larger hospitals and even I don't have as many meds as you do."

Thank you, Dr. Smith.

She put Paul on a course of penicillin, and days later, he was cured.

We spent six days in Tahanea, walking along the deserted beach, foraging for coconuts and fishing in the dinghy. In one of Tahanea's passes, we snorkeled, drifting with the strong current over pink coral, a huge manta ray and some black-tipped sharks. We also scrubbed barnacles off Rosie's bottom, changed the oil and fuel filters, reattached the single sideband radio antenna, and repaired one of the dinghy oars.

As we set sail to Tahiti, I rejoiced that it was a mere 300-mile, or three day passage. But my joy quickly faded. There was no wind and my voice alone begged to motor. We were still buddy-boating with Sueño and neither they, nor Paul, wanted to burn diesel. So we floundered in the South Pacific, our sails noisily rippling with the lack of wind to fill them.

On my midnight watch, I sat in the cockpit, gazing at the stars in the black sky and searching for their reflection on the equally dark, exceptionally calm, ocean. Suddenly, instantly, the sky got brighter - and brighter - as if the sun had risen at warp speed. Puzzled, I stood up and leaned over the lifeline to get a better look.

A glowing green-blue ball with trailing pink and blue flames soundlessly shot past me as it was hurled from the sky. Before I could lunge across the cockpit to follow its trajectory, it was gone. Darkness fell immediately, as if someone had flipped off the light.

Dazed, I slumped on the cockpit bench, wondering what I had seen. Had I seen anything at all? I glanced around nervously; everything was as it had been. A minute or two later, before I had formulated any rational explanation, a deafening explosion rocked me out of my seat. Alarmed, I spun around, looking for its source but found only the same placid, dark and windless night.

That did it.

Spooked, I rushed down below, "Paul, wake up. Did you hear that massive explosion? This ball of fire came out of nowhere and just missed our boat!"

"What?" said Paul, sitting up with an expression of sleepy confusion on his face.

Just then, the VHF radio crackled with Rene's voice; he, too, had heard the explosion.

After a brief chat with Rene, I explained what had happened to Paul. We decided that I had seen a meteorite, and not a mistaken munitions test by the French. The southeastern part of the Tuamotus was still off limits to sailors, as the French had tested nuclear weapons there.

"That ball of fire came so close to our boat; it could've put a hole in our sails!"

Paul corrected me, "No, it would have sunk us."

I hadn't thought of that.

Nor had I thought about meteors before tonight. But I had just witnessed two scientific facts about them. Meteors can travel faster than the speed of sound. And they can generate a sonic boom in their wake. We had narrowly missed being bombarded by one and the fact that countless more meteors lurked in space was not comforting.

The weather continued to becalm us. By the next morning, the wind speed had dropped from 6 knots to 2 knots; ultimately there was none. Bored, Paul mentioned over the radio that he was going to watch the movie, "Coyote Ugly," one of a hundred DVDs we had onboard.

Barbara hadn't seen it.

"Why don't you come over?" Paul asked.

Somehow he convinced Sueño to raft up with us mid-ocean, putting a new twist on buddy-boating. Once our two boats were tied together, with just our main sails up for stability, Rene turned on Sueño's engine and propelled our boats at 4 knots. They came over for lunch and we enjoyed the movie in our "cockpit theater."

Then it was our turn to motor. As darkness descended we alternated the watches between our boats. For the first time, Paul and I slept together while on passage. Well, Paul slept. I rested, feeling uneasy about neither of us being on watch. Around 1 a.m., the waves and wind started to pick up; within an hour, we had 15 knots. We all gathered on deck, sketched out a plan and hurried to separate our boats.

"We've got to release the bow line last," Paul cautioned us. "Otherwise, we might jackknife."

The boats parted. Our relief that Rosie was safe was short-lived.

Tahiti to Bora Bora with our Cat

Society Islands, August 2002

Our arrival in Tahiti on August 21st was heralded by a dozen strong Polynesian men paddling long canoes. Steering Rosie down a narrow channel, I smiled and waved as the men passed us. Then I frowned. The deep water channel markers leading to our anchorage disappeared in a throng of anchored boats. Which way should I go? I maintained our current course while Paul went to the bow to search for the deep water channel as well as any potential danger. As we motored by a cluster of anchored boats, we passed a man on a yacht bearing the French flag.

He gave us a strange look and my instincts tingled. Something was wrong. I leaned over the side of the boat and looked forward: not ten feet in front of us was a barely submerged coral reef!

"Hang on!" I yelled to my errant husband who had been too busy admiring the other yachts to look out for ours, and turned the wheel hard over. Rosie spun around, narrowly missing the coral reef.

Living aboard the boat came with the ever-present risk of sinking. This threat had heightened my observation of our surroundings, which included the boat, the weather, and even – thankfully - a stranger's facial expression.

With a sheepish but now alert husband on the bow, we entered the anchorage in Maeva Beach. It rivaled Georgetown as the largest and most crowded one we had visited. It took us an hour to find a spot to anchor among the hundreds of yachts. Then it took us three attempts to set the anchor so that we wouldn't swing too close to any of our neighbors. Many of them were friends that we had met along the way.

From the boat, we could see our first stop on shore looming ahead of us. I suddenly craved "two all-beef patties, special sauce, lettuce, cheese, pickles, onions -- all on a sesame seed bun." That, and a large order – okay, super-size me – of French fries. Yes, the golden arches of McDonald's beckoned and, heeding the call, we devoured our first fast food fix in nearly ten months.

Then we cruised up and down the aisles of the neighboring French grocery store, the Carrefour where we drooled at the selection of fresh produce, fine wines, meat and warm-from-the-oven bread. I picked up goodies for the next couple of days and it was a luxury to have to think only that far in advance. Provisioning would wait.

That night, we enjoyed a healthier dinner, and went to bed early hoping for a good night's sleep after our passage. No such luck. During the night, the winds kicked up to 40 knots and twice, someone blasted their air horn to warn their sleeping neighbor that they were dragging anchor. Of course, no one knew for whom the horn was intended, until someone on each boat poked his head outdoors and checked. On Rosie, that someone was me.

From the commotion and lights on Scott Free's deck, I gathered that they had sounded the second alarm of the night. A 48-foot Amel had dragged anchor, and had been swept into Scott Free by an unusual underwater river current. There was nothing I could do to help them, so I went back to bed.

In the morning, we called Scott Free on the radio; they had only suffered minor damage and, like us, were continuing their anchor watch. The wind was still blowing 30-plus knots. While there was little activity on the decks of our neighboring yachts, there was a lot of activity in the water.

Throughout the anchorage and out to the reef that protected Maeva Beach, windsurfers and kite boarders were flying across the water like neon bullets and skipping over the white caps. Paul lunged from one side of the cockpit to the other, watching the show and wishing he were part of it. His yearning to go windsurfing in such great conditions finally won over the dull, but necessary, responsibility of keeping an anchor watch.

"Can't you keep watch by yourself?" he pleaded with me, "at least for awhile? Then we'll switch, and you can go out for a play."

I understood how he felt. I, too, was passionate about windsurfing, and it was torture, being stuck on the boat, when there was so much fun to be had. Okay, I said.

In a matter of minutes, Tigger had rigged his board and zoomed off. He darted around our boats, waving at our friends who had come on deck to watch him. While Paul had fun sailing around the boats, my windsurfing time was spent trying to get off a barely submerged coral reef after the wind blew me onto it. Getting off it without damaging the coral underfoot was beyond my ability and Paul finally rescued me in the dinghy.

When the wind died, playtime ended. We had two objectives in Tahiti. Get our two alternators repaired and shorten the length of Howie's upcoming quarantine in New Zealand. Our circumnavigation, based on author Jimmy Cornell's recommendation, included a 6-month layover in New Zealand. During these 6-months, cyclones commonly swept across the South Pacific much like hurricanes did during the summer months in the Atlantic. Further south than the cyclone belt, New Zealand was a safe haven during these months.

We could reduce Howie's quarantine time from six months to one month by obtaining a New Zealand Import Permit in advance. This permit entailed implanting a microchip in Howie, as well as getting a rabies shot and some blood tests performed in advance of our arrival.

Paul had been told to contact Tahiti's Ministry of Agriculture to clear Howie into their country. Another cruiser with a cat on board assured us this was just a formality, a simple phone call. We were thus surprised when the official government veterinarian, a French woman, said that she'd like to come aboard and personally inspect our cat.

When Paul and the vet returned to the boat in the dinghy, I greeted them. I offered her my hand to help her make the big 4-foot step from our dinghy to our deck but she declined. Behind her, Paul smiled smugly. She stood up and I immediately understood Paul's smile. The vet was young, pretty and wearing a very short black skirt that ruffled in the wind. Paul's smile broadened as she threw one leg up onto our toe rail and then lunged aboard.

At my invitation, she headed toward the cockpit while I secured the dinghy. Paul climbed aboard, his grin growing from this bonus display.

I gave him a playful slap on the back and wondered if our guest had intended to make such a noteworthy arrival, or if she had never climbed aboard a boat before.

Despite Howie's protests, the vet gave him a mini-physical, injected him with a micro-chip, and put a flea collar on him. Then she gave us permission to quarantine him on our boat while we were in Tahiti. If needed, he could visit a veterinarian, as long as he stayed in his carrier cage during transit.

When her brief visit was over, Paul took her ashore. As they dinghied past Scott Free, Oreon waved to Paul and the Government Vet, whose skirt continued to flirt with the wind. As soon as Paul returned, Oreon called on the radio and asked who the hot babe was.

Paul filled him in.

"Ummm, do you think I could borrow your cat for a couple of hours?" Oreon joked.

When it was time for his rabies shot, we tricked Howie to get him into his carrier cage and he meowed incessantly as we dinghied him ashore. He liked "le truck" – the name of the Tahitian public bus service – only slightly better. And he despised the vet's office, hissing and whining, as the doctor administered the shots.

"You will need to come back in three weeks to get his blood tested," said the doctor.

"But we can't," I protested.

It was already late August and we still had half of the Pacific to cross before cyclone season started in November. We couldn't afford to waste nearly month of that precious time here. I thought about our cruising plan.

"Is there a veterinarian in Bora Bora?" I asked.

There was and I made an appointment to see him in three weeks.

Paul picked up the alternator. The repair shop had used parts from both alternators to make one good one. I provisioned the boat, adding fresh produce and delicacies such as "Quack-on-a-Rack" (duck), cornichons and Gruyere cheese to our staples. I also bought a case of inexpensive French wine.

We were ready to cruise the Society Islands. Of the four

distinct island groups of French Polynesia – the Marquesas Islands, the Tuamotu Archipelago, the Austral Islands and the Society Islands – the latter are the most known. Its 12 islands are divided into two clusters, with Tahiti and Moorea being in the Leeward group while Bora Bora and Raiatea are in the Windward group. Moorea was the closest, and six easy hours later, we were there.

Like many of the Society Islands, Moorea's spectacular volcanic peaks are surrounded by a turquoise lagoon, which is protected by a barrier reef. We entered the lagoon and anchored near Scott Free, Sueño, Solent Venture and Enchanté. Enchanté was the boat that had dragged its anchor and bumped into Scott Free in Tahiti.

With pride, the locals told us that Moorea was the location for the Bali Hai scenes in the classic 1958 film musical "South Pacific." That prompted us to watch our DVD version of the film. Puzzled that we couldn't easily identify the island in the movie, we read the DVD's production notes. They stated that the principal photography of the movie was shot in Hawaii; the background photography was taken by boat and plane in Fiji and other South Pacific Islands. Given how proud the locals were, we could only assume that Moorea was one of those "other" South Pacific islands.

One day, Carole and Alex on Solent Venture - our friends from the Marquesas who had brought five bottles of wine to dinner – and we rented scooters to tour the island. Barbara and Rene on Sueño challenged us to a race, our scooters versus their thumbs. They hitchhiked to the same attractions and guffawed whenever their ride passed our scooters.

Another day, our friends on Scott Free took us to feed the stingrays. Oreon knew their location and led the way. When we arrived, a dozen sting rays appeared, as if on cue. Oreon and Paul eagerly jumped in the waist-deep, pale green water; the rest of us joined them. Paul gave me some raw fish, and with trepidation, I opened my hand underwater.

Voosh!

A sting ray glided over my hand, taking the fish. Its velvety wing brushed against my arm before it glided to the next proffered snack. After awhile, Paul and Rene grew bored of feeding the sting rays and started to pelt Barbara and me with fish pieces, causing the sting rays to converge upon us.

When I was younger, I had scuba-dived with string rays

in the Cayman Islands and knew that they are usually harmless, unless they are attacked – or stepped on. Trying not to make any sudden steps, while being pelting with fish, was not easy.

I was reminded of something our priest had said before we got married. He asked Paul and me to write down the top five things that we liked about each other. When we had finished, he said, "Read over your list again. These are the qualities that will drive you nuts later in life. Try to remember that this is what attracted you to your partner in the first place."

Top on my list had been: boyish charm.

Ah, yes. My honey had lots of it as I dodged yet another piece of flying fish above the water while trying to avoid the kamikaze sting rays below the water. Reminding myself that I liked his boyish charm – in reasonable doses – I climbed out of the water.

After six days at Moorea Island, we set sail with Sueño to Huahine Island where I surprisingly found my own Bali Hai. Following an easy overnight sail, we anchored off a small village inside Passe Avamoa. We packed a picnic lunch and set off to visit an old archeological site that another cruiser had recommended. We didn't find the burial ruins but we enjoyed the hike nonetheless.

On the way home, we stumbled across a thatched-roof restaurant, nestled between hills in a lush garden. Its menu offered organic tropical fruit smoothies, herbal teas and massages. In this unlikely setting, we listened to New Age music while slurping down our banana mango concoctions. Moorea might have been a film location for James Michener's "an island of loveliness and imagination" but I had found it here, in this perfect spot and moment.

The next morning, we waved good-bye to Sueño as they headed to Bora-Bora; we were going to nearby Raitaea. One of our guide books recommended taking a dinghy trip up Raitaea's Aoppamau River whose jungle-covered banks resembled rivers in Southeast Asia. I was intrigued.

It was late afternoon when we dropped our hook near Enchanté in the otherwise empty anchorage. Eager to get off the boat, Paul suggested that we go up the river immediately. I wanted to enjoy some quiet time on the boat, so Paul set off to "recon" the river.

An hour later, Paul returned with the biggest smile on

his face, and the biggest stalk of bananas.

"Where did you get those?" I exclaimed.

"This old man gave me them, as well as these green coconuts and vanilla beans," Paul said, tying up the dinghy and passing his treasure to me.

Once we carried everything to the cockpit, Howie came out to sniff and inspect the new items. He was particularly taken with the bananas, which had some ants, and at least one spider, crawling on them. We plunged the stalk of bananas into the lagoon to de-bug them before hanging them from the stern pulpit.

Paul held up a bottle of cloudy white liquid. "He also gave me this. It is fermented toddy made from coconut milk, and it tastes disgusting!"

Touched by this stranger's generosity, I asked, "Do you remember where this old man lives? We need to bring him some gifts tomorrow to repay him for all of this."

Paul nodded. "I want you to meet him because he raises fighting cocks. He showed me his prized rooster and, Kel, it had metal spurs on its legs."

I shook my head with amazement, not because I approved of this gruesome sport, but simply because I didn't expect it to find it here, on a remote island in the South Pacific.

The next day, we put together our gift: a six-pack of beer and six cans of Argentinean corned beef, which I had purchased in Panama lest our freezer died again. We dinghied toward the river and were joined by Enchanté.

While we had briefly met Enchanté in the Tuamotus, and had anchored alongside of their boat in Tahiti and Moorea, we didn't really know Carl, Karen and their 6-year-old daughter Rebecca. An hour of navigating our dinghies up the narrow river and helping each other carry our boats over shoals and rocks changed that. Carl, a software engineer and project manager, and Karen, a primary school teacher, started their leisurely circumnavigation ten years ago. Their daughter was born in Aruba, and had never lived on land. They intended to cruise indefinitely,

At a bend in the river, Paul directed our two dinghies to shore. He led us up a small dirt path that was obscured by trees, making me wonder how Paul had met this old man in the first place. The wiry man gave us a broad, partially toothless smile upon receiving our gift. Then he proudly showed us his healthy-looking roosters, who were big, brightly colored and sure enough, wearing spurs.

Once we were headed down the river again, six or seven children saw us on the river bank, waved and shouted "hello." Carl steered their dinghy close to shore while Rebecca and Karen tossed out little notebooks and boxes of crayons to the kids' delight.

Well, all except one child, who shouted hopefully, "Candy?"

Karen laughed, shook her head and yelled, "Bad for your teeth."

After Raitaea, we anchored for one night in Tahaa in 125 feet of water before sailing to busy Bora Bora. With its high twin peaks, towering rock faces and green vegetation, the island is spectacular. A deep lagoon and numerous smaller islets are encircled by the island's barrier reef. Small fishing crafts, outrigger canoes, yachts and cruise ships of varying sizes cluttered the lagoon. We anchored and went ashore to reconfirm Howie's appointment with the vet and to make dinner reservations at one of the hotels. I wanted to see a Tahitian dance show before we left French Polynesia.

The day of Howie's appointment was traumatic for him and me. After my attempts to cajole him into his carrier cage failed, I was forced to jam Howie into it. When I lowered his cage into the dinghy, his paws got wet from the inch of salt water that covered the dinghy's floor which upset him even more. It didn't help that the dinghy was bucking up and down due to the white caps in the anchorage.

After I pumped the water out of the dinghy, Howie and I set off to find the vet's office, which was conveniently located on the beach an inconvenient 20-minute ride away. Howie meowed the entire time and, because I was driving, there was little I could do to console him. Howie's cries could be heard over both the noise of our outboard motor and the howl of the wind.

When we finally arrived at the vet's office, the French vet said his assistant was out of the office but he would manage. I watched as he shaved a patch of Howie's fur, causing Howie to struggle and bleed. I was horrified. The vet called for his assistant, who turned out to be his wife.

She held a crying baby and she impatiently told me to pin Howie down so her husband could take his blood. I refused. I understood that her baby was crying, but my cat was bleeding on their table. I was not a veterinarian assistant; she was.

Her husband agreed with me.

She huffed at me, strapped her baby into a car seat in the corner of the room and held Howie. I couldn't watch anymore and stepped onto the beach for some fresh air.

When it was all over, I cuddled my cat before reluctantly putting him back into the carrier case.

"We're going home, buddy," I whispered, hoping he understood me.

He cowered in the corner of his cage and, after letting out one long wail in protest, was quiet for the bouncy dinghy ride home.

Howie was 11 years old and had been with me before I'd met Paul. I was 25 years old when I picked him out of the feline line-up at a Baltimore County animal shelter. He put his paw on his cage door, as if to say hello. When I asked to hold him, he immediately jumped on my shoulder and walked around my neck.

Purr-purr-achoo!

Purr-purr-achoo!

The poor thing had a cold. Howie put his nose up to mine to smell my breath, then licked my chin. It was love at first lick.

And it was still love, after all these years. Once we got back on the boat, I stroked Howie until his purrs became blissful purr-purr-squeaks. As an extra treat, I popped open a can of albacore tuna and tried to spoon it into his food bowl, but Howie was eating it as fast as I could dish it up.

That evening, Paul and I got dolled-up for our dinner-and-dance reservation. I wore my black pearl necklace, which I had had strung in Tahiti, for the first time. Having endured terrible weather and scary passages, I felt I had earned these pearls and wore them as proudly as an athlete wore an Olympic medal.

Dinner was good, but we discovered that we had become dance critics. While the costumes, and the girls, were gorgeous, the dancing wasn't on par with the Bastille Day dancing we had seen in Hiva Oa. And for entertainment value, the show couldn't compete with the "Big Mamas" show we happened to catch two evenings later at the Bora Bora Hotel.

The hotel was located next to our anchorage and we

decided to have a drink at its beach-side bar. Paul and I were chatting at the bar when a dozen older, larger women appeared, wearing flower printed muumuu (long, loose-fitting dresses), leis and wreaths in their hair.

A man started playing the ukulele and, smiling brightly, the Big Mamas began to swing their ample hips, sway their hands and sing. After a couple of dances, they dispersed into the growing crowd and towed unsuspecting men onto their informal dance floor on the beach.

When Paul realized what was happening, he grabbed his bottle of Hinano beer and ducked behind the rectangular-shaped bar, hoping to hide. But no one got away from the Big Mamas. In spite of his protests and dragging heels, he was firmly led to the dance floor. Soon Paul had the Big Mamas laughing as he tried the Marquesan chicken dance, flapping his bent arms and wiggling his bent knees.

One afternoon, we joined a large group of sailors that were clustered around several cocktail tables at the Bora Bora Yacht club. The conversation focused on the route choice to Tonga that we all had to make. Until now, there had been one primary westward cruising route. While we had ventured off the main route to visit Katiu, and its pearl farms, that had been only a slight detour.

Now a cruiser could opt to sail a more northerly route to Tonga, possibly stopping in the Northern Cook Islands and Samoa; or sail a southerly route to Tonga, stopping in Palmerston Island and Raratonga in the Southern Cook Islands. Knowing that more people chose the southerly route, Paul and I felt inclined to go north. So did our friends on Enchanté and Scott Free. Sueño, Solent Venture and Spirit – crewed by a Kiwi/American couple we had just met – were heading south.

After the conversation broke up, Cathie from Spirit came over. She asked if we'd like to bicycle around the island the next day with her and Stuart.

Sure.

As Cathie left, she said, "Don't forget to slip, slop, slap."

Huh?

She laughed at our expressions. "That's Kiwi for slip on a t-shirt, slop on some sunscreen and slap on a hat." According to her, there was a hole in the ozone layer over New Zealand, causing the Kiwis to be "sun-smart."

Stuart had already completed one circumnavigation

and, having been to Bora Bora before, was a great tour guide. We ate pizza for lunch at a roadside shack aptly called Pizza Hut and we drank cold beer at Bloody Mary's, following in the celebrity footsteps of Marlon Brando, Rod Stewart and hundreds more who had visited this thatched-roof bar and restaurant. When we got back to Rosie, it was dinnertime. I lit the stove just to have the flame die a minute later. We were out of propane.

The next morning, Paul strapped the empty propane tank to the back of his bike and we rode to the propane filling station we had seen the previous day. Unfortunately, the shop could not refill our tank as our American valves and fittings were not metric like the European ones they used.

Paul said he could jury rig a connector and hose so we bought a full, but rusty, European tank. Once he fashioned a connector, using 10 different adapters from his box of plumbing bits-and-bobs, we were faced with the question of how to force gas out of the full tank and into the empty one. Paul hung the full tank from our mast, hoping the afternoon sun would heat the gas. As the sun set, the gas would condense and gravity would force it down the hose, through Paul's connector, and into our tank. That was Paul's theory and – lo and behold – it worked.

Once the rusty tank was hung up, Spirit and Scott Free both called to say that the neighborhood had really "gone downhill." Then they joked that they were going to move their boats in case ours exploded. Our radio chatter must have piqued some concern because we had a couple of dinghies drive by slowly, scrutinizing Paul's contraption.

On Thursday afternoon, the 26th of September, we left French Polynesia and headed toward Suwarrow, a bird sanctuary, in the Northern Cook Islands. Enchanté left at the same time and for awhile we chatted over the VHF radio. A little over a day later, we needed the single sideband radio to communicate because Rosie had zipped away from them during the night.

After fighting to pull down our sails on deck during our maiden voyage, Paul had insisted on rigging all of our reefing and sail lines back to the cockpit. That meant that we could adjust our sails -- taking them in during a storm or letting them out in light winds -- within minutes and without leaving the safety of the cockpit.

By contrast, in order to reduce sail on Enchanté, as on

many other boats, someone had to walk forward to the mast, which could be risky at night -- and dangerous depending on the weather conditions. As a precaution, Enchanté had a boat rule: they reduced sail at dusk. And that gave us a competitive edge, which we didn't know we had -- until now.

John and the Sharks of Suwarrow

Pacific Ocean, September 2002

On the third morning of our passage to Suwarrow, I spotted a whale's tail gliding into one of the frolicking six-foot waves that followed our boat. I searched the gray water for the whale's body; I searched the gray sky for its water spout, but to no avail. The only thing I found was gathering, dark clouds: evidence of an approaching squall that was going to overtake us.

Anticipating its imminent arrival, I woke Paul. With the wind coming from almost directly behind us, we were sailing wing-on-wing. I partially furled our front sail, the jib while Paul reduced our mainsail by putting in two reefs. Within minutes, we were doused by torrential rain which flew horizontally into our cockpit, riding on 40-knot winds.

Suddenly Bob, our autopilot, beeped twice and died.

I scrambled behind the wheel to steer the boat while Paul sat down at our wet instrument panel to assess what had happened.

"The rain must have somehow short-circuited Bob. We need to take off Bob's cover and dry out the circuit board before the moisture rusts or corrodes anything," Paul said, thinking aloud. "Do you still have that can of compressed air for your camera?"

"I do," I said. "But why don't we bake Bob? We can put him in a low temperature oven; make it sort of like Arizona in the summer time. That should dry him out."

When the rain momentarily ceased, Paul removed Bob's cover and popped him into the oven.

An hour later, Bob was back in business much to my relief. It was hard steering the boat when there was no landmark or physical reference point to steer toward. Only the needle on the compass pointed the way to Suwarrow, and that swung like a clock's pendulum with each wave we surfed. Bob was definitely "the man" for the job.

The stormy weather continued throughout the day and into the night.

Around midnight, Bob beeped, and died, again.

Clipping my harness' tether to the boat and shouting to wake Paul, I rushed outside and resumed my position behind the wheel. I looked ahead of Rosie. It was pitch black. I couldn't see anything.

"Keep us on course, Kel." Paul warned me, stepping into the cockpit and strapping on his harness. "We don't want another accidental jibe."

"I know! I know!" I snapped.

Two days earlier, after Rosie had surfed down a wave, she had rounded up slightly so that the wind had no longer been behind us. The wind had caught the back side of our mainsail and would have slammed it and the boom across the boat if it hadn't been for the preventer that Paul had rigged. The damage was limited to a broken shackle and a busted double block on the preventer. Without the preventer, the force might have broken the boom's gooseneck, the standing rigging which supported the mast, or the mast itself. Accidental jibes were to be avoided at all costs.

I had to keep the wind behind us; I had to stay on course. I looked behind the boat to check the direction of the waves; they usually followed the same direction as the wind. I saw a black void. I looked down at the compass to check our bearing. It, too, was black.

"Is there a light for the compass?" I asked urgently. "Or a flashlight?"

"I'll get one," Paul said, bounding below and returning a moment later. He flashed the light on the domed glass of the compass.

As it had done earlier in the day, the needle swung ninety degrees to and fro with each wave we surfed. In addition, I couldn't steer the boat while holding the flashlight. Rosie didn't have power-steering, and it took two hands to turn the rudder against the forceful water that rushed past it. Suddenly a wave sprayed us from the starboard side.

"Bear off," Paul ordered, twisting the wheel out of my hands and narrowly avoiding an accidental jibe. Once Rosie was back on her down-wind course, Paul explained, "When I felt that spray, I knew the wind was on our beam. You need to steer to the wind, Kel. Ignore our bearing. Feel the wind."

"Yeah, right," I muttered.

While Paul pondered why Bob had died again, I pondered the wind. I closed my eyes and concentrated on feeling the wind, and more importantly, its direction.

Wind on the back of my head was good.

Wind tickling my ear was a warning.

Wind on the side of my cheek was dangerous.

I was Woman-with-Wind-in-her-Hair. I was a Native American squaw, steering her canoe, following the whispering winds.

But the winds weren't whispering; they had started to wail. Paul must have heard it, too, because he poked his head outside.

"Look at that!" he said, pointing to the wind speed indicator.

I opened my eyes and looked. We had 60 knots of apparent wind. Given our boat speed of 8 knots, that meant that the true wind speed was 68 knots. Seventy knots qualified as hurricane force, according to the Beaufort Wind Scale. Then I heard the hollow sound of wind blowing in my ear – and hastily altered course.

"Sorry, Woman-with-Wind-in-her-Hair needs to concentrate," I replied, shutting my eyes and trying to feel the direction of the wind.

Paul laughed, and, satisfied that Rosie's reduced sails could handle the nearly hurricane force winds, went down below.

For an hour and a half, I steered Rosie up and down unseen waves in utter darkness, using only the wind as my guide.

And then, thankfully, Bob was back. Paul reinstalled him and then "waterproofed" him by covering Bob with a ziplock bag and a frame of duct tape. It wasn't pretty, but it was functional. On-the-spot ingenuity was essential on the boat and I loved having my own MacGyver on board.

Like the Tuamotus, Suwarrow was only as tall as its

coconuts trees and we were mere miles from the island before it even registered on our radar screen. A half an hour later, on the morning of October 1,st we finally spotted the southernmost atoll in the Northern Cook Islands. Like the atolls we had visited in the Tuamotus, Suwarrow consisted of a ring of sea-level islets enclosing a central lagoon.

We took down our sails and motored into the lagoon's main pass. Paul was on the bow, directing me around coral heads, and toward the charted anchorage off a larger palm-covered islet. There was a single boat, flying the French flag, at anchor.

Behind the wheel, I divided my attention between steering the boat, watching Paul and listening to boat sounds. I heard the bilge pump toggle on and off; the clatter of the diesel engine, and the splash of coolant water as it squirted out of the exhaust pipe and into the lagoon. There was another sound, faint and rhythmic, something not normal. That was bad.

"Paul," I yelled to him, "Would you come back here?"
He did.
"I hear something; it's a faint, tap-tap-tap sound."
He listened, but shook his head; he didn't hear it.
We both listened again.
"It's getting louder," I said, concerned.
"Now I hear it."
Paul descended into the cabin. "It's not coming from down here."
The sound was growing and, we deduced, not coming from our boat.
"There," I exclaimed, pointing toward the partially shaded beach.

Under a palm tree, a wiry man wearing a short sarong around his waist was beating a drum – a hollowed out log - on the beach, welcoming us to his island. It was John, the sole inhabitant of Suwarrow, and the caretaker of this Northern Cook Island's bird sanctuary.

A sailboat that had left Suwarrow yesterday had warned us over the SSB radio: their three-day visit had turned into three weeks. We chuckled, not knowing that our intended four-day stay would slip into 16 magical days.

Behold the power of John.

John, a native Cook Islander who was probably in his late 60s, taught us how to climb a coconut tree, how to make brooms from braided palm fronds and how to tell if we had a tuna or mahi-mahi on the fishing line by the way it tugged.

"Oh, you got a tuna," John said to Paul as he fought to bring in his catch. "See how you got two twitches at a time on your line?"

One morning, we asked John how to catch lobster; according to cruisers on the French boat, they were plentiful.

John waved at the gash on his leg, a shark bite that had been stitched up by a retired doctor on a previously visiting yacht. "I would take you, but I can't get wet for three more days," he said apologetically. "But you find lobsters on the reef. Reach into a hole; pull out lobsters."

Sounded easy enough. Paul and I eagerly walked on the islet's adjoining reef at low tide and, wearing neoprene gloves, Paul reached into a hole. No lobster. We checked another hole and another. There were no lobsters to be found.

The next day, we asked John again. Maybe we had misunderstood him.

"You find lobsters on the reef. Reach into a hole; pull out lobsters."

Once more Paul and I walked around the reef, baking in the sun and discovering even more empty holes.

The third morning, exasperated with his dim-witted students, John led us to the same reef that we had been fruitlessly searching. Instead of going to the lagoon-side of the reef, as we had, he took us to ocean-side. He reached into a hole and pulled out a lobster, and another, until he collected nine from the same hole. Then he took a couple of steps to another hole and pulled out six more. Giving us an appraising look, he repeated, "Reach into a hole; pull out lobsters." How had we failed to follow these simple instructions?

John grilled the lobsters over a coconut-husk fire, and we enjoyed them with him and our Enchanté friends at our nightly potluck dinner at the Suwarrow Yacht Club. We were surprised to find a yacht club on this nearly uninhabited island and were amazed to learn that John had specifically built it for visiting cruisers. The yacht club was housed in the covered area under a stilted thatched hut, which rested on palm-tree trunks one story above the ground. There was a kitchen sink, fed by a hand-cranked water pump, as well as plenty of mismatched plates, glasses and silverware. Colorful signal flags hung next to a beautifully carved varnished driftwood sign that proudly said Suwarrow Yacht Club. It was, by far, the nicest building on the tiny islet.

Before the French boat had departed, the woman had taken me aside. She had quietly explained that the nightly potluck dinner enabled cruisers to share their food with John. The supply boat that carried John's essentials like food staples, gasoline and fishing supplies was over three months late.

At one such dinner, we finally got John to tell us a little about himself. He told us that he had won a Cooks Island competition by diving to 30 fathoms – 180 feet – without scuba gear.

He had also received the British Empire Medal (BEM) from the Queen of England for his charitable giving. It seemed that one day a boat had arrived in Suwarrow, carrying half a dozen Cook Island scuba divers. The divers had come to gather up the atoll's black oyster shells, as there had once been a pearl farm in the lagoon. They were going to take the shells back to Raratonga to carve and sell as trinkets for the tourists. John had listened to their plan and politely accommodated them, but he didn't help them. The divers left empty-handed.

Fearing they might return, John had collected all of the black oyster shells he could find, which had been a sizeable amount. He gave them to the hospital in Raratonga, for which he had received the BEM.

We sat in awe, listening to this incredible man. Naturally, we were all curious about his healing shark bite, which he had gotten three weeks earlier while spear fishing. Paul and I had never been to an atoll with so many sharks; and these weren't the more benign white-tipped or black-tipped ones. These were the gray, "Jaws" variety. Three of them routinely circled our boats in the anchorage; another gang hung out by the pass to the ocean.

John explained how he had fought a shark – and won. He and his nephew, who occasionally visited him, had been spear fishing in the lagoon. Suddenly, a shark that had been circling ambushed them. Stepping in front of his nephew to protect him, John had intercepted the shark. Thrusting his hands into the shark's gills, John had flipped the shark over, onto its back. Belly-to-belly, they had wrestled until the shark had wriggled itself free and disappeared into the deep blue.

If I had to go swimming with sharks, I wanted to be swimming next to John. And that's what I did a couple of days later.

On the beach, I had found a beautiful leopard cowry shell, but couldn't find any more. The guys were planning a fishing trip, so I asked John where I might find some more pretty shells. I figured that Karen and Anne, as well as the women on the two other boats in the anchorage, might be interested in strolling along the beach and collecting shells with me. John said we'd have to take someone's boat across the lagoon to find shells. The prospect of exploring an untouched beach convinced all of the women to join me.

Armed with sunglasses and sun hats, the women, John and I set off on a boat from California. As we motored across the lagoon toward the islets on the other side of the atoll, we came to the edge of a submerged reef.

"Drop the anchor here," John said.

Puzzled, we women looked at each other. Where was the beach?

Then John stripped off his shirt, picked up his mask, snorkel and machete, and jumped in the water. He spun around to face the boat, clamped his machete between his teeth and looked up at us expectantly. What could I do? I shrugged apologetically to my friends, stripped down to my bathing suit, borrowed a mask and snorkel and slid into the water. Everyone else gamely jumped in.

We were in about 12 feet of water over the reef. John nudged my arm and pointed to some coral on the reef below us. He dove down, wrestled a black oyster shell from its coral neighbors and swam to the surface. Then he took his machete, chopped off the barnacles and other bits clinging to the oyster's shell and passed it to me. Clenching his machete between his jaws, he started swimming.

Anxious to stick with my hero, I tucked the nearly one-foot-wide shell in the crook of my arm, and awkwardly swam one-handed beside him. I wasn't about to leave his side as I had noticed two gray sharks lurking behind us like big bullies. They eerily followed us as we circled the mid-lagoon reef searching for shells with John pointing; one of us diving; John cleaning; one of us carrying.

When we were all struggling to swim with the two or three oyster shells we each carried, John led us back to the boat. I was only too happy to leave the sharks behind and anxiously climbed aboard.

Once we got back to John's islet, the guys greeted us on shore. They hadn't caught any fish and they had run out of bait.

"Where do we find some oysters?" asked Paul, a puzzled look crossing his face when all of us women started laughing.

"You should've come to collect shells," I replied, showing him our bounty.

"Wow, where did you find all of these?"

"In the middle of the lagoon."

"I thought you were going to a beach."

"So did I, honey, so did I."

For dinner, John poached the oysters in coconut milk with a pinch of curry powder. It was simply delicious which made allergic Paul pout. I wondered if these potluck dinners were really for John's benefit, as the food he brought to the table was far superior to our frozen and canned contributions.

The next day, John showed us how to make fishing lures from the oyster shells. Using a rudimentary metal blade, he cut a one-inch-wide strip of oyster shell from the center of a half-shell. He hand-drilled a hole in the thicker, hinge-side of the shell and attached a hook, also created from oyster shell, and coconut husk hairs to the other side.

"Cool," said Carl. "We saw fishing lures just like this at a museum in Tahiti."

Paul, Oreon and his son, Michael, were eager to make their own lures, but after they fetched their power tools. With electrical cords stretched across the floor, and drilling-, sawing- and Dremel- stations set up around the room, the Suwarrow Yacht Club was transformed into a work shop, with everyone intently working.

Hours later, after dinner, the Suwarrow Yacht Club transformed itself yet again, becoming base camp for a hunting expedition. The prey: the elusive coconut crab. John had agreed to show everyone how to catch these nocturnal, land-based crabs. The idea of stumbling around mangroves and brush, in the dark, searching for aggressive crabs while swatting away mosquitoes was hardly appealing. I gave Paul a good-luck peck and hitched a ride back to Rosie.

Later, a loud knock on the boat woke me up.

"Kelly, is Paul with you?" Karen shouted from her dinghy.

I groggily looked at his empty side of the bed. "No," I replied, instantly alarmed. Images of Paul sinking in quicksand while being cannibalized by coconut crabs; or Paul falling in an ocean-side crevice and being attacked by sharks;

or Paul lying unconscious, bleeding to death, somewhere, flashed through my head. I threw on clothes.

"Is he there?" Oreon shouted from Scott Free.

"No," responded Karen.

I jumped in her dinghy and we headed back to shore. Scott Free blasted its air horn, rousting the anchorage to help search for Paul.

"Where could he possibly be?" I demanded. "The islet is the size of our back yard in Philadelphia!"

And that was what worried me the most. There was no way he was lost. If he kept walking, he'd hit the beach and then all he'd have to do was follow the shoreline until it led him to the anchorage. No, something terrible must have happened. Behind us, two more dinghies motored to shore and I was grateful to have everyone's support.

Just as we landed, a sheepish Paul appeared from the dark grove of coconut trees.

"Where were you? Are you okay?" I asked, rushing up to him, and followed by Karen and the rest of the anchorage.

"Yeah, I'm fine. I got lost, and it was so dark, I couldn't see anything. When I heard the air horn, I headed toward the sound. That's how I found my way back."

After profuse thank-yous, hugs and pats-on-the-back, the rescue party quickly dispersed.

"So was it fun, hunting for coconut crabs?" I asked when we were back on Rosie.

"Kel, it was great," Paul gushed. "First, John showed us how it was done. After he found a coconut crab, he held it with his foot, whipped out his machete and cut a sliver off a nearby coconut frond. Then he tied a loop around the crab's middle with the frond and hung it on a bush while he kept hunting."

"That doesn't sound too difficult," I said.

"Yeah, well, every time I'd find a coconut crab, there was never a coconut tree within reach. So I couldn't do that frond-tying trick," Paul explained. "I'd try to shuffle the crab along the ground to get near a coconut tree, but that'd turn into a ten-minute football match. Finally I'd win and tie it up. I caught three crabs," Paul said proudly. "Then I switched off my flashlight to look for everyone, but I couldn't see or hear anything."

"Only you could get lost on a postage stamp!" I teased him. "It's a good thing I'm the ship's navigator."

Paul grinned, obviously pleased with the night's adventure.

"Where are the crabs?" I asked, realizing that I hadn't seen them on Paul.

"The crabs started fighting each other because I had to hold them in one hand while I held the flashlight with my other hand. They got so tangled up, I couldn't separate them and I had to let them go," he pouted.

Paul wasn't the only one who lost a potential meal that week.

One afternoon, Paul and I took our dinghy out of the lagoon and into the ocean to do some snorkeling. We anchored the dinghy on the outer edge of the atoll's reef just before it dropped off into deep, blue oblivion. Too excited to put on his snorkeling gear, Paul hopped in the water with his mask, snorkel and fins in his hands.

I finished getting ready and slipped into the water with our bright yellow Hawaiian sling spear-gun. It was essentially a blunt-tipped metal rod with a large rubber band attached to it. It was less accurate than Paul's pneumatic spear-gun, and it seldom speared anything. Paul thought that if I carried it, I might be less afraid of swimming with sharks.

As was my habit, I held onto the side of the dinghy, put my head under water and did a 360-degree sweep of the water, looking for predators before checking on Paul who had drifted 12 feet away.

Head down, he was putting on his first fin; he already had his mask and snorkel on.

Suddenly an 8-foot gray shark appeared out of nowhere and swam directly toward Paul, flipping a u-turn just three feet away from him and swimming away. Before I could react, the shark came barreling back, swimming closer to Paul, sizing him up, then retreating as before.

Shit. That was two drive-bys! I thought, terrified.

Paul wasn't even aware of the danger; he was still putting on his fins.

In that split second, I considered scrambling into the dinghy for self preservation – but if I did that and the shark attacked Paul, I wouldn't be able to live with myself.

The shark was returning!

There was no choice. A jolt of adrenaline and 12 years of competitive swimming ignited me as I shot to Paul. I jammed the spear into his hand and frantically pointed.

Paul looked up, and reflexively thrust the spear at the hurtling shark, grazing its nose. The shark spun around and swam away.

We did too, fear ejecting me into the dinghy while Paul stayed in the water, covering me, watching for the shark. Then he pulled himself aboard.

After I regained my composure and explained what had happened, Paul scooted next to me, and putting his arm around me, said, "Thanks, gorgeous."

Paul was clearly not as shaken up as I was because the next day he suggested that we go back to the same place to snorkel with Scott Free. He said that, while waiting for me to climb into the dinghy, he had glimpsed the drop-off wall.

"It was stunning, Kel, I know you'd want to see it."

"How can you even think about snorkeling there after yesterday's drive-bys?" I demanded.

"Because I don't have to swim faster than the shark, I just have to swim faster than the guy next to me. There'll be more people in the water today: better odds."

"Paul, that's terrible," I said, laughing and playfully slapping his arm.

Armed with the Hawaiian sling, I reluctantly went along and was glad that I did.

The side of the submerged volcano plunged steeply and disappeared into clear sapphire water. Splotches of pink-, red-, blue-, purple-, violet-, chartreuse- and yellow-colored coral covered the wall like a vertical perennial garden. Fan-shaped coral gently swayed, as if caught by an invisible breeze, while elk-horn coral loomed above the smaller coral like garden statues.

The coral was perfect, as if someone had been religiously watering and fertilizing this garden. This garden had never been beaten up by a storm, or damaged by careless anchoring. It was spectacular, and humbling in its enormity and beauty.

Just as the coral underwater was untouched, so were the birds on the islet aptly named Bird Island. Suwarrow was, after all, a bird sanctuary. So it was a bit amusing that its caretaker wanted to treat us to roasted bird for lunch. Yet I understood John's desire.

His supply boat was three months late. Other than seafood, breadfruit and coconuts, birds were a natural and plentiful food source on the atoll. In addition, he was a proud man and a proud host. This was another way he could contribute to our daily potluck dinners.

One day John announced that we were going to Bird Island. Paul and I, as well as Carl, Karen and Rebecca from Enchanté, hopped aboard Scott Free. So did four young men from Chile who had just arrived on a canary-yellow yacht. They were planning to pay for their cruising trip by making television documentaries as they sailed, and by the amount of gear they lugged on board Scott Free, they were serious about it.

Once we arrived at Bird Island, Paul and I jogged to keep up with John, who swiftly walked to the heart of the islet. Red-tailed tropicbirds blanketed the ground and decorated the shrubs like fluffy Christmas ornaments. Everywhere birds sat, flew, roosted, preened, ate, slept and cawed. An acrid stench from bird droppings matched the size of the bird population.

John walked up to two birds sitting under a bush, pulled out the smaller, juvenile one and whacked it over the head before putting it into a bucket. Once he had collected – and that's what it was – enough for our group, he sat down on a patch of grass and prepared them. Within three minutes, he had cut off their wings and feet. Plucking was way too inefficient. John just pulled off the birds' skin as if they were wearing down T-shirts. This, too, was accomplished within a matter of minutes.

Almost everyone else missed this demonstration because the dinghy had not yet returned with the second load of people. Two of the Chileans managed to film the latter part of the process; they had missed the beginning because the weight of their gear had slowed them down. After two weeks of being in Suwarrow, Paul and I had learned to stick close to John.

Other than birds, scrub and small bushes, Bird Island was barren, so we walked to a neighboring islet, covered with coconut trees, to cook the birds. As we made our way across the connecting reef, I threw chunks of coral to scare away small, encroaching sharks. They congregated in the reef's shallow tidal pools and had no fear of us.

Once on land, John chopped down some palm branches, shaved off all of the fronds and used them as spits, roasting the birds over a coconut husk fire. Forty five minutes later, Bird-a-la-John was done. Beaming, he passed out lunch. To me, the meat tasted like salty duck; someone else thought it tasted like lamb.

John smiled and said, "Tastes better than chicken."

For dessert, John cut open several germinating coconuts – seedling trees - and we sampled their sweet, spongy center. Who knew that the humble coconut could be consumed in three forms: as an effervescent drink, a meaty fruit and a marshmallow?

To repay John for his hospitality, we built raised flower beds around the Suwarrow Yacht Club and planted them with flower seeds that Scott Free had on board. When John complained about being awoken at dawn by buzzing mosquitoes, Enchanté donated a mosquito net and hung it around John's cot in his little hut.

The next morning, John complained that the mosquito netting blocked the wind, making his bed too stifling for sleep. We gave him one of our spare 12-volt fans. Paul installed it above John's bed, wiring it to the existing 12-volt system that appeared to be fueled by solar panels on the hut's roof. When Paul flipped the switch, neither the fan nor the lights worked.

Instead of the quick one-hour job Paul had envisioned, getting the fan to work took most of the day and required troubleshooting John's entire electrical system. In the process, Paul discovered that the solar panels weren't producing any output, and upon climbing on the roof, found that they weren't even connected to the system.

While Paul fixed the electricity, I went with John to his radio room which was housed in yet another little hut. Every week, John had a scheduled SSB radio chat with the Prime Minister of the Cook Islands.

He chatted awhile in Cook Island Maori and suddenly passed me the transmitter. "The Prime Minister wants to speak to you."

I took the mic and introduced myself, saying what a wonderful time we were having in Suwarrow and what an asset John was to the Cook Islands, both as a caretaker and good-will ambassador. I also inquired about the supply boat, reminding the Prime Minister that it was already – ahem! – three months late. He assured me the ship was on its way which was a relief.

Because most cruisers sailed south to New Zealand or Australia to avoid the November-to-April cyclone season, we figured we might be the last boats to visit John's atoll for the next six months. Before we left, I went through our food lockers and filled four grocery bags for John, and so did Karen and Anne. We also gave John whatever gasoline we could spare. He needed it to run his small generator and for his fishing boat's outboard engine. Smiling, he said that he didn't need anything because his friends, "the yachties," took good care of him. We knew the opposite was equally true.

Before we departed for Tonga – we had spent too much time in Suwarrow and were forced to skip Samoa -- Paul and I handed John our passports and the park entrance fee. He refused to take our money, saying that we had already paid in other ways, and stamped and signed our passports. Next to his signature, he wrote BEM.

With lumps in our throats, we sadly walked back to our dinghy, passing a sign noting that Tom Neale, a New Zealander, had lived alone on this island for three long stretches from 1952 to 1978. While his 1966 book, "An Island to Oneself," had made Tom Neale and Suwarrow famous, Paul and I knew that Suwarrow was really John's island.

As John beat his drum for us, we left Suwarrow with Enchanté and Scott Free. Scott Free was headed to the Haapai group of the Tongan islands while we, and Enchanté, were going farther south, to Nuku'alofa, the capital of Tonga. Tonga would be our last stop before sailing to New Zealand for the upcoming cyclone season. Paul, Howie and I were all seasick before we lost sight of Suwarrow's coconut trees, but Rosie took good care of us, completing the 860-mile trip in seven days.

Our welcome to the Kingdom of Tonga on October 22nd was less than hospitable.

Spin Cycle to New Zealand

Tonga, October 2002

"Bring your gun and bullets to this office within 24 hours," the Tongan Customs officer gruffly told Paul. "If we don't have them by this time tomorrow, you will be forced to leave the country."

Surprisingly, Tonga was the first country that wanted to retain our shotgun.

The next morning, we toted the "harmonica" to the Customs office, which was located in a little shed on an abandoned lot near the waterfront. Three huge Polynesian men in black satin skirts, the official uniform of the Kingdom, greeted us at the door and ushered us into the dimly lit room. One of the men opened the case, pulled out the gun and fondled it while the other two men silently watched.

"Where are the bullets?" the man holding the gun asked.

Paul unzipped his backpack and pulled out the plastic bag containing the slugs, "Here."

"How much did you pay for these?" the man asked.

Puzzled, Paul asked, "Why? Are we going to have to pay Customs' duty on them? Because I don't remember how much I paid."

"No," the man replied. "I want to buy some."

Paul and I glanced at each other uneasily. All of our guidebooks said that it was illegal to sell ammunition to the local people. Even Customs officers in previous countries had given Paul the same warning. Two of the intimidating men stepped closer to Paul. So did I, hoping to give Paul a little moral support. Paul hemmed and hawed.

Frustrated, the man waved us out of the office, "We'll discuss this when you pick up your weapon."

Perhaps it was the hostile welcome, or the prospect of a hostile passage – our upcoming sail to New Zealand had been likened to the spin cycle of a washing machine – that made us consider Tonga more as a pit stop and less of a cruising destination. We worked on the boat and listened daily to the marine weather forecast out of New Zealand on the single sideband radio. We also went provisioning.

It had been nearly a month since we had last seen fresh produce in Bora Bora, and the market in Nuku'alofa was a haven of inexpensive fruit and vegetables. Native women, wrapped in large burlap blankets and fastened with rope belts, sold baskets and handbags. They also sold tapa cloth, fabric made from the bark of the mulberry tree and painted with natural dyes. Several shops offered carvings in whalebone, oyster shell and driftwood. We even saw lures similar to the ones John had taught us to make in Suwarrow.

Carl accompanied Paul to the Customs' office when it was time for us to leave ten days later and, thankfully, the intimidating officer who had wanted to buy Paul's ammunition had the day off. Later that day, we set sail with Enchanté. While our destination was New Zealand, there were two large mid-ocean reefs that Carl wanted to visit. We were happy to stop. Paul was hoping to find more lobsters while I welcomed any break to a potentially rough passage.

We agreed to meet at North Minerva Reef, 300 miles away, and as soon as our anchor was up, the race was on. Because Enchanté had an hour's head start, we tried to shave a couple of miles, and half an hour, off our trip by taking the South East Pass out of Nuku'alofa. Enchanté had taken the recommended route out of the North West Pass.

As we pounded into a 25-knot headwind, covering a measly 6 miles in three hours, we realized we had made a classic beginners' error. We had never considered the direction of the wind! Instead of saving time, we added another two hours to Enchanté's lead. In eight months, we had become cruisers but we still weren't sailors.

As we approached Minerva Reef, the wind died, the seas became sloppy and something was burning. I had retreated to my berth, and was fighting off waves of nausea, when suddenly I smelled smoke. I called Paul, who jumped down the four companionway steps in a single bound. He yanked up the floor boards over the engine, and black smoke poured into the cabin. He hastily turned off the engine. The muffler had cracked and spilt acrid exhaust fumes into the boat. And that was the end of me.

We were six miles away from the entrance to Minerva Reef and a storm was brewing; it was expected to bring 40-plus knots of wind that night. It didn't matter that we wanted to be safely anchored inside the reef before the storm hit. With no wind and no engine, we couldn't reach the reef before it was dark as it was already late afternoon. And there was no way we would attempt to enter the pass without good light. Reluctantly, Paul adjusted the sails so that we were hove-to, stalling the boat and readying it for the storm.

With the sun still shining and the boat going nowhere, we tried to fix the muffler by filling the crack with underwater, quick-drying epoxy. Paul was now feeling queasy, so I volunteered to help. There was no point in both of us being seasick, and I hoped to keep Paul well in case the storm struck.

Lying on the floor, I stuck my head into the smoky engine compartment and scrubbed the muffler's crack with acetone. Paul applied the epoxy as quickly as he could, before he, too, needed to lie down. With both of us ill, it was a relief that Rosie was already hove-to, and ready, for the storm.

From our lee-beds, we alternated our watches as usual, checking the horizon for boat traffic and the pending storm, which thankfully skirted us. At 3 a.m., Paul reset the sails and by sunrise, Rosie was at the entrance to Minerva Reef.

The wind and the current were working against us in the pass; we needed the engine. With our fingers crossed, Paul flipped it on and our repair held – for 10 minutes. Then the smell of exhaust fumes permeated the cabin, and once again, Paul was forced to turn it off. With me working the jib and Paul handling the mainsail, we tacked, and tacked again, trying to make some headway in the pass but to no avail. We turned Rosie around and let the wind, and water, sweep us back into the ocean. It was time for Plan B.

Plan B was to wait for high tide and ride the current into the pass; but that was at least three hours away. As we prepared to heave-to for the second time, Plan C materialized as an approaching boat offered to tow us into the lagoon. Over the radio, Magic Dragon explained that they, too, had been waiting for daybreak to enter Minerva Reef. Paul made a bridle for Rosie and tossed it to our new friends. Once we were safely through the pass, Magic Dragon released us and we sailed 3 miles across the lagoon to join Enchanté.

This was our first time anchoring under sail. Prudence dictated that we anchor away from the other boats, and far away from the reef, just in case we dragged anchor. Without the safety net of an engine, we'd have to sail away from any danger. Paul and I "planned our work, and then worked our plan," successfully anchoring without any unkind words, or hand gestures.

As we sat in the cockpit, congratulating each other on our anchoring job and sipping our beer, a classic gaff-rigged wooden sailboat coasted past us. We had heard about this boat and its single-handed captain. The boat didn't have an engine, a windlass, electronics -- not even a GPS or a fridge. And the 27-year old captain read literature. While we sat and watched, he dropped his sails, then walked forward and dropped his hook with practiced ease. My beer suddenly didn't taste as deserved as it had a couple of minutes ago. Why were Paul and I toasting each other? We should be toasting this bygone-era captain.

Paul agreed, but not for the same reason. "Think about it, Kel, he actually found his way to Minerva Reef, into the 100-foot wide pass, by using just his sextant."

Paul was impressed. In Philadelphia, Paul had taken a course in celestial navigation and used a sextant, while standing on a stable shoreline – and not a rocking boat. Under these ideal conditions, his calculated position had been within a couple of miles of his actual position. Finding the narrow pass to Minerva reef required an accuracy that was magnitudes closer than several miles.

"On one of our future passages, I'm not going to use the GPS. I am only going to use our sextant," Paul promised. Or was that a threat?

Okay, I said, knowing that there was nothing to stop me from checking our position with the GPS. GPS was much more accurate than a sextant – one article said within 20 meters – and didn't require keen concentration, college-level mathematics or three-inch-thick almanacs. But if using a sextant made a passage more fun for Paul, he could knock himself out.

That afternoon, after a solid nap, Carl, Karen and little Rebecca dinghied over to our boat and asked if we wanted to catch some lobsters on the reef with them. Paul wasn't ready to face the muffler, and I longed for a walk on terra firma, so off we went.

Minerva Reef turned out to be part-time Lobster Haven; part time because the reef is completely submerged at high tide and protrudes from the water by several inches at low tide. Unlike Suwarrow's "reach into a hole and pull out a lobster" technique, catching lobsters on Minerva Reef required a wet suit, mask, snorkel and spear-gun.

The lobsters still hid in holes, but these holes were located at the bottom of eight-foot-deep ravines that were carved into the ocean-side of the reef. Paul had to dive into icy-cold water to spear them. If that weren't enough of a challenge, the timing had to be exact. Just after one wave crashed and before the next one clobbered the reef, and any unsuspecting hunter.

When it came to catching lobsters, I was definitely a fair-weather friend and there was nothing fair or friendly about those pounding, freezing waves. Karen and I took on the role of Bucket Babes, holding the lobsters that our strong men caught in our buckets and shouting out warnings whenever a wave was about to crash.

While I watched Paul dive in one of these ravines, a lobster in my bucket crawled over his mates and climbed out of the bucket, making a dash for freedom. I scurried after it and tossed it back into my bucket. But the damage had been done. I had failed to notice a wave, which was beginning to break on Paul.

I shouted a warning as the wave flipped him over and washed him ashore. Before I could dash out of the way, the wave swept him into my legs. I fell onto the unforgiving coral reef, ripping my wetsuit and gashing my leg.

As I gingerly stood up, I noticed my overturned bucket. The lobsters were making a break for it, scurrying across the reef in all directions. Paul, I knew, would forgive me for missing that wave; he would not be happy if I lost an hour's worth and probably 10 bruises' worth of lobsters. I scrambled around the reef, retrieving as many as I could.

Our lobster dinner was so good, we came back the next day. Paul and Carl were diving while Karen and I chatted about the things we planned to do in New Zealand. Suddenly, in the distance, a vision of Tongan muscular beauty appeared. Clad only in bathing trunks, the man jogged across the reef toward us. He had six-pack abs, well-defined biceps and triceps; rippling thigh muscles and cut calves. He was simply gorgeous.

Our conversation faltered, and died, at this unexpected apparition.

As he sauntered closer, and saw us unabashedly gawking at him, he flashed us a huge smile. Karen and I started to giggle and twitter like two schoolgirls.

Apparently he was used to this sort of reception, because he confidently came up to us and introduced himself.

"Hello, my name is Moeaktola Taufaahou."

Our smiles must have fallen as we both struggled to repeat his name. We wouldn't be cooing it anytime soon.

His smile, however, grew even wider as he confessed, "But my friends call me Mighty Fine."

At that, Karen and I burst into laughter.

"I bet they do," Karen said, and we both cracked up again.

He was indeed Mighty Fine.

It turned out that Mighty Fine had been a bouncer for a popular bar in Tonga until he had met his Kiwi fiancée. They were crewing on a single-handler's boat in exchange for passage to New Zealand. And that was how he ended up on Minerva Reef, inadvertently transforming two grown women into silly adolescent girls. We pulled ourselves together, welcomed him to Minerva Reef -- what there was of it as the tide was coming in -- and introduced him to our husbands.

Without any hesitation, he jumped into the icy water and dove down with Paul, bringing up his fair share of lobsters without any gear at all. Having caught 30 lobsters, we invited the entire anchorage over for dinner on Rosie.

We fully extended our salon table and set 10 places around it, nine for people and one for Howie. We feasted on lobster sautéed in garlic and butter, steamed lobster with cocktail sauce, lobster legs covered with Old Bay seasoning and Mexican lobster casserole. Accompanied by a freshly baked French bread, a green salad and several types of cheese, it was a feast by any standards, and a special one for being in the middle of the ocean.

Catching lobsters was interesting; fixing the muffler

was not. But it had to be done. One afternoon, while the tide was low and the anchorage was calm, Carl and Paul cut strips of fiberglass and epoxied them to the muffler, making a solid repair. While they worked in the cockpit, I stowed our things in preparation for our spin-cycle trip to New Zealand. Like the other boats, we were waiting for a good weather window before starting our trip.

A cruising guide stated, "Pick a good weather window and expect a gale anyway." Heeding this warning, we were relying on a reputable weatherman to dictate our departure time. Days later, he gave us a green light for our southbound passage. Within 30 minutes, all of the boats in the anchorage – there were six of us – up-anchored. The race was on.

Halfway across the lagoon, our cabin erupted with black smoke. Paul killed the engine and we anchored under sail for the second time.

Discouraged, and swearing that his repair job wasn't leaking, Paul pulled up the floorboards. He was right. It wasn't the muffler. The rubber hose leading into the muffler had split. Paul dug through one of our lockers and pulled out a replacement hose. We weren't known as the floating West Marine – a supermarket of marine parts – for nothing! After Paul securely clamped the new hose into place, we ate lunch before rejoining the race in last place.

Our weatherman recommended that we head to a fictitious waypoint, approximately mid-way to New Zealand, and wait there for another good weather forecast farther south. His theory was that it would be better to wait a day or two in pleasant weather, allowing any gale farther south to pass, rather than getting caught in crappy weather. It was an interesting concept, sort of like waiting on a street median for a break in traffic before crossing the road. Who wanted to get run over by a car? Or a gale?

After we left Minerva Reef, the first part of our 800-mile trip was marked by light to no winds. With our asymmetrical spinnaker up, Rosie was averaging 4.5 knots. Twice a day, we tuned into the single sideband radio and swapped positions with the boats from our anchorage.

During one of these radio sessions, we heard another boat complaining that their starter motor had broken. Rosie had the same engine, a Perkins 4-108; and, true to our nickname, we had a spare starter motor on board. Because By Chance was 100 miles ahead of us, and en route to our fictitious waypoint, Paul volunteered to drop off our spare. They gratefully accepted.

The next night, at 2 a.m., we motored alongside By Chance. Paul put the starter motor and two hot cinnamon rolls I baked in a covered plastic bucket. He attached it to a line and let it trail behind Rosie. By Chance hauled in the bucket and took out the goodies, and we departed as soon as we retrieved the bucket. The next morning, we were heroes on the morning radio chat, not so much for the starter motor but for the homemade cinnamon rolls.

A day before we were due to arrive at the fictitious waypoint, the weatherman said, "Go, go, go!"

We altered course to New Zealand.

The next day, the wind picked up. A day later we were On-the-Nose-Cherokee-Rose, with our sails close-hauled in 40-knot winds and 10-foot seas. I woke up to the sound of a horrific crash as Rosie flew off one wave and slammed down on the next.

Over the sound of rushing water, rattling cans and Rosie's beating, I yelled, "What the heck is going on?"

We were heeled more than 40 degrees and I had to use my rock climbing skills just to climb out of my berth. Howie, who had taken refuge at my feet, meowed in protest.

Paul poked his head down below and proudly told me that he had tweaked Rosie; we were now doing 7 knots with reefed sails. I was ready to tweak him as Rosie crashed down on another wave.

The gale lasted for four days.

No matter how hard I tried, I could not convince Paul to slow Rosie down. Crests of waves crashed over the dodger. Two slides on the mainsail broke and a block on the staysail sheered. The radar, bilge pump and refrigerator balked at our steep heel.

So did the floorboards on the windward, high side, of the mast. They were squeezed so tight, they no longer lay flush, but were pushed up like cracked concrete around a tree's roots. Paul tried to stomp the floorboards back into place, but with no success.

"I wonder if the mast is attached to the keel of the boat?" Paul wondered aloud. "Perhaps the bolts have rusted away."

The aluminum mast and mast foot were bolted to a stainless steel plate on the keel. Corrosion, we had discovered, was more severe when different metals were in contact with each other.

"Thanks for that added worry," I said sarcastically. "Can't you see that we are straining Rosie, and her rigging? Everything is starting to break under these forces. And if you don't care about Rosie, what about the strain you're putting on us? And on our marriage?" I stomped my foot in frustration. "Slow the boat down."

While this passage had made me tired, and scared, it seemed to have affected only Paul's hearing because he didn't listen.

And, as if my nightmare weren't bad enough, one of the shrouds -- the wire ropes that held the mast in place -- became unattached during my midnight watch. Its metal turnbuckle banged against one of our cabin's Plexiglas windows with every jolting wave.

Fearing the beginning of the end for Rosie's rigging, I woke Paul and handed him his foul-weather gear. Tethered to the boat by his harness, and carrying a flashlight, Paul waded out on the deck – yes, the rail was under the water -- to investigate. All of the leeward, or low side, shrouds were very loose. Crouching, he tightened their turnbuckles while the waves washed over his chest.

Then we tacked the boat – a daunting task in 10-foot seas – so he could adjust the shrouds equally on the other side. He looked like a drowned rat when he returned to the cockpit, and considering that I held him responsible for a lot of this wear-and-tear, this pleased me immensely.

The next morning, after I relayed our nighttime events to Karen during our scheduled radio chat, she told Paul off while I gloated.

Paul finally relented – I think all of our mishaps were finally starting to worry him -- and slowed Rosie down to 2 knots. She rode up each wave, and then gently rode down the back. The boat had only a slight heel. I could sleep. I could eat. I could hear myself think. I even stopped complaining.

The slower speed had the reverse effect on Paul. He started grumbling that we'd never reach New Zealand at this rate, and that it would take us three or four days to travel the remaining 60 miles, a distance we could easily do in a day. His protests got louder the next day when we learned that Enchanté had sped up, pounding into the waves, so they could reach landfall by afternoon.

While they were enjoying cocktails at the Opua Cruising Club and getting a decent night's sleep, we spent another night creeping over the waves. But I didn't care. At least we would arrive safely, and on Rosie – and not in her life raft – which was worth an extra night at sea.

Paul and I were overjoyed, and proud, when we finally tied Rosie up to the Quarantine dock in Opua, New Zealand the next afternoon. As soon as our feet touched land, our trying passage was instantly forgotten. We hugged each other and danced around the dock, our faces beaming with ear-to-ear smiles. We had crossed the Pacific Ocean; we had actually SAILED to New Zealand. Yes, of course, that had been part of the plan, but somehow the fact that we had done it still surprised us.

Within five minutes of tying up the boat, two things happened. First, the light on our satellite e-mail system flashed. My dad congratulated us for reaching New Zealand. The timing of his e-mail was spooky. How did he know that we had just arrived? Big brother – or, in this case, big daddy – was definitely watching us.

And second, New Zealand officials besieged us. The Ministry of Agriculture and Forestry promptly whisked Howie away to "Pussycat Lodge" for his one-month quarantine. Immigration cleared us in, stamping our passports and issuing British Paul a 6-month visa, and American me a 3-month visa. The Police unleashed their dog, who sniffed the boat for drugs then they confiscated the harmonica for the duration of our stay.

Customs searched our food lockers, taking the clover honey, almonds, pine nuts and sesame seeds I had on board, as well as our remaining fresh and frozen food. When I asked why New Zealand was so stringent on food items, the Customs officer gave me an example of a biosecurity threat: honey. He explained that honey is not sterilized, and as it is produced by bees, it can potentially carry bee diseases. With more than twenty million dollars of bee products produced annually by New Zealand, any threat to the local bees was a threat to the Kiwi economy, as well as to their unique horticulture. I willingly acquiesced to everything, except when the officer took a pan of frozen lasagna.

"Please don't take it," I begged. "That's our dinner tonight."

He asked its ingredients and I told him: cheese, tomato

sauce and noodles.

He paused, obviously trying to decide what to do.

"I've just spent 10 days at sea, four of them in a gale," I pleaded. "You've taken all of our fresh and frozen food, and I don't know where the nearest grocery store is."

He shifted his weight from one foot to the other. "You'll eat it tonight?"

I nodded vigorously.

He relented.

After everyone left, we took a nap, ate my hard-won lasagna, and went to the Opua Cruising Club for a drink. Enchanté was seated at a long table with a dozen cruisers we didn't know.

As Karen introduced us, a woman suddenly said, "Oh, you're the cinnamon roll people!"

Everyone at our table and the adjacent one turned to look at us, including the crew of By Chance, who gave us a welcoming smile and a promise to return our starter motor.

We sat down and ordered a couple of beers.

We learned that Scott Free had responded to a mayday call on the single sideband radio. They sailed to South Minerva Reef to help the distressed boat. Anne and Oreon found the cruisers standing forlornly on the submerged reef. Their boat had hit the reef and was irreversibly wedged in one of the deep ravines. As water had filled the cabin from a resulting hole, the electrical system had shorted, causing a fire. Because they didn't have a life raft and their dinghy wasn't inflated, the couple was forced into the water, seeking refuge on the very reef that had claimed their boat.

Like many cruisers, this couple did not have boat insurance, so their loss was both emotional and financial. To ease the financial loss, Scott Free and two other boats spent the following week helping the owners dive on the wreckage and retrieve anything of value, including winches and blocks.

The couple had used their electronic chart to plot their course from North Minerva Reef to New Zealand, but had neglected to magnify the chart to see that their course ran over South Minerva Reef. At the end of this somber story, someone pointed out that eight or nine boats had sunk year-to-date while crossing the Pacific, and once again, I was reminded how lucky we were.

Boat Work and Body Work

New Zealand, November 2002

Opua was the largest city in the Bay of Islands, which, with its beautiful beaches, vineyards, and warmer climate, was a popular vacation destination in northern New Zealand. But we didn't have much time to explore the area, as we had to sail south to Auckland.

That was where my Dad would be arriving in a week and that was where we had reserved a slip for Rosie at Gulf Harbour Marina. While Rosie was set, we weren't quite as ready for the three months of back-to-back visitors we had lined up. Everyone in our families, it seemed, had wanted to visit us, and we had enthusiastically agreed. But having just one week to prepare was a daunting task. We had to sail south overnight, open a bank account, buy or rent a car, find the grocery store, and clean up passage-weary Rosie and ourselves in a city we had never seen.

Thankfully, we had some help from Paul's two uncles, who had immigrated to New Zealand some twenty years earlier. They found a car dealer who promised to buy back our vehicle in six months, when we would be setting sail again. We bought a Nissan Mistral, a 4-door SUV that could comfortably haul us, our guests, and our toys – bikes, windsurfers, rock climbing and camping gear. We figured half of our time in New Zealand would be spent touring the country with our guests and the other half would be spent working on the boat.

Tears filled my eyes when Dad arrived at the marina and climbed out of the airport limo. Throughout our entire journey, from looking at boats to buy, to helping out on Sundays in Charleston, to researching alternators via satellite e-mail, Dad had been there for us. I threw my arms around him, giving him an enormous hug. Dad's expression said that he was equally pleased to see us.

We regaled him with stories from our trip, answered his questions and introduced him to our friends on Enchanté and Spirit, who were berthed in the same marina. We spent three days riding our bicycles up and down the vineyard-covered hills of Waiheke Island, eating at gourmet restaurants and sampling the local wine.

Closer to home, we climbed sheep-dotted hills and enjoyed stellar views of the Hauraki Gulf and Auckland in the distance. We shooed away the peacocks that roamed the beach area, and laughed at the Pukekos – dark blue birds with bright red beaks and orange legs – who preferred to run everywhere rather than fly. We hiked through a semi-tropical forest, marveling at the tall tree ferns and green parakeets.

With the America's Cup regatta, the premier international sailing race that was being held in New Zealand a couple of months away, we explored Auckland's Viaduct where the high tech, super expensive racing yachts were housed. That's when we learned that we could race on one of the older America's Cup boats.

The day before Dad was due to leave, Paul's mum, Mavis, arrived. We greeted her at the airport with big hugs and a thermos of hot tea. She was going to need it. Two hours later, despite her feeble protests about being jet-lagged, the four of us – and 12 other people – stepped aboard one of the two 1994 America's Cup yachts. Another 16 people climbed aboard the sister yacht.

Dad, Mavis and I were "grinders," working the massive winches that resembled giant coffee grinders. Paul handled the mainsail traveler and – unbeknownst to me – pumped the captain for racing tips.

After a short warm-up on the Hauraki Gulf, we crossed an imaginary start-line and the race was on, us versus the other America's Cup boat. We pounded into the waves, trying to eek every bit of power out of the 12 knots of wind. Overfilling the sails, the boat heeled so steeply that I slid down its deck. But we were flying along at 13 knots in this neck-in-neck competition.

My back and arms ached as I turned the winch handle as fast as I could. Between bursts of grinding, I watched with fascination and dread as our captain zigzagged our boat in front of our competitor. We nearly collided with the other boat in an exhilarating, and exhausting, game of chicken which reminded me of Bahamian Family Islands regatta.

After we won the race, Dad and Mavis took turns steering the boat. While Dad looked very comfortable behind the wheel, Mavis looked like the little bitty that she was, her head barely poking over the top of the four-foot-tall steering wheel.

She kept shaking her head, and repeating to herself, "But I've just arrived from England."

I might have been worried about whisking an average 60-year-old woman off a 24-hour flight and onto a careening boat, but this was Mavis. Tigger's mother. And the huge, albeit dazed, smile on her face said that she loved it.

Several days after Dad flew home, Paul, Mavis and I celebrated the southern hemisphere's biggest summertime holiday, Christmas, with Cathie and Stuart on Spirit. Then we loaded up the car with our camping gear and headed south to Rotorua.

Rotorua is situated over a superheated underground lake, as evidenced by the natural, steaming holes scattered across the ground. Some were simply vent holes, others bubbled and gurgled with boiling water – or nearly boiling mud. And, oh, the stench! The town smelled like rotten eggs. In some areas, it was just a faint odor and in other areas the smell was so strong we wished we were wearing chemical respirators.

The campground we had chosen in Rotorua boasted the "only heated campsites in the world, and they were right. At night, the tent was toasty warm from the superheated lake buried deep below our sleeping bags, but rather than lulling me to sleep, I found it disquieting. The "blub, blub, blub" sound of popping mud bubbles from a nearby hole didn't help.

Pushing aside my fear of being stewed alive in boiling mud, I agreed to try a therapeutic mud bath, which was – not surprisingly – common in Rotorua. As Paul, Mavis and I wallowed in our private mud pool, Paul's single comment was that the mud bath would have been more fun if his mum weren't chaperoning us; no offense, of course, to his mum.

Rotorua had more than mud holes and steam vents; it also had its share of adrenaline rushes. We went on a warm-weather version of the luge, which consisted of steering a one-man go-cart down a mountain path, embanking on the curves and speeding down the straights. At another attraction, Mavis sat shotgun while Paul drove a sprint car and tried to best his own time. We all tumbled down a hill in a Zorb, a gigantic, clear, inflated gerbil ball made for people.

Back at the campground, Paul grilled our dinner of chicken and veggies on the communal barbecue while I cooked a simple sauce of cream and Dijon mustard. As I stirred the sauce, I watched a nearby woman uncover her dinner from a hangi, a Maori word which referred to a native underground oven. The Maori people, who are the original New Zealanders, have used this technique to cook their food for centuries, adapting it to their local environment. In Rotorua, these underground ovens use the natural geothermal steam to slowly cook food; in other regions, wood is burned and buried to produce heat.

After several fun-filled days, we returned to Auckland, and to Rosie. As always, our time with Mavis zipped by, and before we knew it, she was on a plane back to England and we were on our own. With a couple of weeks before my sister and her husband were due to arrive, we spent our time drawing up our boat "to do" list, which got longer with each passing day. The big items included pulling out the mast to inspect its base; finding and repairing the leak, or leaks as the case may be, on our worn teak decks; fixing the wind vane and the wind generator.

We tackled a couple of small jobs, which inevitably meant running to one of the marina's boat supply stores. I was surprised – and grateful – when one of the sales clerks directed me to a competitor's store because she didn't have exactly what I needed. Similarly, when we took several pieces of our wind generator to a repair shop, the Kiwi man behind the counter said that they could fix it, no worries, but if we wanted to save money, he'd tell us how to repair it ourselves. Astonished, Paul and I looked at each other. We were definitely in a foreign land!

If the daily cultural differences didn't remind us how far we had come, then the world map mounted on the ceiling above our bed did. With a dry-erase marker, Paul had drawn our route thus far. At night, lying in bed, I'd gaze at the map and dream of the exotic islands that we might visit once we started cruising again. Given a free moment, I'd pull out our guidebooks and read about these faraway places: Fiji, Vanuatu, Solomon's Islands, Palau, Kiribati, Philippines, Vietnam, Thailand, and Papua New Guinea.

When we had dinner with Enchanté, Carl and I would swap possible cruising routes and destinations with gusto, discussing the merits of snorkeling in the sandy atolls of the Louisiades (off Papua New Guinea), seeing the orangutans in Borneo or visiting Kapingamarangi, one of the few islands in Micronesia that was settled by the Polynesians.

In January, Suzanne and Kevin arrived, ready to explore the strangely different South Island of New Zealand. While the North Island had been created by volcanic activity, the South Island had been formed by shifting tectonic plates, so its topography was mountainous and dramatic. In fact, one of the reasons Peter Jackson chose to shoot the "Lord of the Rings" trilogy in New Zealand was due to the variety of locations its two islands presented.

Somehow I managed to convince Su that she'd love camping – she typically stayed in five-star resorts – so we packed our tents, sleeping bags and hiking boots before heading to the airport for our flight.

Once we landed in Queenstown and picked up our rental car, we toured the area's campgrounds so that Suzanne could take her pick; it was a small price to pay for a happy camper. As we drove to inspect the sixth campground, the winding mountain road gave us gorgeous views of pristine Lake Wakatipu below and scantily snow-capped mountains in the distance.

On the lake, a couple dozen small sailboats raced around a buoyed course, which caused Paul to pull the car over to the side of the road for a better look. As we watched the regatta on the lake, Suzanne unexpectedly hopped out of the car and started to run down the nearest driveway. Puzzled, I got out of the car to follow her, to see what she was doing, and then noticed the sign "Luxury condos for rent" next to the drive.

"That girl is shameless," I said, getting back into the car and pointing at the sign.

Kevin started to chuckle while Paul said nothing. I knew what he was thinking because I was thinking it, too. Camping fit our budget; luxury condos did not.

"They have vacancies, and whirlpool tubs in their condos," Suzanne coaxed us, minutes later. She added, "It's our treat. What do you say?"

It was the tub that got me. Granted, I had had the mud bath in Rotorua, but the idea of soaking in a hot tub and emerging clean was very appealing. Sheepishly, I slid out of the car without saying a word. Then Su and I raced down the hill as fast as our legs could take us, laughing at the spontaneity of this coup.

The three-story apartment was gorgeous and had a generous balcony overlooking the lake and the mountains. Later that evening, as we sipped wine and watched the sun set behind the Erye Mountains in plush, comfortable chairs, Su said that she really liked camping.

The next day, we explored quaint Queenstown and prioritized the things that we wanted to do while we were here. There was a lot to choose from, as this town catered to "adrenaline-junkies." If one could die doing a particular activity, then it was readily available to do so. And one could readily enjoy the breathtaking view of the Remarkables and the Erye Mountains while doing it.

From the menu of available activities, the guys decided to bungee jump – apparently the bungee is a Kiwi invention – from "the Ledge," which was a platform suspended a quarter of a mile above Queenstown. Suzanne and I opted for a massage. We all agreed to go canyoning – a exhilarating combination of scrambling over boulders, floating down river rapids and zipping on lines suspended over waterfalls. We also careened up the Dart River on a jet boat and placidly paddled downriver in a canoe. Every activity afforded spectacular views of snow-topped mountains, dense pine forests, and pristine rivers.

Happy and worn out from our South Island adventures, we flew back to Auckland and home-sweet-Rosie. Even though Rosie remained in our slip, in the protected marina, Su felt queasy on the boat. She seemed almost relieved when it was time for them to fly home, where her bed didn't rock.

After they left, we started our boat work in earnest. Our first job: tackling the leak in our teak decks. Because we didn't know where the leak was coming from, it ended up being cheaper and wiser to simply remove the teak decking, seal the underlying fiberglass and coat the deck with non-skid paint. If we were going through the hassle of painting the deck, we might as well do Rosie's hull. Paul estimated that it would take us a week to chip off the old teak planks, remove the 2,000 screws that had held the wood in place and fill the remaining holes with epoxy. We forgot we were dealing with a B-O-A-T.

Boats always take longer than expected. Three weeks later, we were done. We figured it would take us a week to remove the hardware – winches, cleats, travelers, etc - on our decks and cabin top to prepare for the non-skid painting. It took us three weeks. The boat painter estimated that it would take four to six weeks to paint our boat; it took nine weeks once we pulled the boat out of the water. We figured it would take two weeks to put the hardware back on the boat. After all, we had taken it off, so technically it should be easier to put it back on. Wrong. Five weeks later and we were still putting the boat back together.

The boat wasn't the only thing we were trying to fix. In the midst of living on an exceedingly dusty boat, supported by metal boat stands, in the middle of a paint shed, we were also undergoing in vitro fertilization (IVF). Let me rephrase that: I was undergoing IVF while Paul held my hand – and tried not to squirm.

For several reasons, we had finally decided to try IVF after an almost two-year break from fertility treatments. First, we had not given up the hope of having a baby. And now that our friend Barbara on Sueño was pregnant, our conversation kept drifting back to children. If the excitement of our life at sea – all of the preparations, the repairs, the storms, the remote islands, the camaraderie – hadn't diminished our desire for kids, then nothing would. In terms of diversions, how could we possibly top the past year?

During Mavis' visit, Paul had told her about our struggle to have children, breaking the silence we had had on the subject. Mavis suggested that we fly back to England as IVF was covered by the National Health Service. I thought we should check locally before we considered leaving Rosie and flying to England. With the favorable exchange rate, we discovered that IVF in New Zealand was less than half the cost in the States. So we could afford to try a couple of rounds which alleviated Paul's financial concern.

I was still ambivalent about undergoing IVF; why would a healthy person willingly have surgery? I also didn't want to hope for a baby if we couldn't have one. I didn't think I could handle the disappointment if we failed again. But IVF was the only treatment we hadn't tried; it was our last chance. I agreed to an initial consultation. When Dr. Miller, our Kiwi fertility specialist, said that we had a reasonable chance of getting pregnant with IVF, my worries vanished. I was on board.

Over the next two months, in the midst of sanding the boat – we were always sanding something – we took periodic breaks to go to the doctor's clinic. A week after our initial consultation, our unsmiling nurse showed Paul how to give me an injection in my belly. I was to have one injection a day for two weeks, followed by two injections a day for two more weeks. The first hormone injection controlled my ovulation so that the doctor could effectively manage the timing of my cycle; the second hormone injection promoted multiple egg formation.

Paul had squirmed when he had given his orange a shot in Dr. Smith's office; he certainly wasn't any better when faced with my stomach. He fidgeted in his chair, insisting that he hated needles and that he couldn't give me a shot.

The nurse put the syringe and needle in his hand, and unsympathetically told him to give me an injection.

"Go on, you can do it," I nodded encouragingly.

In a brief moment of resolve, Paul brought the syringe to my stomach and timidly pushed. When the needle met the resistance of my skin, he freaked out. He dropped the syringe on the table, jumped out of his chair and danced around in a circle, holding his stomach and shaking his head. Seeing how hopeless he was, Charlotte redirected her attention toward me and showed me how to administer my own injection. Then she gave me my first shot.

The next morning, it was just the two of us standing in our galley. Paul got the syringe ready without any issue then he gingerly laid it down on the counter.

"Okay," I said, sitting down on one of the companionway steps and pulling up my t-shirt to expose my never-seen-the-sun tummy. "Give it to me."

"I can't," Paul said, laughing nervously, and holding his stomach.

"Come on," I said, "I just want to get this over with."

Still he refused.

Impatiently, I grabbed the needle. "Fine, I'll do it myself." I took the syringe, held it next to my stomach and froze. My bravado vanished. "Oh, Paul," I said, exasperated. "If you want a baby, you've got to give me this shot."

That did the trick, though he shut his eyes when he jabbed me with the needle.

It wasn't much easier the next morning, especially when Paul saw the black and blue bruise on my belly from his first administration. But as the days went by, Paul got better at giving me shots and after awhile I was even bruise-free.

Three weeks later, we were still sanding – and living on – the boat in the paint shed. My mom had just arrived for her two-week visit; and I was having mood swings. Except I didn't know it.

Every afternoon, I lassoed my mom and Paul into helping me clean the cabin. By this time of day, every horizontal surface was covered with at least a millimeter of white paint dust and even the vertical surfaces – the walls, cabinet fronts and speakers – were draped with veils of white powder. It looked like an interior winter wonderland.

We had just started cleaning when Paul announced, as he did every day, that this was a pointless task because we were still sanding the boat. I lashed out at him, bitter that he could count on my help with every boat task but I couldn't count on him to help me clean anything.

As I stormed out of the boat, I turned around in the cockpit and screamed down the companionway hatch, "I hate you!"

I knew I was overreacting, but I just couldn't help it. I had never felt such raw anger and it consumed me. Out of the corner of my eye, I saw my mom cringe at my outburst. Paul looked genuinely pained. And the hired painter who just happened to hear my final jab quickly turned away when I spotted him on the ground.

I climbed down the ladder that led from the cockpit to the concrete floor of the paint shed and marched to one of the two nearby pay phones. I didn't know what time it was in the States, but I didn't care. I called Suzanne and started sobbing on the phone as soon as I heard her voice, my anger evaporating as quickly as it had come.

She calmed me down, pointing out how stressful my life was, sanding and painting the boat while undergoing IVF. She didn't think I was crazy, but she thought I should talk to my doctor. As soon as we hung up the phone, I called Dr. Miller. His receptionist informed me that he was in a meeting but did I want to talk to Charlotte, our nurse?

"By any chance do these drugs cause mood changes? I asked her. "Because I haven't decided whether I want to push Paul off the boat, or jump off myself," I said, trying to make light of how I felt.

"No, they don't," she said brusquely. "But if you are thinking about suicide, you need to see a counselor. There are several good ones in Auckland. I'll get their numbers."

I hastily hung up the phone, tears in my eyes. Maybe I was mentally ill.

Crying, I called Suzanne back. She answered on the first ring. When I told her about my conversation, she was shocked. She assured me that she, too, would be shouting at Paul if her home were covered in a blanket of dust and if she were working the long hours we were – never mind going through something as emotionally difficult as IVF. Su almost made me feel normal.

After I washed my face and apologized to Paul and my mom, we found a furnished two-bedroom townhouse for rent adjacent to the marina and we moved in later that day. Despite the unexpected expense, Paul had decided that it would be good for us to live in a clean, dust-free, environment for a couple of weeks.

I loved it. I loved being able to pee in the middle of the night without having to climb down a steep ladder and walk across the parking lot to get to the bathroom. I loved having dust-free bed sheets, a dust-free couch and a dust-free kitchen. No puffs of dust when I sat down. I loved not leaving white footprints everywhere I went. And I really loved having a dishwasher, washing machine and dryer. Life on land was easy.

A couple of days before we were to go to the hospital to harvest my eggs, I was given another injection – another hormone – to trigger ovulation. Then my dreaded surgery day arrived.

In his office, Dr. Miller explained how he was going to harvest my eggs and Paul perked up, listening attentively and asking lots of questions. He loved biology. I, on the other hand, didn't. I tuned them out; I didn't want to know the gory details.

I just wanted to know if the drugs I had been on could cause mood swings. They could; according to Dr. Miller. Bloating, abdominal pain, headaches and mood swings were common side effects of the fertility drugs. I felt validated, vindicated. He promised me that he'd enlighten the unenlightened Charlotte.

After our briefing, Dr. Miller showed Paul to a private room where he was left to produce a semen sample. I sat in the adjoining waiting room. When Paul emerged with his sample cup in hand, his face wore an expression of distaste. Ejaculation-on-demand was not fun, he informed me, and some randy bloke had stolen the inside pages from the girlie magazines, leaving only the magazine covers on the coffee table.

Dr. Miller led us into the operating room and I was relieved to see that it looked just like any other hospital room with an ultrasound in it. He gave me some good drugs that left me awake, but in a relaxed, dream-like state. I didn't feel a thing. During the operation, Paul held my hand while straining to see the ultrasound screen. Charlotte held the ultrasound paddle over my stomach, and ovaries, while Dr. Miller harvested the follicles for eggs.

It was over quickly and, once the light anesthetic wore off, Dr. Miller explained that they had centrifuged Paul's sperm to concentrate them. He was going to put my eggs in a Petri dish along with Paul's sperm so that the eggs could be fertilized. He'd give us an update tomorrow.

As we walked past the reception desk, Charlotte called out, "You're a good hen. We got 20 eggs."

The next day we were dismayed to learn that my eggs had stayed on one side of the Petri dish while Paul's sperm had stayed on the other side. Nothing like paying all of this money to bring the two together, only to find out that they were wall-flowers at a dance. Perhaps this was the reason why we couldn't get pregnant!

Dr. Miller recommended that they inject one sperm into each egg manually; the technique was called Intracytoplasmic Sperm Injection, or ICSI. While they couldn't scientifically force fertilization, if the two were shoved together, perhaps they might dance. We agreed to go ahead with ICSI.

The next day, Dr. Miller called again. The process had been successful. Because I had been such a good hen, to quote the charming Charlotte, we now had five fertilized eggs. I did not want five babies. Dr. Miller suggested that we consider taking the embryos to the blastocyst stage. Normally, embryos are transferred back to the womb two or three days after cultivation and fertilization. Leaving the embryos to grow for another day or two in the lab meant that they could transfer the most advanced one or two embryos. Apparently "survival of the fittest" extended to the Petri dish. We followed his recommendation.

Two days later, Do, Re and Mi were painlessly implanted in my womb. We had decided to give the embryos names because calling them blastocysts seemed so clinical. "The Sound of Music," which we had recently watched, had inspired our naming system. Fertility did not appear to be an issue with the von Trapp family.

Now Mi was a surprise. Paul and I had agreed to implant two embryos, figuring that if I had roughly a 30% chance of getting pregnant with one egg given my age, maybe we could increase our odds with two eggs. And this was the logic that saved Mi, but distressed me later that afternoon when I contemplated the possibility of triplets for the first time. What in the world had we done?!

Paul was pretty good at diverting my attention with yet more sanding that needed to be done. At the last minute – the paint crew was standing by and waiting on us – we realized that we needed to sand our dorades and get them painted along with everything else. The boat would look unfinished with powdery, peeling dorades mounted on a gleaming boat. And given how much effort we had put into Rosie, nothing short of perfect was allowed.

I was standing in line at the marina's boat store, buying more sanding paper, when Dr. Miller appeared on the store's television.

"Hey, there's my doctor!" I exclaimed to the nearly empty store. He was the fertility expert on the Kiwi version of "Good Morning America." I was impressed; apparently, I had a good doctor.

Mom was very tolerant of our hard work schedule and of our frequent doctor's visits. While Dr. Miller had cleared me for "work as normal," I took this chance to take Do, Re, Mi and Mom out. We toured a local pottery manufacturer, visited a couple of incredible waterfalls, went to a couple of vineyards and olive groves, and saw the giant Kauri trees, which rivaled the American Redwood. We hiked the hills at Shakespear Park and played Scrabble in the evenings. We cooked together.

All in all, I felt pretty good. Perhaps a bit tired, which

caused a little voice inside of me to wonder if I weren't pregnant? That little grain of hope grew, despite my best efforts to squelch it.

Sixteen days after the embryo transfer, I went to a clinic in nearby Manly and had my blood drawn for a pregnancy test. The next day, I got the news. I was not pregnant.

I found Paul at the paint shed and my expression said it all. He gave me a huge hug and said he'd tidy up and walk me back to the house. I felt pathetic, standing in a paint shed full of guys while silent tears ran down my face. I left. When I got to our house, Mom tried to console me, but there was nothing she could say to make me feel better.

As the news sank in, I became angry. Angry at myself for hoping that we were pregnant. Angry at my body for rejecting Do, Re and Mi. Angry that I was on this damn emotional roller coaster again. I hadn't considered failure when I had agreed to IVF, and now here I was, mentally and emotionally unprepared.

When Paul walked in the door 10 minutes later, I was heading out.

"Where are you going?" he asked, concerned.

"For a run," I said. I hadn't run in years, but I felt like punching someone, or something. No, Charlotte, I didn't need a counselor, but I did need to vent my frustration, my a-n-g-e-r.

"Hold on a sec," Paul said, "I'll come with you."

I nodded impatiently. It would be safer to have Paul with me since it was already becoming dark outside. Given how mad I felt, though, Paul would have to protect any would-be thugs from me.

We ran silently, my furious pace slowing down as the miles passed underfoot. We ran almost six miles before I stopped, and burst into tears. Paul pulled me next to him and hugged me tightly. He, too, was crying.

"Why is this so hard?" I asked him, burying my face in his chest.

Paul was too choked up to reply, but he squeezed me even tighter.

In for a penny, in for pound. In our case, we decided we were in for US$10,000, which was the approximate cost of one round of IVF in the States with health insurance. Here, with the current exchange rate, that would get us two rounds without insurance.

After my mom left, we repeated the same cycle again. Clucking like a hen, I produced 10 eggs, three of which made it through the blastocyst stage. We implanted Fa and So; La was tossed into the deep freezer for another day. No terrifying triplets this time.

From the States, Suzanne was optimistic.

"I've got a good feeling about Sofa," she said.

"About who?" I asked, puzzled.

"SoFa. You know, it's backward for Fa and So."

I laughed.

When I called her a couple weeks later to tell her that this round had failed, she tried to cheer me up. "Well, who'd want couch potatoes anyway? So and Fa would have sat around all day, watching TV and fighting over the remote."

I laughed lamely, clutching the receiver in my pay phone booth, and thanked her for her help. This time I was better prepared for bad news.

But our friends weren't.

Enthusiastic – and hopeful – at the beginning of our IVF course, we had told our friends on Enchanté, and Sueño, in addition to Mavis, Suzanne and my mom. They had been excited for us and had routinely asked us for updates. Like us, none of them had been prepared for bad news. For them, it was like being at a poker table with a friend who was losing her life's fortune. It was sad to watch.

And it was painful to face their disappointed expressions when we felt so dejected ourselves.

But I was too worried about Paul to take on anyone else's feelings. La had just crashed and burned.

Neither of us shed any tears. Our hearts were now well-shielded, but we were despondent. I could feel myself starting to retreat into my "don't-want-what-I-can't-have" mental state. And I wondered how Paul was going to cope with this latest failure. I was concerned about him and about our marriage.

As in Philadelphia, no one had warned us about the difficulties that unsuccessful IVF could cause in a marriage. But I figured one of them out for myself. I knew that Paul really wanted children and we couldn't have any. Together. That didn't mean that he couldn't have children with another woman – the reason for our infertility was still unknown --

and I needed to know where I stood. If we still had a future together.

The day was as gray as our moods, but it had just stopped raining, given how quiet the paint shed had become after the constant beat of raindrops on its corrugated fiberglass roof.

"Let's take a break and go for a walk," I suggested, thinking I'd rather have this conversation outside where there was plenty of air to breathe.

Paul shrugged, "Okay."

Low clouds swept across the sky and the wood docks glistened with small puddles of rainwater. An occasional loose halyard clanged against its mast in the wind and the smaller boats rocked side-to-side in their slips, their masts drawing invisible arcs in the sky.

As we walked, it took me awhile to broach the subject. I wasn't sure I wanted to know Paul's answer. If I didn't ask, I wouldn't have to deal with possible rejection. But that would simply postpone the inevitable if he didn't want to stay with me. No, it was better just to ask.

And why was I worried? He was my soul-mate, my best friend. Who else would sail around the world with him? Who else would save him from a shark attack?

"Honey, how badly do you want children?" I blurted. "Do you still want to be with me if we can't have children? Because you might be able to have kids with someone else."

I held my breath. I had expected him to answer immediately with "of course I want to stay with you," but he said nothing.

We kept walking.

Shit.

This was clearly a "the first person who talks loses" situation. I had learned this in sales training years ago. At the end of a sales call, if a sales person asked a difficult question, such as "Can I have your order?" a pregnant pause or an uncomfortable silence usually followed. To relieve the mounting tension, an inexperienced sales person might say, "Oh, that's okay. You can tell me later." But then that sales person just lost the answer to his question; he still didn't know where he stood. And I needed to know exactly where I stood, as I had just asked for the largest order of my life.

After a couple of excruciating minutes, Paul finally acknowledged, "I want to stay married to you."

Whew.

He continued, "You are more important than having children. But I think we should adopt."

Adopt? We had never considered adoption before. Disregarding Paul's offhanded attempt to ask for a baby in the Marquesas, I hadn't thought about adoption since our chat with Rupert and Judy in the Galapagos Islands.

"I don't know how I feel about adoption," I confessed. "I don't know anything about it. Let's do some homework, find out what options are available, how much it costs, how long it takes. Then we can talk about it."

"Good idea," Paul said, squeezing my hand.

"Now that we have that settled. What took you so long to answer my question?" I demanded. "I can't believe you had to think about it!"

Misadventures of Howie and the Engine

New Zealand, May 2003

It was mid-May and our six month layover in New Zealand was almost over, or so we hoped. Rosie was gleaming with her three coats of shiny two-part polyurethane paint, and our friends Claire and Bruce had just flown in for a five-week visit. Days before they had arrived, I had had to reset their expectations. They had hoped to sail with us to Fiji for the start of the cruising season. Bruce had been really excited; while he had sailed with us on Rosie's maiden voyage, most of his sailing had been confined to Lake Michigan. A passage from New Zealand to Fiji was real sailing.

But Rosie wasn't sailing anywhere on her metal chocks in the paint shed. The painting was done, but now we were laboriously screwing on all of the deck hardware. Bruce chuckled when he saw the buckets of deck parts waiting to be reinstalled. He gamely grabbed a cordless drill and started screwing. Claire, who was my best friend, also pitched in.

While everyone was hard at work, I was letting my fingers do the walking in the yellow pages. Claire and Bruce had flown halfway around the world for an adventure, not to fix our boat. Bruce seemed keen to go camping, so I found a local company that rented camping vans. Two days after their arrival, they were hiking and camping their way around the North Island.

Paul and I worked frantically putting Rosie back together again. Paul was more adept at power screwing without shredding the threads and, after many botched attempts on my part, relegated me to other work. One of my jobs was to clean the mast foot as, once Rosie was back in the water, we would step – or reinstall – her mast. We had taken the 60-foot-tall mast off the boat in order to fit Rosie inside the paint shed.

On our passage to New Zealand, the floor boards had refused to lie flush on the floor next to the mast. At the time, Paul had wondered if the mast foot was even attached to the boat. It was time to find out. I pulled up the floor boards and looked at the aluminum mast foot. It was covered with paint dust, as was most of the fiberglass, plumbing and electrical cords that were hidden under the floor.

I brushed the majority of the dust off the mast foot with my hand, revealing the deep groove that held our mast firmly in place. I called Paul and we inspected it, pleased to note that it looked good, and that its bolts were firmly attached to the stainless steel plate and keel.

I pulled out the vacuum cleaner, ignoring Paul, who rolled his eyes at what he considered a waste of time in our dusty environment. Then I vacuumed up the remaining dust on top of the mast foot, inadvertently banging it with the vacuum's plastic adaptor in the process. The mast foot crumbled into a dozen pieces!

With visions of our mast falling over under full sails and ripping a hole in our boat had this happened at sea, I was simultaneously horrified and thrilled that I had taken the time to vacuum it. Cleaning did pay.

Claire and Bruce arrived back from their two-week camping trip, just in time to see sparkling Rosie "splash." Once Rosie was back in the water, we led her over to the adjacent gantry – or manual crane – so we could install her mast on her new, custom-made, mast foot. Being in the water, with her mast on, Rosie looked like she might be able to sail one day soon. But first we had to attach all of the shrouds, and halyards; attach the boom; re-rig the running lines that controlled the sails as well as the preventer; refit the sails; install the clutches and winches...the list went on and on.

What to do with our friends? Hoping that we'd be ready for a sail when they returned, I booked Claire and Bruce on a flight to Fiji. It was the only way I could guarantee that they'd see it. There they spent a glorious 10 days on Ma Lo Lo Lai Lai Island, sailing a catamaran, snorkeling and enjoying an unexpected second honeymoon.

We were not having a honeymoon, or anything remotely like one. Paul and I worked doggedly, getting Rosie ready, while several docks away, Carl and Karen on Enchanté cheered us on. They fixed dinner for us every other night, it seemed, saving us from our usual fast food dinner of burgers and fries at Ripples, the inexpensive marina café.

The cyclone season was over and most boats were leaving for Fiji, Tonga or New Caledonia. Without saying so, I think Carl and Karen – like Bruce and Claire – were waiting to see if we could get ole' Rosie sail-worthy. If we could get her ready within a month, they'd wait for us. And we really wanted to go cruising with them; they were just our "speed."

When Claire and Bruce arrived back, tanned and relaxed, from their Fiji holiday, we figured we could set sail. Not for an ocean passage but for a 4-hour sail in the Hauraki Gulf. We would take them to Great Barrier Island, a nearby island that had a couple of all-weather anchorages; it would give them a taste of the cruising life.

I went grocery shopping and loaded up the fridge. Paul and Bruce double-checked the decks. Claire stowed items. Paul pulled up our electronic charts of the Hauraki Gulf, and pulled out our harnesses and tethers. We were ready.

Paul fired up the engine and it ran well – for about an hour – when suddenly there was the now familiar but deafening sound of the high-temperature alarm. The engine was overheating. Then smoke filled the cabin; the exhaust manifold had snapped off. Water leaked from the badly corroded engine coolant reservoir. The heat exchanger was blocked. The injectors needed to be replaced. And to add insult to injury, the fan belt flew off, disappearing into our bilge, never to be found again. Apparently Rosie wasn't ready for a 4-hour trip, and she made it abundantly clear.

Our friends were also disappointed; they had come all this way to go sailing. They had even brought along their foul-weather gear, and their harnesses. Leaving Paul and Bruce crouching over the engine, I popped into the marina office to use their internet connection. I found a charter boat company on the Great Barrier Reef in Australia; got prices for renting a 36-foot sailboat as well as airfare prices for the next day. I returned to the boat and proposed this new adventure to Claire and Bruce. I felt guilty that they had already spent so much money on this trip and that we couldn't take them sailing. Claire shook her head when I mentioned the price, but Bruce pointed out that they'd never be in this part of the world again; they should do it. So off they went.

And so did Carl, Karen and their daughter, Rebecca, as Enchanté set sail for four months in the Fijian Islands.

Once everyone left, our morale plummeted. The engine needed more than some TLC - it needed to be rebuilt. But before it could be rebuilt, we had to get it off the boat. Paul rigged a block-and-tackle system from the boom through the companion hatch to the engine; and together we hoisted the Perkins 4-108 engine off its mounts under our floor. Once the engine was lifted out of the cabin, we swung the boom over the dock and lowered the engine into a cart, to the marvel of several bystanders. Even I was impressed with our work.

"Where did you learn how to do that?" I asked Paul when the engine was safely in its cart. Paul shrugged, "It's just physics."

I shook my head and smiled, glad to have such a handy honey on board.

The engine mechanic said that he could do some of the repairs but some of the parts needed to be sent away to be fixed. As it was June, we had to face the possibility that we might not be ready to go cruising before the next cyclone season arrived. That meant we'd be staying in New Zealand for an extra 10 – 11 months, until the following April or May. That presented several immigration issues.

First, we had to explain to New Zealand Immigration why we couldn't leave the country and why we needed them to extend our visas. We also needed to let New Zealand Customs know that we intended to leave New Zealand, with our boat, so that they didn't charge us a boat import tax. And lastly, we needed to deal with US Immigration.

Despite marrying American me, it had taken us three years to get Paul's green card. Shortly after we had bought the boat, I had discovered there was a little caveat with the green card. Paul was not allowed to be out of the United States for more than two years or he'd risk losing his permanent residency. And he could be gone for two years only if he applied for "parole," which we had done. His parole commenced on July 6, 2001, when Immigration gave him permission to leave, not when we actually left for the Bahamas the following February. Those months working on the boat, the time spent sailing across the Pacific plus our now seven months in NZ meant that his parole was about to expire.

Were there any extensions for good behavior, for cooperating with the warden?

I called and asked US Immigration from my pay phone at the marina, explaining our situation to the Immigration officer who answered. She informed me that there were no extensions after two years. Paul had to return to the States before his Reentry Permit expired, and she could not guarantee that he'd be given parole again.

"What do you think the chances are that he'll be granted parole again if he returns before his permit expires?" I pressed the officer.

"For something as frivolous as sailing around the world?" she said. "Not likely."

"But what are we supposed to do?" I asked her. "I can't sail the boat by myself and if Paul isn't allowed to return to New Zealand, then our boat will be stranded here."

"Well, that's not our problem," she said. "If he doesn't return before his Reentry Permit expires, he'll have to apply for a visa at the nearest US Embassy when he wants to return."

I hung up the phone, discouraged that all of our efforts to retain Paul's green card were for naught. We had no choice; we would have to apply for a visa when the time came.

Thankfully, New Zealand Immigration and Customs were more understanding and allowed us to stay, tax-free, until the next cruising season began in 10 months. That gave us plenty of time to get the engine rebuilt, reinstalled and tested. Testing it simply meant taking Rosie out for a drive. Given that we ended up rebuilding the engine three times, we had plenty of opportunity to cruise the North Island, and the Hauraki Gulf.

On one testing trip, we finally made it to Great Barrier Island where we had hoped to take Claire and Bruce. The island has a protected deep-water bay with several coves. Two passes on either side of Kaikoura Island lead into the bay. We entered through the narrower Man of War pass. Towering cliffs on either side of the pass formed a dramatic tunnel which hinted at the beauty that lay beyond. The tight confines of the pass abruptly ended and we were suddenly in the sparkling blue water of the bay, surrounded by verdant rolling hills which were covered with shrubs and pastures of grazing sheep. It felt like we had found a secret spot.

Once we were through the pass, we anchored at Smokehouse Bay. On shore, there was a shack that held a smokehouse and, of all oddities, a clawed-foot bathtub. Cruisers could smoke their fresh catch in the smokehouse and take a bath while they waited. The fire that generated the smoke also heated the water for the tub.

We dinghied ashore to check it out. Paul disappeared into the smokehouse while I found the bathroom. Even from the doorway, it was clear that I would not be taking a bath in this tub. Its white porcelain was mottled with cream-colored age spots; bizarre-shaped rust stains freckled and flecked its interior surface; discolored scratches and gouges in the porcelain completed its patina. The tub needed a vigorous scrub with bleach and a good spritz of phosphoric acid to remove the rust stains. Thanks to Rosie, I had become a bit of a pro at rust removal.

"That is one skanky tub," I said to Paul as he entered the room. I kept my distance in case the tub could somehow infect me.

"Oh, come on," said Paul, hugging me from behind and wrapping his arms around my stomach. "Where's your sense of fun? Let's take a bath together."

He released me and turned on the faucet. Brown water sputtered out.

"No, thank you," I exclaimed. "My last bath wasn't that long ago!"

Paul laughed and said, "Come on, let's go. I want to catch some snapper so I can smoke them."

Unfortunately the snapper did not want to be smoked, or caught.

Paul switched his focus to easier prey: mussels. There were several mussel farms in the bay and while the mussels that grew on the farms' lines were off-limits, there were plenty of mussels that grew on the buoys that marked the perimeter of the mussel farms. According to a Kiwi cruiser, these were fair to pick and tasty when smoked.

While Paul was allergic to mussels, he was excited at the prospect of harvesting and smoking them. Carl, who decided to join us, and I were excited to eat them. It turned out to be a lot of work for not a lot of food. Thank goodness for a fully stocked fridge!

The next afternoon, I was washing dishes and absent-mindedly staring out the porthole when a plume of water spewed out of the bay, rising on the back of a whale. Not just any whale but a killer whale, and not just one whale but a pod of them. Excited, I pointed them out to Paul who, in turn, hopped on the VHF radio and called Enchanté. Camera in hand, we jumped in the dinghy and chased after the whales. Carl, Karen and Becca joined the pursuit.

As we got closer, we saw that there were two adult Orcas as well as a baby Orca. They were gorgeous with their black backs and white bellies – and huge.

Paul steered us near them so I could take a photo.

It was weeks later when I realized how foolish we had been, chasing after killer whales. On a BBC television program, we watched an Orca whale kill a seal. The whale threw its body on top of the seal, pushing the seal under the water, where it drowned. And there we had been, sitting in our inflatable, gray dinghy, next to a mama killer whale and her baby.

We were soon to have another encounter with the wicked sea world. After the second engine rebuild, we motored overnight to Whangaroa, a large bay north of Opua. Shortly after we dropped the hook off Milford Island, the wind started to blow consistently. Paul rigged two of our windsurfers and we excitedly set off, zipping between Rosie and nearby Ohauroro Island.

As usual, I was getting a better workout than Paul because I fell often and had to manhandle the sail while treading water. As the afternoon progressed, the wind increased and I couldn't get up despite my valiant efforts. Even belting out Helen Reddy's "I am Woman" didn't help.

Like a real pal, Paul sprayed me with his wake as he zipped past me, heading toward Rosie on his board. I forgave him when he returned in the dinghy and pulled me into the boat. As we dinghied back to Rosie, windsurfer in tow, we passed a large motor boat. On the stern a man was fighting to pull in a large fish while his boat mates cheered him on.

Two smaller powerboats were drifting nearby, their skippers watching the show. Paul put the dinghy in neutral as we watched the fisherman reel in a 13-foot shark. The shark was longer than the width of the motor boat and fought violently, ripping a piece of fiberglass off the stern dive platform, as it was dragged on board.

"That shark was in the water while I was floundering about on my board?!" I exclaimed. "That does it! I'm not going windsurfing until we are in clear water. I want to see what's swimming in the water with me."

"Yeah, but sharks don't like to eat people."

"Hrrumph," I said, "Tell that to the shark that fancied you in Suwarrow." I was fed up with these scary bullies.

I was fed up with our engine, too. As its woes continued, so did the engine repairs – and the payments. Our cruising kitty, or sailing budget, was dwindling quickly. On a previous trip to Waiheke Island, I had scouted a couple of gardens for possible publication and was overjoyed when Better Homes and Gardens accepted one of them for a 10-page spread. While one article would hardly cover our expenses, every little bit helped. Besides Better Homes and Gardens, Blue Water Sailing, another national magazine, also agreed to publish a couple of my articles.

With spring upon us, we made a couple of trips out to Waiheke Island so I could check on the garden's status. The photo shoot had to occur when the garden was at its flowering peak.

We were anchored off Waiheke Island on one such trip when Howie peed on our salon settee, prompting us to take our diabetic cat to the vet. I chucked a protesting Howie into his cat carrier and climbed into the dinghy while Paul started the outboard. It was dusk and we had to surf the dinghy over the beach's breaking waves in order to land. Howie meowed frantically as we whizzed down the back of one wave.

In the brief lull between crashing waves, Paul lifted the outboard out of the water to clear the beach while I jumped in the four-inch deep ebb to hastily pull the heavy dinghy to shore. I wasn't fast enough. The next wave caught the dinghy and threw it forward again, yanking its painter – or line – out of my hand and soaking me from my feet to my thighs.

After dragging the dinghy 15 feet up the beach, we walked to the vet's office. It once had sounded so glamorous to live on a yacht, but there was nothing glamorous about arriving at the vet's office wearing clinging, wet pants that dribbled on the floor.

Our multiple trips to Waiheke paid off, as the photographer and I caught Stephen and Linda's garden in its full glory. Using my scouting photos, the editors had put together a photo order, listing the photos they'd like us to capture. Matt, the photographer, brought his technical knowledge, experience and bags of gear. I brought editorial focus, props and Paul. Paul wasn't sure he wanted to be there but I had sweet-talked him into it. Once I saw that Matt hadn't brought an assistant, I was glad my husband had come.

We got to work immediately. While Matt set up his gear and lined up the first shot, I styled it. When he thought he had a good shot, I peered through the viewfinder to make sure the shot told the story that the editor wanted. Then I ensured that the shot was as pretty as it could be and that all of the elements in the shot were easily identifiable. That meant twisting a container around; moving a table a couple of inches away from a chair; pulling a troublesome branch out of the way – all of which Paul did while I directed him from the viewfinder. Once I was satisfied, Matt checked his settings, directing Paul and me to angle bounce cards into a particularly dark patch of greenery. Then he shot it.

It had taken us over an hour to get the first shot and Paul was flabbergasted. Eight hours later, he was knackered. Nine hours later, he was sipping a glass of wine and eating peanuts with Stephen and Linda in their living room, chatting about Rosie and the mail-order pharmacy. When the shoot was finally over, we trudged back to the dinghy.

"That was hard work," Paul said.

"I know. Why do you think you always used to cook dinner on shoot nights?" That made me pause. Who was going to cook dinner tonight? "Let's order in dinner," I suggested, wishing Domino's Pizza offered door-to-boat service.

"Dream on," said Paul.

Just as my sister had given us a reason to tour the campgrounds of Queenstown, Howie gave us a tour of Kiwi veterinarian clinics. After his unfortunate peeing accident in Waiheke, we took him to our local vet's office for a check-up. The vet examined him and told us to leave Howie for the day so that he could clean Howie's teeth.

When Paul picked up the cat later that day, Howie's chest was covered in blood. I was upset when I saw our beloved cat and unimpressed with the vet. While Howie rested on the couch in the salon, I prepared dinner. Paul was collecting garbage on board.

Splash!

Unbeknownst to me, Howie had followed Paul outside and had fallen into the water. He was frantically paddling around Rosie. Paul jumped down to the dock and pulled him out of the water.

"Why did he fall in the water?" I demanded, worried for the safety of our cat. He had never fallen in the water before.

Paul thought he was still drugged from the vet's.

I agreed and we decided to keep Howie locked in the cabin for the night.

After dinner, I boiled some water on the stovetop burner and brewed some tea. As we sipped our tea, we got a whiff of wet fur followed by the pungent scent of something burning. I jumped up from the table and spotted Howie. He had just walked across the burner, singeing his fur. To protect him from himself, Howie spent the rest of the night in his cat carrier with his favorite black-and-white mouse toy.

Unfortunately, this was not Howie's last mishap in New Zealand. At the beginning of May, after an excruciating year's worth of engine repairs, we motored overnight to the Bay of Islands. This was the third time we had rebuilt the engine and we needed to thoroughly test it. Howie thought he'd test us by eating the bait off Paul's fishing line after we had anchored in Assassination Cove.

As is the principle of a baited hook, the hook got firmly stuck in the roof of Howie's mouth. He yowled and hissed; he flicked his tongue at the hook, trying to remove it. Paul quickly cut the fishing line off the hook to release our "catch." I scooped up our poor cat as he darted toward one of Rosie's dark crevices to hide. With pliers in hand, Paul peered into Howie's mouth.

"It's embedded too deeply," Paul said. "I don't think I can get it out."

I felt sick to my stomach, looking at my little buddy who was struggling in my arms, vainly trying to spit the hook out of his mouth. I tried to calm him down with soothing words and by stroking his head, but he would not be calmed.

And who could blame him?

"We have got to find a vet," I said firmly, looking around the placid anchorage surrounded by sheep-dotted hills. Without the internet or a local phone book, I was stumped. A year and a half of these land-based conveniences had spoiled me. I had forgotten how to be a cruiser.

Paul hadn't. "Let's call on the radio. Maybe one of these yachts lives around here, or has a pet."

A boat responded and said that there was a vet in Opua. We put Howie into his carrier so he couldn't hide while Paul and I readied Rosie for an immediate departure. After plotting our course, we hoisted the anchor and motor-sailed two hours to Opua. As we got nearer, we called the Opua Cruising Club on the radio and they gave us the phone number of the vet.

When I called the vet, I explained Howie's situation and the fact that we were on a boat and did not have a car. He agreed to pick us up at the bottom of a hill, near a small beach where we could land the dinghy. Paul would dinghy us to the beach and return to Rosie, as we were anchoring in open water without wind and wave protection.

The vet arrived in his battered white pickup truck and took us to his house; his concrete garage served as his clinic. In the middle of the garage was a gigantic stainless steel operating table, suited for his usual patients: horses, cows and sheep. The able vet fixed Howie up in a matter of minutes and returned us to our little beach with some antibiotics. Within an hour of being back on Rosie, he was purring and squeaking from all of our extra attention.

The engine was also purring – albeit noisily – from all of the attention we had lavished on it over the past year and we were relieved that it was working well. As it had in Charleston over two years ago, our focus shifted from boat repairs to preparations for leaving. The cruising season was almost upon us and we would soon depart New Zealand for Fiji.

While our days had been busy since our arrival in New Zealand, 18 months ago, the absence of television or Internet on board had given us ample time to read at night. And read we did -- about Harry Potter, cruising destinations, and advanced sailing tactics, especially for stormy weather.

The rough seas that separated New Zealand from the islands of the South Pacific, including Fiji, awaited us. We had heard stories of yachts capsizing, boats sinking and cruisers mysteriously disappearing on these waters. I was worried because we hadn't completed any ocean passages over the past 18 months. We were out of practice and about to sail through the spin-cycle again.

We unburied Rosie's sea anchor from one of our lockers and inspected it. In life-threatening seas, one could toss out a sea anchor. This resembled an underwater parachute and, if properly deployed, forced the boat to face into the wind. If the wind and the waves were coming from the same direction, and they usually were, this allowed the boat to safely ride up and down each wave without speed. While we didn't test the sea anchor – it would take forever to collapse a parachute full of water -- we did rig it so that we could launch it from the safety of our cockpit. If the seas were so violent that we needed a sea anchor, I certainly didn't want Paul running forward to the bow to set it.

We also tested our Epirb, an emergency satellite beacon; inspected our life raft; and reassessed our "grab bag." Besides Howie, this was the only item we'd grab if we had to abandon ship. It contained bare necessities like a hand-held desalination water maker; fishing line and hook; a Leatherman, a pocket knife with a dozen retractable tools; photocopies of our passports and some cash; a basic first-aid kit; sunscreen, hats and old sunglasses; a collapsible bucket; our camping GPS and spare hand-held VHF radio.

All of this was to prepare ourselves for our passage to Fiji. For ten days, we waited, at anchor in Opua, for a good weather forecast. While we waited, I provisioned the boat. Paul worked through Bruce's pre-departure checklist, which we had continued to use ever since our maiden voyage. Half a dozen yachts left before we had finished our preparations. Four of them limped back to Opua after gale conditions thrashed their boats. Two boats had broken forestays, another boat had broken its gooseneck and the catamaran had cracked its superstructure between its two hulls. It was rare to have one boat return to port with some damage, but four? We had never witnessed such widespread carnage and it did not bode well.

Praying that we had reassembled our boat – her mast, rigging, deck hardware, lifelines and engine - correctly, we departed on May 18th for Savu Savu, Fiji, with reports of southeasterly winds and a moderate sea. Before we were even out of sight of land, Paul and I were seasick. We set the egg timer, flipped on the radar and alternated watches from our berths. After a couple of days, Paul recovered; it took me six days.

I was lying on my berth on the sixth day while we motored through a calm. The engine was humming along, albeit with a new vibration, when all of a sudden it made a horrific clang. I bolted upright at the noise, and Paul, who had been in the cockpit, rushed down the steps. We listened. The engine no longer hummed, it clattered. Paul promptly turned it off.

Damn it. After a year of engine repairs, we deserved a working engine.

We consulted Nigel, via our well-used diesel engine repair book, and we tried the easy fixes while we were at sea but to no avail. Other possible causes, which included a broken head gasket or a broken crankshaft, were intensive repairs that would have to wait until landfall. Utterly discouraged, we altered course to Suva. According to our guide book, Suva had the best repair facilities in Fiji, and it was 200 miles closer than Savu Savu.

From Soggy Suva to So So Bay

Fiji, May 2004

Without a working engine, we anchored far from shore and away from the other boats as a safety measure. Then we got a good night's sleep before facing the engine. The next morning, we hoisted the engine out and propped it on two floor joists that spanned our 6-foot-deep bilge. Paul climbed into the bilge and dropped the sump from the engine above his head to inspect the crankshaft. It was cleanly snapped in two. With the engine and transmission out, only the prop shaft remained.

The prop shaft was rotated by the engine's transmission and turned the propeller, which was snugly located between our keel and rudder in the water. Suspecting that the engine's new vibration might have been caused by a bent prop shaft, now was the time to pull it out and inspect it.

In the murky green water of Suva Harbor, Paul dove under the boat and removed the propeller while I passed him tools from the dinghy. That was the easy part.

The next step, pulling out the prop shaft, meant that we would have an underwater hole in the boat for as long as it took Paul to shove a bung – a cone-shaped piece of wood – into the hole. According to Nigel, a 2-inch diameter hole located three feet under the water, as we would have, would let in 136 gallons of water per minute.

On the count of three, I pulled the shaft out of its hole. Before Paul could slam the bung into the hole, salt water exploded into the boat, slamming into Paul's chest with shocking force and spraying the bilge. Fighting the water, he jammed the bung into the hole. The water stopped.

Like an un-caged cork in a bottle of champagne, I eyed the bung with trepidation. How could that puny bung withstand the pressure of the ocean outside? If it popped out when we weren't on the boat, Rosie could easily sink. At my urging, Paul reinforced the bung by strapping it in place with wire.

A local machine shop verified that our prop shaft was out of alignment.

That was to sum up June, our first month in Fiji: searching for crank- and prop- shafts, waiting for them to be delivered before rebuilding, realigning and retesting everything.

Not surprisingly, our morale was low, low, low. It didn't help that Suva was rightfully known as "Soggy Suva" because it rained all the time, and not just a drizzle, but torrential downpours. We filled our 200-gallon water tanks in less than 15 minutes by using a bunched up towel to puddle the rain water around the water tanks' inlets on deck. We were never short of water in Suva, but we were in dire need of some sunshine. Because we weren't getting it literally, I begged Paul's mum, Mavis, to come for a visit.

Mavis always cheered us up, and her trip to Fiji was no exception. With her, we laughed at the rain that soaked us to our underwear; we guffawed as she climbed over the engine that divided the salon from the galley; we joked about the decrepit fishing boats, or "rust buckets," anchored next to us. While we waited for our parts, we toured Suva, ate delicious Indian curries and sipped Fiji Bitter at the Royal Suva Yacht Club.

It was on one of those rainy days at the Yacht Club when I suddenly remembered that we had accidentally left the deck-top hatches open in the salon.

"Oh no," Paul responded. "The laptops!" He didn't have to explain. They were under the open hatches.

It was pouring as we scrambled to collect our shopping bags and dashed toward the dinghy. Before we darted out of the Yacht Club's protective cover, a French woman, with four kids in tow, grabbed Paul's arm. She quickly explained that she was on the catamaran anchored near us.

It seemed that their boat had dragged the night before

and, with the wind picking up, she was concerned that their boat might drag again. But she couldn't leave her four children on shore to make sure her boat was okay; would we check it for her?

"Yes," said Paul hurriedly, and we sprinted to our dinghy.

In the anchorage, four- and five- foot waves made the ride a scary obstacle course as their breaking tops broke over our dinghy, and us. After flying off their peaks, our inflatable dinghy landed flatly in the waves' troughs, spanking the water. Mavis and I clutched the flimsy lifeline so we wouldn't topple overboard.

The catamaran had, indeed, dragged and was just a foot away from hitting another sailboat. The French woman had told Paul how to start their engine, so he drove directly to her boat and leapt on board. I quickly flipped the dinghy around and Mavis and I pounded our way to Rosie.

Once we were alongside, Mavis timed the waves to get aboard our wildly bucking boat. There was an eight-foot difference between the dinghy and Rosie's deck at one instant; in the next, there was just a foot. She scrambled aboard and ran forward to shut the hatches from outside.

I tied up the dinghy, leapt aboard and unlocked the companionway doors. Mavis hurried down. She slid across our wet varnished floor to check on the computers. One was saturated; the other looked okay. I left her to dry the one computer while I went back to help Paul.

Another cruiser was using his inflatable dinghy to buffer the errant catamaran from the sailboat it was trying hit, while the sailboat's captain fired up his engine, up-anchored and motored out of harm's way. Paul, in the meantime, had let out more anchor chain on the catamaran, hoping it would stop the anchor from dragging. By the time the catamaran was secured, it was no longer next to Rosie but halfway across the anchorage.

An hour later, the wind and seas were placid. The only evidence of the squall was our laptop drying in the oven. Sitting in our cockpit, we watched the French woman, and her four children, as they dinghied to their catamaran.

The sight of them prompted a discussion about children, and our plans, if we had any. Having steered us toward IVF, Mavis had followed our attempts and was equally grief-stricken when they had failed. Paul explained that we planned to adopt children when we finished sailing around the world. As much as we wanted to adopt a baby now, while both of us could be full-time parents, we were going to wait.

As promised, I had done some homework in New Zealand. We were dismayed to learn about the lengthy wait times associated with adoption; the exhaustive legal requirements which included home, police and FBI checks as well as the actual court proceedings; and the wallet-traumatizing expense associated with it. There were additional immigration issues, if we adopted internationally.

Nothing about adoption sounded easy.

Of course, sailing wasn't easy either and that hadn't deterred us. But now the question wasn't one of ease but one of finances. For the past three years, we had been unemployed, spending our savings on living expenses, boat repairs and IVF. We had just enough money to finish our circumnavigation - or adopt - but not both. If we postponed adoption until we returned the States and found jobs, we could have both: our sailing trip and a baby.

While we had set sail as a response to our life crisis, our goal to sail around the world had taken on its own life. We had sacrificed our jobs, sold our house and cars and spent our hard-earned money for this. Equally taxing was the daily effort it took to make this trip possible, from fixing the engine at sea, planning our next route, maintaining Rosie's systems, monitoring the weather, sailing in all conditions to repairing our current problem, the broken crankshaft. We were committed to our circumnavigation, just as we were committed to becoming parents one day. If we could do both, then we would.

Better than anyone else, Mavis understood how we felt. She had experienced the cruising life in the Bahamas, marina-living in New Zealand and now the frustration of repairing Rosie in Fiji. She was sharing the adventure with us and today's storm was just another chapter.

After the day's excitement, we ate a quiet dinner and went to bed early

That night, I tiptoed past Mavis' bed in the salon to get a glass of water.

As I crept past her, she whispered urgently, "Kelly, I hear water."

We had warned her to tell us if she ever heard anything unusual, especially dripping, trickling, pouring, or gushing sounds that might indicate a leak. We still had the bung in the prop shaft hole. I froze and listened to Rosie's usual sounds: the bilge pump toggling on and off, water lapping at Rosie's bow, a distant ship's engine. I didn't hear anything, unless –

"Do you mean Howie?" I asked. He was peeing in his litter box.

We both listened for a moment and then Howie pawed at his kitty litter, indicating he was done.

"Oh dear," Mavis said, laughing self-consciously.

I laughed, too, relieved that it was just our cat. It was unlikely that his leak would sink the boat.

Two days before the new crankshaft arrived, Mavis flew back to England. With the help of Clive on Hannikin, a friend and a fair diesel mechanic, the installation of the crank- and prop- shaft went smoothly. The engine was installed by the end of the day. The next morning, Paul dove back into the water and reinstalled the propeller. We were anxious to test the engine and fired it up immediately.

Bang! Clang! Clang!

We knew right away what was wrong. We had forgotten to remove the screwdriver from the transmission! We had strategically jammed the screwdriver to stop the transmission from turning while reinstalling the propeller. The damage was disheartening, as the screwdriver ripped out all of the control cables and shredded the rear transmission seal. I consulted Nigel, but "forgotten screwdrivers" was not covered.

Another week of engine repairs finally ended, and we motored overnight to Malolo Lailai Island, and Musket Cove, a hotel resort that also catered to cruisers. We declared ourselves on holiday and spent two weeks snorkeling, windsurfing and hiking. We even played a couple of rounds of golf on the resort's oceanfront course. At US$5 for 18 holes, why wouldn't we?

Our fun ended when one of our two laptops died. It was the one that had gotten soaked in Suva, where, after futile attempts to dry it, we had had it repaired. Because we had switched to electronic charts for navigation, we wanted a working laptop as a backup, especially as we intended to sail north from Fiji, where repair facilities were nonexistent. We prudently set sail to Lautoka to get it repaired again.

While we were there, Hannikin sailed into port. Jean and Clive were going to rent a van and drive inland to visit a remote, traditional Fijian village; did we want to come? Other than Suva, we hadn't seen much of Fiji, so we tagged along, carrying a foot-tall cone of kava roots that we had purchased in the local market.

Our guide book said that it was customary for arriving visitors to present kava roots, which are mildly narcotic, to the village chief. The villagers then grind up the roots and stir it into water to make a drink called grog. At the ensuing sevu sevu ceremony, the chief and his guests sit in a circle around a big bowl of grog. The chief passes his guest a small bowl of grog, claps three times and then waits for his guest to drink it in a single gulp. Then his guest claps three times. The bowl is refilled and passed to the next person, and the process is repeated until the grog is gone.

When the chief accepts your kava, he is welcoming you into his village and agreeing to look after you. In bygone days, I guessed that meant that his village wouldn't eat you; the Fijian ancestors were cannibals. What the guidebook neglected to mention, and what we soon discovered, was that Fiji was torn between their ancestral customs and the modern day need for an income.

After two and a half hours of driving over unpaved mountains roads, we arrived at Navala, in the highlands of Fiji at what our guide book called the most picturesque, traditional village in the country. We hadn't even closed the van's door before a villager appeared and demanded a $15 per person admission fee. So much for a traditional village! We paid our dues and, upon hearing that the village chief was not there, left our kava in the van.

The village was gorgeous. As I was busy taking photos, I quickly fell behind the "guided tour." As a result, one family invited me into their bure, their thatched hut, and proudly showed me their home and its centerpiece: their kava bowl. Meanwhile, the tour guide turned to Paul, Clive and Jean and explained that it was customary for tourists to pay her $10 because she wasn't at home, cooking and cleaning, as she would have been had we not come. That soured the experience for Paul and we left shortly thereafter.

We had recently re-watched Tom Hanks in "Castaway" and, as the credits rolled, I noticed that the movie had been filmed on Monuriki Island in Fiji. Like a kid on a treasure hunt, I searched our electronic charts and guide books for Monuriki Island but could not find it. Where was it? Further digging finally revealed that the people of Yanuya Island owned uninhabited Monuriki Island. Because we were still waiting for our laptop to return from Suva, we set off to visit Tom Hanks' island.

When we arrived, we went to the village on Yanuya to present our kava to the chief. The chief was gone, but his grandson accepted our gift and muttered a Fijian prayer to us and our ancestors. When his prayer was finished, he pointed to another thatched hut. Seeing our puzzled faces, he explained that we needed to go to that hut to pay a landing fee for Monuriki.

Monuriki was an idyllic tropical island. We searched for Tom's cave and climbed to the top of the mountain where Tom's character had tried to commit suicide. As we half-slid, half-climbed down the mountain, we scared away a herd of miniature goats, the island's only inhabitants.

We returned to Lautoka. By now, we had been in Fiji for two months and we were anxious to leave, but not without our laptop.

Going to town to check on its progress, Paul hopped in the dinghy and started the outboard. He was zipping away when an amphibious four-foot-long black-and-white banded snake slithered out of its hiding place under the dinghy's removable floor.

We had heard that the venom of these sea kraits (laticauda colubrine) was ten times more poisonous than a rattlesnake and could kill a man almost instantly. Scared stiff, Paul altered course to the nearest boat and, to the stunned surprise of the couple on deck, jumped on board their boat.

"There's a snake in my dinghy," Paul cried.

"I'm terrified of snakes," the husband shrieked, "I don't want to hear about this." He clapped his hands over his ears and started humming.

The wife grabbed their boat hook and together, she and Paul shooed the snake out of the dinghy.

Paul gingerly stepped back in the dinghy and headed to Rosie. No sooner had Paul stepped out of the dinghy when another snake wrapped itself around the outboard and started inching its way into the dinghy. The snake must have heard our exclamations because it slithered back into the water.

When Paul finally made it ashore, we were dismayed to learn that our computer repair was on 'island time;' it was not going to ready for another two or three weeks.

With more time to burn, we decided to cruise the

Yasawa Islands, a chain of islands north of Musket Cove. Kela, a boat we hadn't seen since Tahiti, also wanted to go, so we set off together for Soso Bay on Naviti Island. And once again, with two boats setting sail for the same destination, it was a race to see who could drop their anchor first.

Kela had a huge advantage in this race. It was called 22 feet. On sailboats, speed was proportional to the boat's length, and so it was no contest between our little Rosie and their lovely 64-foot Sundeer ketch. To even things out, we rushed to up-anchor and took off an hour earlier than Kela. As we entered Soso Bay, Kela breezed past us.

In a last-ditch effort to win the race, Paul rushed to the bow and threw out our anchor and chain. As he glanced up to check on Kela's progress, he lost track of how much chain was going over until it was all over. As in ALL overboard. The bitter end of the chain had not been fastened to the boat and now our anchor and 300 feet of chain were lying some 50 feet below us.

Oops.

Paul shouted for me to push the man-overboard button on our GPS to mark the spot. Then he hurriedly put on his mask and snorkel to see if he could retrieve the chain while I kept Rosie clear of the reefs surrounding us. It was dusk. Paul dove down, but it was already too dark to see our chain. Kela suggested that we raft up with them for the night and, because the night was so calm, we did.

I should've seen the storm coming; after all, they always seem to follow a calm. But I didn't, nor did anyone else. Instead, we relaxed. We had dinner and played Pictionary on Kela with Kirk and Debbie, and their nearly teen-aged sons, Braden and Grady. Howie eagerly explored their spacious boat.

At 1 a.m., I woke up because the wind had picked up. I nudged Paul. We got up and played the "what if" game. What if the wind got stronger? What if we needed to break free from Kela, what would we do? How would we anchor with our primary anchor on the bottom of Soso Bay?

As we analyzed the growing waves and wind, Kirk joined us on deck and we all agreed it was time to cut ties. Within 10 minutes, the waves had grown from one foot to four feet. With Rosie upwind and rafted to Kela's hip, it looked like our bow was trying to smash onto Kela's deck. The boats rocked and rolled, and the motion threatened to tangle our rigging, which would be catastrophic.

Paul and the Kela crew were fending off our two boats and somehow, in the confusion, I ended up behind our wheel. While Paul tried to figure out which lines to drop first, I watched with horror as Rosie pitched against Kela.

Then Paul shouted over the wind, "Kel, when I release this line, steer Rosie clear."

As if our engine was a match for the now 6-foot waves and 40 knots of wind! Kirk pulled our stern close to Kela. For a second, the wind funneled between our boats, pushing Rosie's nose briefly away from Kela.

It was now or never.

Kirk released the stern line, Paul tossed the spring line and I threw the engine into gear, revved up the throttle and kept the wheel straight.

Vrrroomm! We were off!

But there was no time for relief. We were now slamming into the six foot waves, in utter darkness, with shallow reefs all around us and no rigged anchor. While we had been rafted to Kela, we had set our stern anchor to keep our boats from lying sideways to the swell. In our haste to separate from Kela, Paul had cut off the stern anchor. Now there were two Cherokee Rose anchors on the bottom of Soso bay and neither was attached to us.

Our last anchor was at the bottom of our cockpit locker, below six feet of fenders, cans of varnish, dinghy wheels and fishing gear. The only rope long enough to anchor the boat was still tied to the sea-anchor.

Because the storm and nighttime limited our visibility, I relied on the radar screen to guide me as I tried to keep Rosie in the middle of the bay. Next to me, Paul emptied the cockpit locker and uncovered the spare anchor. Then he pulled apart our sea anchor and attached its line to the spare anchor. Before he chucked it overboard, I stopped him. Was the anchor attached to the line, and was the line attached to Rosie? We couldn't afford to lose this one.

It was 3 a.m. when we finally went down below to sleep. The sea was so rough; we slept in our separate sea berths, with our lee cloths up to prevent us from rolling out of bed.

The next day, despite the still turbulent seas, Kirk and Brayden helped Paul search for our anchor and chain. They used the dinghy anchor as a crude hook and dredged the bottom, thinking the dinghy anchor was bound to snag some part of our 300-feet of chain. But it didn't work.

After a couple of wasted hours, Paul came back to the boat to dig out our scuba gear. I passed him the handheld GPS with the man-overboard position to help him locate the anchor. The guys motored to the spot and Paul dove down, finding the chain within a foot of the GPS position. We winched the chain and anchor aboard, attached the bitter end to Rosie and re-anchored.

We hadn't intended to visit the village at Soso Bay, but after spending two days and nights parked in their backyard, we felt we should. As captains of the boats, Paul and Kirk presented kava to the chief, who gladly accepted it and gave them a blessing. Paul plucked up the courage to ask him if he would invite us to a sevu sevu ceremony, as we had never been to one.

Bill, the chief, graciously agreed. He invited Paul and Kirk to come back that evening, telling them to bring their families and a couple of cans of beer. When we came to shore later that day, children ran to the beach to meet us and asked for candy. We didn't have any and their disappointment was obvious.

The sevu sevu ceremony was pretty much as we expected it to be, and the grog, which looked like muddy water, tasted as bad as it looked. What we hadn't expected was the kava-induced tingling and subsequent numb sensation in our lips. We didn't experience any other side effects. After the chief drank his bowl of grog, he asked for a beer to wash away the taste of the grog!

Before we left Soso Bay, a Kiwi sailboat pulled into the bay and anchored. Awhile later, its captain called us on the radio. It seemed his anchor chain had just snapped and now his anchor and chain were resting on the bottom of the bay. Did we have a spare shackle that he could borrow?

We cruised the Yasawas for another week before we received a satellite e-mail from my sister. Dad had been in a serious bicycle accident in France. He had broken his pelvic bone, his hip and his shoulder.

We rushed to the nearest resort. On shore, I asked to use their phone only to learn that it was a radio-phone and couldn't make long distance calls. If we were looking for remote, we had truly found it in the Yasawas.

We left Kela and spent the next four days sailing back to Lautoka, and to long-distance telephones. En route, the wind picked up and blew 30 knots on our nose, forcing us to seek shelter for a day. While the wind howled, we listened to the SSB radio with growing concern. A dive boat had taken an English couple out to scuba dive in spite of the rough weather and the couple hadn't resurfaced. Ultimately the dive boat had left them.

While we listened to the radio, four planes searched the area while the rescue team called for any yachts in the area to help. We checked our charts but we were too far south to help. Friends on another boat joined the search but to no avail. They were presumed dead. I was shocked, and angry, that the dive boat captain had departed, knowingly leaving people in the water. I imagined how the couple felt, floating in the water together, knowing that drowning or being eaten by sharks was far more likely than being rescued – and I was scared for them.

When we arrived in Lautoka, I was relieved to hear my dad's voice. He was in good spirits despite the fact that he would be in traction for three weeks. Paul and I offered to fly home to look after him, but he declined; Lynn was taking good care of him. Paul and I put together a slideshow of our time in Fiji, complete with narration, and mailed that to him along with a care package of DVD movies that we bought.

We also picked up our laptop, which was finally repaired.

After three months in Fiji, dealing with engine and computer issues, we were now ready to leave. While most cruisers set sail for Vanuatu, New Caledonia, Australia and then pass through the Torres Strait for the Indian Ocean, we had decided to take a less-traveled route. We were going to head north to Tuvalu, and Kiribati, then sail west through Micronesia. We would follow Magellan's route through the Philippines before sailing to Hong Kong.

Our trip to Tuvalu started with a stressful departure from Fiji. Rather than leaving Fiji through a tried-and-true route, I had the brilliant, or not so brilliant, idea of sailing north through Fiji's Bligh Waters, a coral-littered sea, then entering the ocean through the Round Island Passage, just north of the Yasawa Islands. This "shortcut" would save us 12 hours with the added bonus that we'd be sailing through protected waters. As long as the sun was shining, we would be able to see and avoid the submerged reefs. Our cruising guide suggested an anchorage off one of the submerged reefs; we would anchor there for the night.

The problem was, once we got to the so-called anchorage, the reef wasn't there. Obviously our charts were wrong. And that was a big "yikes!" because the sun was starting to set and poor Rosie was surrounded by fiberglass-eating coral. I was frantically searching for a suitable place to anchor but was getting discouraged, and scared. If the sun set and we weren't safely anchored, what would we do? We couldn't move the boat because we'd hit a coral reef and we couldn't motor in place all night. Paul wasn't helping matters.

"Slow Rosie down. I've caught a fish," Paul said excitedly as his fishing reel whizzed out of control.

I looked at the coral reefs around us and the sinking sun. Who cared about fish?!

Once Paul had pulled his beloved 40-pound trevelly on board, we motored cautiously with Paul on the bow and me driving, constantly checking the depth sounder.

Finally, three Fijian Indian fishermen bailed us out. In their rowboat, equipped with a small, rusty outboard engine, they pointed us in the direction of a deep, submerged reef and we dropped the hook as darkness settled around us. Relieved, we collapsed into bed just to wake up before dawn as Rosie bounced in the now choppy water.

Our friendly fishermen knocked on the boat to say goodbye. In the dark, they proudly showed us their night's catch and told us that it would yield Fiji $300 at the market. Minutes after they left, they were obscured by the rough seas.

Curious about their motivation, we did the math. That was F$100 per

person. Each person spent 12 hours that night plus, say, four hours commuting; that worked out to F$6 an hour, or US$3 an hour, not including the price of gas. I was once again reminded of how fortunate we were, not having to risk our lives for three dollars an hour. And they *were* risking their lives, spending the night at sea in an unseaworthy open boat, without any sign of VHF radio, flares or lifejackets.

The trip to Tuvalu was fast, with 15 to 20 knots of wind and a pleasant beam- or broad- reach the whole way, but it continued to be as stressful as it had started. Howie wasn't well. One of his eyes had been watering in Fiji for a couple of days. The day before we left, we had pulled a hair out of his eye, which we had assumed was the culprit. Instead of getting better, his eye got worse. On the second day at sea, it started to ooze bloody pus. The next day, it was bleeding and half-closed.

Via our satellite e-mail, I contacted my sister, Su, and she called her vet on our behalf. After e-mailing her with our list of antibiotics, the vet told us to divide one of our pills into 16 portions and to feed Howie one portion a day. The antibiotic worked wonders and, two days later, he was back to being his usual purr-n-squeak self.

But our stress spiked again when we approached Funafuti, the capital of Tuvalu. Because it was almost dusk, and we didn't have sufficient sunlight, we wouldn't be able to navigate the pass into the protected lagoon. We decided to anchor in the ocean by dropping our hook on the atoll's outer reef. Once the engine was off, and the sky got darker, we could hear the rumble of thunder and see multi-pronged flashes of lightning in the distance.

The storm barreled toward us.

Celebrations in Tuvalu

Tuvalu, September 2004

As during the lightning storm off the coast of Ecuador, our 60-foot tall metal mast was significantly higher than the water and coral reefs around us and seemed to beg for a lightning strike. But unlike the previous storm, when we had been sailing, we were now anchored. Sitting ducks.

According to Nigel, whom I immediately consulted, if lightning struck, it would travel the path of least resistance to ground. In our case, ground was the ocean. The strike might reach the ocean by traveling through the engine (which was grounded by its propeller shaft and propeller) or through the anchor chain or through one of our copper through-hull fittings.

Of course, that meant it might damage the engine's bearings, or blow a hole through the boat. It might even travel along the boat's electrical lines – which looked like a mass of spaghetti under Rosie's floorboards – and destroy our electronics.

Following Nigel's recommendation, Paul attached strips of copper to our standing rigging and dangled these strips into the ocean, providing a quick and easy way for lightning to find ground. While he did that, I unplugged all of our electronics. I put our laptops, portable radios and GPS into the stainless steel oven. Paul figured the oven would act as a faraday box – everyone should have a Paul on board – and protect them from any stray current.

Then we lay down in our sea berths, rolled with the ocean's swell and waited for the inevitable. Paul counted the seconds between the thunder and the lightning. When it hit one second, I started to pray. After 10 anxious minutes, the electrical storm passed. All that preparation and worry, and the worst hadn't happened. We weren't complaining. Torrential rain immediately followed. We dashed outside with soap and scrubbed the decks, cleaning them before filling our water tanks with cool rainwater.

The next morning, we entered the pass and anchored off Funafuti. Tuvalu had been featured recently in a BBC program. Some scientists believe that because of global warming and rising sea levels, Tuvalu is doomed to become another submerged coral reef. Like Suwarrow, or the Tuamotus, Tuvalu is only as tall as its coconut trees.

We saw people in Funafuti drive motorcycles and scooters on the paved roads and buy their food from the two small grocery stores, and yet, from what we observed, they didn't have jobs. To be fair to them, there wasn't anything to work at. But we had to wonder; where did they get their money? For the first time on our travels with Rosie, there wasn't another yacht to turn to for answers to our questions. We were the only sailboat in Funafuti.

Walking through town one day, we met a young woman who was working on her doctoral thesis in environmental anthropology in Tuvalu. Over dinner, she explained that there were three main forms of income in Tuvalu. First, the government licenses its fishing rights to other countries, such as Taiwan, Japan, Korea, New Zealand and America. Second, 15 percent of the Tuvaluan men worked as seamen on container ships – there was a maritime academy in Tuvalu - and they sent their earnings back to their families. Third, and most profitable, is the lease of the Tuvalu's internet domain. Just as the United Kingdom's websites end with a ".uk", Tuvalu's end with a ".tv". In 2000, Tuvalu leased the .tv country code top level domain to a North American company for millions of dollars in royalties to be paid out over 12 years. This company, in turn, markets the .tv top level domain names as ideal web addresses for media-rich content sites. These three forms of income were apparently enough to pave the roads and provide canned corned beef for the local people.

Two hours was plenty of time to see all there was to see in Funafuti and, after spending four days there, we were ready for a change. I suggested that we sail to one of the neighboring islets to visit the Maritime School. Paul thought this was going to be a big yawn, but he didn't have a better idea, so we went.

Jonathan, an ex-Brit and ex-Aussie, ran the school. A retired supertanker captain, he kindly gave us a tour of the facilities and answered our questions with a good deal of sarcasm and wit.

At the end of our short tour, our clothes were clinging to our bodies like second skins. Located at eight degrees south of the equator, Tuvalu was notably hotter than Fiji. Jonathan saw our discomfort and invited us to his house for gin-and-tonics. With ice! Wild horses couldn't keep me away. There he entertained – and frightened – us with tales of ships running over yachts.

The next day, we returned for dinner at Jonathan's invitation. In preparation for the meal, he led us through the coconut grove on "his" private islet. Thriving in the partial shade were hundreds of bird's nest ferns. He stopped at one, snapped off one of the leaf's curly, bright green ends and told me to try it. The new growth crunched and tasted like a raw snow pea. The three of us gathered a large bowlful for our evening's salad. After a lovely roast dinner at Jonathan's house and watching the school's dress parade in the morning, we sailed back to Funafuti to clear out of Tuvalu.

We asked Immigration if we could officially check out of Tuvalu but have their permission to stop at one of the Tuvaluan atolls farther north. Normally, one would have to sail back to Funafuti after visiting any of its atolls to clear out, but that meant sailing against the prevailing wind and waves, not an attractive option. We were hoping our award-winning smiles would convince Immigration to make an exception for us.

But there was no one to smile at. The one man who could make this decision was sick. After fruitlessly waiting three days for this man to return to work, we checked out. We decided that we'd stop at the atoll, ask the local authorities if we could stay for a couple of days and act accordingly.

With an early morning start, we sailed north for 60 miles to Nukafetau. Late that afternoon, we went to the village to seek permission to stay. We were immediately surrounded by children of all ages. Unlike Fiji, none of them demanded sweets, they just followed us, saying "Hello, how are you?" as they tried to practice their English.

They led us to the local police officer. Wearing a towel wrapped around his waist and holding his two-year-old daughter in his arms, he was buying some rolls from an old lady in a thatched hut. We introduced ourselves to Seeorsay and explained our situation. He hesitated when we admitted we had already cleared out of Tuvalu but then said it was okay for us to stay. With that business concluded, he invited us to his house. That wasn't the only invitation we got.

Everywhere we went, people waved and said "Talofa," Tuvaluan for "hello." Teua and her husband, Evanglia, offered us drinking coconuts, showed us how to make coconut toddy – a fermented drink – and invited us to lunch. Salani gave us a bunch of bananas and a loaf of bread baked in the village's communal, coconut- husk-burning, oven. Vaitupu, the headmistress of the school, invited us to her sister's wedding on Wednesday and everyone invited us to their Independence Day celebrations on Friday, October 1st.

In return, Paul fixed the Protestant pastor's computer and showed him how to work his video camera. We went to the school where we gave Vaitupu, the headmistress, stacks of used school books that a Kiwi charity had given to us to pass out. We learned that the school had five used computers, donated by an Australian charity, but no one knew how to set them up. Paul volunteered to set up a network for them, and Vaitupu was thrilled. Then her face fell. She explained that she didn't have a table to set the computers on nor the needed power strips, but she'd ask around – after her sister's wedding.

While we were there, she asked Paul to fix their photocopier; another person asked Paul to repair their CD player and a third person asked him to fix his VCR. In their mind, all electronics were the same. Because Paul knew computers, he could obviously repair these other items. My husband gamely tried but, without the needed replacement parts or tools, had limited success.

I wasn't exactly idle myself. I took photographs of everyone: the newlyweds, the 3-day old baby, the children, the parents, the sports events, the wedding and the dancing. On the boat, I'd print out the photos on our color printer and pass them around when we were in town. Before we left, I saw these photos hanging on the otherwise bare walls in these people's homes. Paul was doing the "important" stuff, but I was definitely more popular.

We arrived at Vaitupu's house for the wedding reception and were surprised to see crowds of "peeping-toms" huddled around the glassless windows. Vaitupu ushered us past them.

Inside was a riot of color. As in Fiji, the women we saw dressed modestly in their muumuu and lava-lavas but in immodest colors: turquoise blue, hot pink, neon orange, race-car red and spring green. The men were equally vivid in their sarong skirts and printed shirts. But even the vivid tropical prints couldn't compete with the kaleidoscope of food that carpeted the floor.

Vaitupu told us that half the women in the village were related to either the bride or the groom and that they had spent the past two days preparing food for the celebration. There was roasted pig, fried fish, boiled breadfruit, rice, rolls, raw fish in coconut milk, sweet fritters, bananas, taro cooked in banana leaves, sliced papaya, fried breadfruit chips and numerous dishes I didn't recognize.

Because there wasn't a table in the room, the food was spread buffet-style on the floor in the middle of the room. Everyone sat several feet away from this feast with their backs against the house's cinder block wall. Vaitupu asked some people to move down, and she signaled for us to sit along one of the walls. Near us, the wedding couple beamed while chatting with the procession of well-wishers. Someone said several words, and dinner began.

The wedding couple served themselves first while everyone watched. Then Vaitupu gestured that we were to get our food next. I started to protest, but seeing Paul's stern glance, wisely shut up. While we thought we were the least important guests there, they obviously felt otherwise. So Paul and I self-consciously helped ourselves and sat down. Then it was a free-for-all as the rest of the room, and the people watching outside, swarmed around the food.

As we had discovered along our trip, music was always appreciated. I had wrapped a couple of our used CDs as a wedding gift and we had planned to just slip them the gift. When we went to do so, the room quieted. The wedding couple stood up and suddenly we were co-stars in a ceremony that we hadn't rehearsed. Despite our lack of grace, everyone applauded. Afterward, there were three speeches – we didn't understand a word – and then everyone broke into small groups to play cards. That's when we quietly exited.

Independence Day was sunny and, as usual, hot. The celebration started at the school yard with competitions of all sorts: volleyball, running, coconut husking, high-jump, long jump, sack and three-legged races. We joined a group of people standing in the shade of a breadfruit tree to watch the festivities, but Seeorsay coaxed Paul into doing the three-legged race. I begged off, saying that I'd take photos. Paul was paired with another woman, who told Paul to hold her close. When the gun went off, Paul practically carried his partner, and ran to the finish line while the crowd cheered them on. By comparison, everyone else seemed to be running in slow motion.

It wasn't long before Seeorsay was back, urging Paul to join him in the high-jump – but it was a high jump with a twist. no mattress or landing pad. I watched, surprised to discover that my honey could jump. The competition continued with the stick moving up, notch by notch, and the competitors dwindling in numbers.

There were six men left when Paul missed his first attempt. In this event, everyone got three chances before being disqualified. When Paul's second chance came, he dove headfirst over the pole and somersaulted upon landing. While not legitimate in the Olympics, it was apparently allowed here. The village laughed and clapped at Paul's antics; even the referee stopped to shake Paul's hand. And so it continued until Paul's dive-and-tumble combo beat the island's best, and proper, jumper.

Later that day, we learned that there were cash prizes for all of the competitions and that Paul had won AUS$18. The award ceremony would be held in the afternoon and we, of course, were expected to attend. Eighteen dollars was a lot of money for these people and inadvertently Paul had taken it away from the villagers.

We found the game coordinator and insisted he give the high jump prize money to the real winner, the man in the red shorts. Because Paul had won the three-legged race with this other woman, he asked that his half go to the school.

The game coordinator, who happened to be the pastor of the one church on the island, raised his eyebrow and clarified Paul, "Give it to the school? Not the church?"

Paul coughed and hastily corrected his request.

The pastor beamed.

The Independence Day celebrations continued that

evening with a traditional dance competition, held in an open-air, thatched-roof meeting hut. Seated on the hard concrete floor, and wearing green clothes, the north side of the village was competing against the south side of the village, clad in orange. While the women's dancing was a modest version of Polynesian dancing, it was the men who captured our attention.

Four men sat on the floor around a wood box, one man per side. They drummed the box with their hands and sang in unison. Another man beat a crude piece of sheet metal with drumsticks. As the song continued, the tempo quickened and the men beat their hands faster and faster.

The villagers, who wore their team's colors, were seated around their respective drummers. When their team sang, they clapped their hands in time and sang along, faster and faster. I couldn't help but wonder if Ravel had gotten his inspiration for "Bolero" in Tuvalu. Unlike Ravel's refined orchestra, the Tuvaluan beat was raw and primitive. It conjured up images of a tribe beating their drums before the hunt. And we were in the center of the pulsating beat, having been seated behind the sheet metal drummer on the green team.

While we were seated, a man walked up to us and spritzed us with perfume. Then he moved on, spraying everyone on the green team before moving onto the orange team. Another man followed with a different fragrance. A third man wove through the seated crowd, spraying every woman twice strategically across her bosom. I stifled my laughter when it was my turn.

We, and the entire room, stank.

We later learned that it was a Tuvaluan sign of respect to spray someone with perfume and, had we done our homework, we would have known to have brought some perfume, too.

Throughout the ceremony, I discreetly took photos and, hoping to capture some of the evening's primitive magic, I also took a couple of video clips. Suddenly the lead man on our side stood up and pointed at my camera. He gestured that I should take his photo. Flustered for being singled out in the crowd, I saluted without thinking, causing everyone to laugh. He gyrated to the pulsing music, and to my camera.

Observing the man and his obvious excitement, Paul leaned over and whispered, "Remind me not to wear a skirt when I dance."

As usual, Howie waited in the cockpit and greeted us as we stepped aboard that night. He took one sniff of fragrant us and retreated to the cabin with a pained meow. Paul started to follow him down below when I halted him. There was no way our smelly clothes, or our smelly selves, were going down below. Leaving our clothes down-wind of the cabin, we stripped, and showered in the cockpit. But the stench of cheap perfume lingered in our nostrils for hours.

The next day, the wind blew and we spent half the day windsurfing in the lagoon. The other half of the day we spent showing our new friends our boat. Paul ferried groups of people out to the boat where I handed out cups of fruit juice and gave them a tour of Rosie. Everyone was surprised to see Howie on board, but the children were especially taken with him, following him around and petting his soft fur.

With a good weather forecast, we said our goodbyes and motored out of the lagoon. It was 650 miles to Tarawa, the nearest port of entry for Kiribati, and its capital. We estimated the trip would take us five to seven days, depending on the wind. The seas were smooth, the wind was light but steady and the sun was shining. For the first time, I wasn't sick on passage, but another crewmate was.

Sorrowful Goodbye, Sudden Hello

Pacific Ocean, October 2004

    As we sailed to Kiribati, we realized that Howie was definitely ill. His appetite had steadily diminished. Paul and I begged him to eat during our watches, offering him trevally, tuna, salmon, and milk. But he shunned even his favorite foods; he flatly refused his specially-formulated cat food which regulated his diabetes. As a result, his diabetes flared up.

    Within a couple of days, he had visibly lost weight, stopped purring and couldn't stand by himself. I sent Su a frantic e-mail. She contacted her vet, who told us to syringe-feed Howie a mixture of his wet food and water. We did and, at first, it seemed to help.

    Suzanne searched on-line for a veterinarian clinic in Tarawa or Majuro, the nearby capital of the Marshall Islands but there weren't any. After a couple of phone calls, she found an American nurse in Majuro who had treated animals. In light of Howie's condition, we decided to skip Tarawa and sail directly to Majuro. Meanwhile, Howie's health deteriorated.

    Then Howie went into convulsions and even satellite e-mail wasn't fast enough. I yanked out our Merck Manual of Medical Information and read that human diabetics sometimes suffered from hypoglycemia if they didn't eat. Howie's symptoms matched. We found glucose in our first aid kit and, not knowing how much to give him, gave him two dilute doses before his convulsions subsided. We continued to monitor him.

For once, I was thankful for our watch schedule and the fact that one of us was always awake. At around 5 p.m., Paul joined me in the cockpit, where we had created a little nest of towels for Howie.

"How's he doing?" Paul asked quietly.

I shrugged my shoulders helplessly. I didn't know.

At the sound of our voices, Howie lifted his head, looked up at both of us, meowed and died.

In disbelief, I scooped him up and clutched him in my arms. "Howie?" I cried.

Paul silently shook his head at me, his eyes reddening as tears formed. He put his arms around me and Howie, and pulled us close. "He's dead, Kel."

I shook my head and burst into tears.

"We've got to bury him," he said gently.

"He's not dead," I said angrily, pulling away from Paul's comfort. Through my tears, I demanded, "Get the stethoscope. I don't believe you."

Paul looked at me sadly before retrieving the stethoscope from our first aid kit.

No heartbeat.

Howie was dead.

"Kel, we've got to let him go."

"Why?" I demanded. Howie had been my faithful friend for 14 years. What was I going to do? Throw him overboard? He was still warm, and soft.

I sat down, sobbing, and cuddled Howie. Paul reappeared, gently took Howie from my arms and laid him down on a sheet of wood. It was one of the locker covers from our settee.

"There," he said, "now we need to say our good-byes and bury him at sea."

Howie looked so lonely, so sad on that piece of wood. I couldn't bear it. "He needs his favorite toy."

Paul nodded and brought back his black and white toy mouse. He put it next to him.

I looked at my cat, lying forlornly on the board, and sobbed, "I can't do this. There are sharks out there. He'll get eaten."

"It's the cycle of life," Paul said gently.

I knew Paul was right; I knew we needed to bury Howie. "We need some sort of service," I said.

Taking Paul's hand, we bowed our heads as I prayed for

Howie. Then we told each other our favorite Howie stories, half chuckling, half crying as we remembered all of his adventures. With Eva Cassidy playing in the background, Paul draped an American flag over Howie and his favorite toy. Then he tipped the board.

Splash!

I lunged to the side of the boat to look overboard but couldn't see my beloved cat. Paul pulled me away from the side and hugged me. Still in disbelief over Howie's sudden death and the equally sudden burial-at-sea, I slumped down in the cockpit. Paul went below to make us a cup of tea.

For the first time in days, I glanced around us. In the far distance, to our right, was Onatoa Island; to our left, the sun was sinking on the horizon with shades of gold, pink and orange. Behind us was Howie. As I gazed gloomily at Rosie's wake, at the distance that was growing between me and my beloved cat, a star emerged on the horizon behind us. As the bright star rose, seemingly out of the ocean, I declared it "Howie's star." While we sipped our tea, I found his star in our book of constellations. It was Canopus in the southern hemisphere constellation Carina.

Paul changed the conversation to a more practical one. "We don't have to go directly to the Marshall Islands now. Do you want to stop in Kiribati?"

I sighed, "Sure. Why not?"

That decision changed our lives.

Fighting the outgoing tide to enter Tarawa's lagoon, the last two miles of our passage took an hour. The lagoon was unlike any other we had seen. It had only three shades of turquoise, indicating an almost uniform and shallow depth, and the water was not clear. The sea floor was obscured in only eight feet of water which was unnerving with our six-foot draft. We dropped our hook at the recommended anchorage off Betio, a town in Tarawa. Other than a small Kiribati Navy ship and a couple of decrepit rusty fishing boats, we were the only boat there.

Following the directions in our guide book, Paul tried to call Tarawa Radio on Channel 16 to announce our arrival, but the radio just buzzed. The channel was jammed. So Paul went ashore to clear in. He returned a half an hour later with two hefty Customs officers. After I offered them some fruit juice, they asked about our food stores, including any alcohol and cigarettes we had on board. I admitted that we had a case of wine and a scant case of beer.

"We'll have to charge you import tax on the alcohol," said the male officer.

"It's not worth paying tax on," Paul said. "You can take it."

The two officers shifted in their seats and, after a long pause, the man asked if it was for our personal use.

It was. And we could keep it tax-free.

After a couple more questions about meat, eggs, nuts and seeds – they must have been trained in New Zealand! – we were allowed to keep our stores. We took the officers back to shore and headed toward Immigration.

The Immigration office was located in Bairiki, a bus ride away. But we didn't have any Australian dollars, the currency used in Tarawa, for the bus fare. After walking past the tired Customs building, which looked like a warehouse, we were pleasantly surprised to find an automatic teller machine on the dirt road. Voila! We were solvent.

We asked a passing woman which bus would take us to Bairiki, and she hailed one for us. She shouted something over the mini-van's deafening music. Apparently she told everyone to move over, as its occupants reshuffled themselves to allow us to sit down. And we were off, with boom-ba-da-boom blasting from the mini-van's subwoofer and some golden oldie – Linda Ronstadt? – that had been remade into a rap song blaring from the speakers.

Once our visas were granted, we returned to Rosie for our after-passage cold beer and a good night's sleep.

But a good night's sleep was not to be had. That evening, it rained heavily and the wind picked up to 25 knots. The Navy ship had re-anchored and was now 100 feet – about two boat lengths – ahead of us. As the wind continued to blow, the Navy ship drifted back on her anchor chain until she was just one boat length away. Taunting us, she swung side-to-side in front of our bow. Behind us, a coral reef ominously waited; it had already claimed two fishing boats, judging by the visible debris.

We flipped on the radar, and our instruments. We ran up and down the companionway steps, checking that the Navy ship hadn't drifted any closer. How did one fend off a naval ship? Or a coral reef? With great difficulty. The best solution was to prevent contact with either, so we spent an uneasy, but thankfully uneventful, night on watch.

The anchorage was not much better in good weather, as we quickly discovered. There were two inherent problems. First, by the time the prevailing northeasterly winds swept across nine miles of the lagoon, there was an uncomfortable chop. It was common to have three-foot waves in the anchorage, which turned Rosie into a non-stop see-saw. Day-to-day living was unbearable as we slept in our sea berths, ate simple foods and popped seasickness medicine. The second problem was that these same winds turned land into a lee shore. If our anchor dragged, the wind would push Rosie onto the coral reef or the shore in mere minutes. The anchorage was, to say the least, less than ideal.

After a couple of days of putting up with at-sea conditions while being anchored, I had had enough. We hopped on another ear-splitting minivan, and headed east to survey the lagoon for a better anchorage. Half an hour later, encouraged by the significantly flatter lagoon we saw, we hopped off the bus at the Otintaai Hotel for a cold drink.

Given that Tarawa atoll was shaped like a greater-than sign (>), with Betio at the open, southwest end, the Otintaai Hotel was snugly located near the armpit of the atoll. The hotel had a floating dock – perfect for tying up the dinghy – and the lagoon was flat. We had just found a new home for Rosie.

We ordered two Victoria Bitter beers and toasted Rosie. While we sipped our cold drinks, a British man and his beautiful Kiribati wife sat down near us. They told us a bit about the Kiribati language, which is written with just 15 letters. To compensate for the lack of letters, some letters are combined to make different sounds. For example, the combination of "ti" makes the "s" sound, thus Kiribati is pronounced "kiribas."

A person from Kiribati is called an I-Kiribati; the prefix "I" before a place refers to a person from that place. When white people first arrived in Kiribati, they were called I-Matangs, meaning people from Matang, the land of the gods. They must have figured out that we were far from godly as today I-Matang simply refers to a white or European person.

Our conversation with David and Uatara lasted through dinner. The topic turned to the subject of kids. We were surprised to hear that they had adopted Uatara's sister's baby.

David explained that adoption was common in Kiribati. As in many of the Pacific Islands, adoptions usually occurred within the extended family or within the community. Uatara's sister had allowed David and Uatara to adopt her daughter for financial reasons; they could better provide for her.

With an economy similar to Tuvalu, Kiribati's receives a large portion of its income from its fishing licenses and from the money the Kiribati seamen send home. Like Funafuti, Tarawa has a marine training school. Unlike Tuvalu, however, Kiribati does not have a desirable upper level domain to lease and the phosphate deposits from the island of Banaba, which once accounted for 80% of Kiribati's export earnings, were depleted 30 years ago.

Less than 8% of Kiribati's population has paying jobs, and those jobs don't pay much. We heard that maids and shop keepers made AU$1 an hour. And this meager wage often supported the worker's extended family. In a country where subsistence living – fishing and growing bananas and papayas - was the norm, David and Uatara were wealthy. After all, as a retired British businessman, David had a pension.

Paul was less interested in Kiribati's economy and more interested in its adoption process. David said that it took three hours.

Three hours? Paul glanced at me across the table; hope lit up his face and shone in his eyes.

Oh no, I thought with dismay, nothing about adoption was easy. That's what I had learned when I had spoken to an adoption agency in the States. But this wasn't America, a hopeful voice inside of me said. Maybe Kiribati was different...

David must have seen our glance because he quickly pointed out that he was married to an I-Kiribati and that they had adopted their neice. He thought the process would be different for I-Matangs and suggested that we talk to a Bulgarian couple who lived in Betio. The husband ran the Maritime Training Center, and they had adopted a Kiribati baby. Paul said we would.

The next morning, I was on a mission to learn everything we could about Kiribati adoption. If it wasn't possible for us to adopt, I wanted to know immediately, before our hope and subsequent disappointment grew any larger.

The security guard at the Marine Training Center directed us to the Bulgarians' home. Dolly answered the door, puzzled to find strangers on her doorstep. I introduced ourselves and explained that David and Uatara had suggested we talk to her about adoption.

Dolly had been a lawyer in Bulgaria and she was well-versed on Kiribati adoption law, which was based on the British Adoption Act of 1958. The British influence in Kiribati was not dead despite the fact that Kiribati, previously known as the Gilbert Islands, was no longer a British protectorate. Kiribati had gained its independence in 1979.

Dolly explained that the process took either three or six months, depending on our nationality. Because Paul was British, it might take only three months to adopt a baby. She suggested that we ask at the nearby People's Lawyers office, which was run by the Kiribati government..

We did.

Jennifer, the lawyer on duty and a volunteer from New Zealand, was very polite but looked at us a little strangely when we asked if we could adopt a child.

"Yes," she said. "But where is the child you want to adopt?"

Startled, Paul and I stared at her. I quickly explained that we were trying to understand the process before we committed ourselves to anything.

"Oh," she said. "Well, first you find a baby that you want to adopt. Then you ask the baby's mother go to Births, Deaths and Marriages to get a birth certificate, because the baby probably won't have one. Then all of you come here, and I will explain the adoption process to the baby's birth mother and to you. If you both agree, then we'll start the paperwork."

"How long does the process take?" I asked, explaining our conversation with Dolly and our hope that, because Paul was British, it might only take three months.

"Hmmm," she said, thoughtfully. "Let me look into that and get back to you."

The time it took to adopt a child affected our cruising plans, as did any associated costs. Jennifer stepped us through the legal fees and we discovered that we could afford to adopt, and cruise, at the same time.

Paul and I beamed.

But our smiles were short-lived as we left her office. We were still stymied by the first, insurmountable step. Find a baby. Good heavens. Were we back to trolling for a baby? Or should we post a "Baby Wanted" sign on a coconut tree?

We returned to our adoption ally, mentor and friend.

We summarized our meeting with Jennifer, and Dolly smiled knowingly when we mentioned our first task. She said she'd see what she could do to help us. We thanked her and left, certain that we had hit a dead-end.

We dinghied back to rockin' Rosie. With a great deal of trepidation, we motored Rosie from Betio through the shallow lagoon to her new home off the Otintaai hotel. Paul wisely turned on our GPS so we could track our exact path. If we managed to avoid running aground, or hitting something, we could use our path to back-track through the lagoon. We anchored in 15 feet of water off the hotel, and it was bliss to be aboard a level boat again.

A couple of days later, Paul dinghied ashore to go to the Internet café. He returned unexpectedly minutes later, his face flush with excitement.

"Guess what?" He said as he bounded down the companionway steps. "There are two babies available for adoption, a boy and a girl!"

I looked at him bewildered.

"There was a message from Dolly at the hotel's reception desk, so I called her," he explained, then blurted, "Kel, can we adopt both of them? Please?"

"No," I said firmly, shaking my head at his beseeching smile. "We are on a boat in the middle of nowhere. We know nothing about babies."

That was true. Before we left to go sailing, none of my girlfriends had children; neither did my sister or Paul's sister. While Barbara on Sueño gave birth in New Zealand, we had rarely seen her. Her days were occupied with the baby, ours with boat repairs. I mentally counted: it had been more 20 years since I last babysat! Figuring out what to do with one baby would be enough of a challenge.

Besides that, thanks to our IVF experience, we knew that having twins or triplets caused additional marital stress, and even ruin a marriage. If we adopted two children at once, wouldn't that be the same as having twins?

Paul was still grinning at me, hoping for two children.

"No, no, no," I added, just to be really clear.

Paul's smile drooped for a second and then brightened again. "Okay, which baby do you want? Maybe we should go see them first. Dolly said she could arrange for us to visit them."

While it was tempting, it felt wrong.

"No," I said, sitting down to collect my thoughts. "We are not window-shopping for a baby. How would we choose? And, after we visit them, how would we tell one set of parents that we don't want to adopt their child? That's not how it's done -- " my voice faltered. Who was I kidding? I didn't really know how any of this was done.

"How old are the babies?"

"They are both two months old."

"Why are the parents offering their babies for adoption?"

"Dolly said both cases were for financial reasons. They want their children to have a better life."

I thought for a moment. "Well, if we are going to have a baby, I've always wanted a daughter."

Paul beamed and rushed to the companionway door.

"Whoa!" I rose out of my seat, alarmed. "Where are you going?"

"To tell Dolly that we want to meet the baby girl."

"Isn't this a bit fast? Sit down," I ordered him, pointing to the settee next to me.

Paul reluctantly sat down.

"Have you thought this through? What will we do if the baby isn't healthy?"

Paul took my hands in his. "Kel, you're worrying too much. There won't be anything wrong with the baby."

I tried a different tack, "We don't know how long the adoption process will take. What will we do if it takes six months instead of three?"

"Simple: we'll change our cruising plans. We can stay here longer," Paul said. "There aren't any hurricanes or cyclones on the equator."

I sat back, trying to digest all of this.

"Can I go now?" Paul asked excitedly, standing up.

"Are we ready for this?" I asked him, searching his face.

"We are," he said, leaning down to give me a peck on the cheek before he rushed off the boat.

What were we doing? I asked myself. It was all happening too fast. Didn't these people know about island time?

Apparently not, as two days later we went to meet the baby. En route, we stopped by Dolly and Svilen's home. Dolly had asked if they could come with us to see the baby, but only if we were certain that their presence wouldn't spoil our first precious moments with our prospective daughter.

Was she kidding me? I was relieved to have their moral support.

Svilen drove the four of us to Bairiki to meet the cleaning lady who knew the birth mother and baby. It was she who led us through the village and down its dirt paths.

Paul eagerly pulled my hand, practically skipping, while I dragged my feet. My unease only grew when we saw the crowd that had gathered around the baby's hut. It seemed the entire village had shown up to watch us meet the baby and now I was panicking.

What if we didn't like the baby? What if the baby didn't like us? How did you say, "Thanks but no thanks" to a mother, never mind to a whole village? I wanted to run away, but Paul was tugging on my hand, pulling me toward the hut.

We paused awkwardly outside the hut's door before someone guided us through the first room and into the scantily furnished second room.

A pillow rested on the floor, which was carpeted with pandanas mats. Lying on the pillow and wearing a blue dress that engulfed her, was a little baby with big brown eyes. A woman – presumably her mother – picked up the baby and passed her to me. I sidestepped, nudging Paul forward. I didn't know how to hold a baby. Paul understood.

He took the baby with ease and held her while I peered around his shoulder. The baby stared at Paul while he cooed and smiled at her.

Then he turned to me and whispered, "Hold the baby's head with one hand and her bottom with the other hand."

And just like that, I was holding the baby. As I looked at her, she smiled at me! I beamed at her, relief washing over me. She was gorgeous – and obviously smart, saving her smile for me.

I could be her mom.

Oh baby!

Kiribati, October 2004

"Okay, you take her now?" asked the Kiribati woman, breaking the awe and the smiling spell that had overcome Paul and me as we gazed at this beautiful baby.

"Now?" Paul and I exclaimed in unison. We weren't ready for a baby today. Rosie wasn't ready for baby, either.

"Can we come back Monday morning to get the baby?" I hastily asked. It was Friday.

"Okay," she said. We took our last looks at the baby and left as the village silently watched us go.

Dolly and Svilen lent us some primer books on baby care. We began our two-day crash course in parenthood, reading until the wee hours of the morning and preparing Rosie during the day. On Saturday, I sewed baby sheets and made a lee cloth for the baby's bed, while Paul constructed a folding, diaper-changing table next to the washing machine. On Sunday, we went to Betio and bought baby bottles, formula, wipes, diaper pins and a stack of cloth diapers. Getting rid of garbage was always an issue on the boat, so the luxury of disposable diapers was out of the question.

After a lot of searching, we found a cloth baby carrier that strapped the baby to one's chest, essential if this baby was going to live with us on the boat. Not only did climbing aboard Rosie from the dinghy require both hands, so did dragging the dinghy ashore when we weren't near the hotel's floating dock.

We returned to the village on Monday morning, not even two weeks after we arrived in Kiribati, to pick up the baby and her mother. We had a full day ahead of us: Births, Deaths and Marriages for that birth certificate; the Peace Corps for a medical checkup and finally the People's Lawyers' office.

We were greeted by the same overwhelming crowd of staring people. When Paul whipped the baby carrier out of our new diaper bag and strapped it, and the baby, to himself, everyone pointed and laughed approvingly. Paul smiled good-naturedly. We had agreed that he would carry the baby until I became more confident, and comfortable, with my mothering skills. Then Tiana, her mother, led us down the road so that she could register the baby's birth.

Once the office typed up the birth certificate, we finally learned the baby's name: Timateta Tetika. Our soon-to-be daughter's first name was pronounced Sim-a-te-ta. Her last name was pronounced Tes-i-ka.

After we had the unofficial looking, but officially stamped, birth certificate, we hopped on one of Tarawa's trademark loud minivans for the 35-minute journey to the Peace Corps office. Although there was a hospital on the atoll, we didn't know how qualified the doctors there were. I felt more comfortable visiting the American medical practitioner, Tara, who had kindly agreed to give Timateta her first check-up.

"She looks like a healthy Kiribati baby," Tara declared after examining her.

After lunch, we paraded into Jennifer's office at the People's Lawyers office. She grinned when she saw the tiny baby strapped to Paul's chest and said, "I see you've found a baby." She explained that the adoption process would start once Tiana gave us custody of the baby. I was surprised to learn that we'd have custody of the baby before the adoption was finalized. Jennifer explained that this gave the villagers a chance to see how we were as parents. If there was any cause for concern, the villagers could notify the court and stop the adoption process.

An I-Kiribati translated Jennifer's explanation so that Tiana clearly understood what was occurring, and that, unlike a local adoption, once this adoption was final, she may never see her baby again. I held my breath and waited as Tiana looked at the form and thought about it. Then she picked up the pen and signed. Paul and I were now Timateta's legal guardians. This fact was driven home when Tiana got off the bus in Bairiki, while Paul, the baby and I stayed on. We were really doing this…no, I corrected myself as I glanced at my husband with the baby strapped to his chest. We *had* really done it. We were now parents.

That evening, we tucked our baby into her little bed and she quietly fell asleep. Fifteen minutes later, I crept into our cabin to check on her, still amazed that she was here, with us on Cherokee Rose. Paul tiptoed behind me.

"Is she alive?" I whispered anxiously. "She isn't moving. Her chest isn't rising and falling; and I can't hear her breathe."

Paul retrieved his contact-lens mirror from his wash kit and held it in front of her nostrils. Steam appeared on the worn mirror.

Whew.

Two hours later, Timateta woke up and cried for milk. After a couple of sips of formula, and four rounds of out-of-tune "Rock-a-bye Baby," she went back to sleep. For two hours. Then it was time for some more milk, some more songs and back to bed. Paul and I were up every two hours that night, unaware that our newest crew member had just rewritten our watch schedule for the next year.

The next day, we wrote a sure-to-be-surprising e-mail home to our family, announcing that we were in the process of adopting a gorgeous baby girl. We had had no warning; neither did our family. We also asked everyone for name suggestions, and for the verses to any lullabies. One night, and I was already tired of "Rock-a-bye Baby."

Thrilled with our news, everyone had a strong opinion on Timeteta's name. Some thought we should keep it; others suggested Mattie, Simeon and Teta as variations on her first name. Some family names were also offered.

No one knew any baby songs.

In the end, my opinion prevailed on the subject of her name. I didn't want to use Timeteta because no one would pronounce, or spell, it correctly. But I wanted to keep some semblance of her Kiribati name, which was how we came upon Jessica, a single consonant sound off her last name.

For the baby songs, we watched "The Sound of Music" again, replaying a couple of songs over and over again until I had mastered them. Gazing at the beautiful baby in my arms,

I didn't mourn – or even think about – Do, Re, Mi, Fa, So and La. I had Jessica.

One of our baby books said that it was common for a new mother to feel like her baby was a stranger, despite the baby having spent nine months in her womb. This feeling was perfectly normal. I was a new mom, and admittedly my baby was a stranger. But sometime during our second week together, she ceased to be. I was cradling her in my arms in the salon, rocking her and gazing at her intelligent brown eyes when I was overcome, overwhelmed, struck by the enormity of what we had done. Of what I had become.

I was Jessica's mom. Forever. I'd be there to clean her up when she fell off her bicycle and scraped her knee. I'd be there to wipe away her tears when her teenage boyfriend broke her heart. I'd be there when she graduated from university; when she won a heat at a swim meet; when she had her own baby. Throughout her life's ups and downs, I was going to be there, protecting her, encouraging her, loving her. It might take the courts months to decide upon our adoption petition, but my heart needed only two weeks to rule on the case. Jessica was my daughter; and I loved her unreservedly.

The days and weeks passed in a blur as we developed a routine around Jessica's needs. How an immobile, tiny person could create so much work was mystifying, and yet we had no time for contemplation. We were too busy sterilizing her baby bottles in the pressure cooker; boiling water for her formula; disinfecting her diapers in bleach-water before washing them and hanging them up to dry on Rosie's lifeline.

Our water and power consumption soared, forcing us to become experts in "resource management." Whenever possible, we collected rainwater to bolster our water tanks, but unfortunately Mother Nature wasn't as consistent as our water usage. In order to make water, we had to motor an hour across the lagoon and anchor off one of the small ocean passes. When the tide brought in clean ocean water, we flipped on our desalination water maker and made six gallons an hour. We could make about 25 gallons before the tide changed. But there was a cost; we had to pay for the water with electricity.

Running the water maker cost us 12 amps an hour, which could be generated by either one hour of peak sunlight on our solar panels, half an hour of 20-knot winds with our wind generator or fifteen minutes of running our engine and its alternator. Our day-to-day chores required a daily water – and power -- assessment. Washing a load of diapers in the washing machine took 20 gallons of water and 20 amps. Making baby food cost one-fourth of a gallon of water to cook the vegetables and 6 amps to run the food processor and subsequent vacuum packer. The freezer, where the baby food was stored, required 20 amps at least twice a day.

Since the engine – we hoped - was more reliable than the sun or wind in terms of generating power, Paul routinely maintained it with oil and filter changes. One morning, after checking the engine's oil level and preparing Jessica's bottles, we popped Jess into the baby carrier and climbed on deck to head to shore. Our dinghy was gone! Where was it? And how would we get ashore? We were trapped on the boat.

Anchored by the hotel, we were isolated from any boat traffic. No chance of hitching a ride to shore. We motored Rosie back to Betio, zigzagging our way across the lagoon and roughly following our previous GPS track. We hoped that the Kiribati Navy Ship, or some small fishing craft or out-rigger, would be there to give Paul a ride to shore. Once we dropped the hook, Paul tried to use the VHS radio to call any of the anchored boats for help. But Channel 16, the international channel for hailing boats, was still jammed, and still buzzing, as it had been when we first arrived in Tarawa.

We had no alternative. We stood on deck, waving, whistling, and shouting at any passing boats. One fishing boat finally came over to ask if we needed help.

Once on shore, Paul filed a claim with the police and asked the local fishermen if they had seen our dinghy. No one had. Discouraged, he hitched a ride back to Rosie.

Help came with an unexpected knock on the boat. Svilen had heard about our missing dinghy. Once we were all seated in the cockpit, he suggested that we place an advertisement on the local radio station. One of his trainees could write the ad for us in the Kirbati language and deliver it to the radio station office. We were willing to try anything.

Within a day of airing the notice, a woman called Svilen at the Marine Training Center. She had seen our dinghy. Paul and Svilen, escorted by a couple of protective seamen, went to her house. Our dinghy was in her neighbor's yard. Several thatched huts away they found the outboard engine. At yet another home, they found our gas tank and my pink sequined flip-flops from Target. We never figured out if our dinghy had been taken, or if the dinghy had been found adrift.

After our dinghy was retrieved, and before we had a chance to leave the bumpy anchorage in Betio, another sailboat arrived, followed by three more! While the small Tarawa ex-pat community had welcomed us wholeheartedly, it had been over a month since we had seen another sailboat. We instantly resumed cruising life, agreeing to join the other sailboats at Abaiang for a Thanksgiving potluck dinner. Abaiang, a neighboring atoll, lay some 20 miles north of Tarawa.

This would be our first time sailing with Jessica on board, and it required some extra preparations. When their daughter had been a baby, Carl and Karen on Enchanté had mounted two car seats on their boat, one in the cockpit and one in the salon. Karen's reasoning had been sound. If they were sailing, or if there was an all-hands-on-deck emergency, she could strap Becca into one of the car seats and concentrate on the boat, knowing that her daughter was safe.

Someone in the expat community lent us a car seat and we strapped it in the cockpit. Then we buckled Jessica up and set sail for Abaiang on November 13th. Jess snoozed most of the way.

We anchored in the lagoon, off a beautiful uninhabited islet nestled between two ocean passes. For once, we stopped thinking about adoption proceedings and the necessary home study, police- and FBI- background checks. We concentrated on having fun. Paul went spear-fishing and climbed coconut trees daily. I snorkeled and walked on the deserted beach. The three of us went swimming, with Jessica comfortably seated in a mesh sling that Paul had rigged in our life ring. In the evenings, we entertained on Rosie or went to someone else's boat for dinner. It felt like we were on vacation.

For the first time in years, romance crept back into our lives. Since we were now parents, our love-making no longer involved doctors, calendars, goals or high stakes. It was simply love. And what a relief!

Our marriage, our gorgeous daughter, our sailing adventure and supportive family – we had so much to be thankful for this year. It was only fitting that we celebrated two Thanksgivings. On Thanksgiving Day, another couple came over to our boat for a quiet celebration. Dinner consisted of sautéed grouper and parrotfish that Paul had speared that morning with a spicy Thai sauce, freshly baked French bread, curried coconut chips, carrot salad, potato salad and an apricot almond tart for dessert. A couple of days later, when all of the boats had arrived, we celebrated Thanksgiving again with a potluck dinner on the beach, a roaring bonfire and a competitive game of bocce ball.

After two relaxing weeks in Abaiang, we returned to the rocking anchorage in Betio to celebrate Svilen and their adopted daughter, Celestine's birthdays. We dinghied ashore and had a great time at their joint birthday party, meeting more members of the ex-pat community and showing off our gorgeous daughter.

The next morning, Paul complained that he had headache. I figured he had drunk one too many cans of Victoria Bitter. His headache got worse as the day continued, and as the days passed. After I found him moaning in the fetal position on our bed, begging me to turn off the lights which weren't on, I realized that something was seriously wrong.

Killer Kiribati

Kiribati, December 2004

I consulted our Merck Manual and started Paul on a course of amoxicillin, thinking he might've gotten a sinus infection from spear-fishing. The antibiotics didn't seem to help as much as the three pain-relief tablets he took every four hours.

And then, after a couple more days, even the tablets ceased to be effective.

On Friday, after Paul had been sick for nearly a week, I went ashore to buy some stronger painkillers and to call a doctor. Paul was incapable of looking after Jessica, so I strapped her to my chest, hopped into the dinghy and headed towards shore.

As I dodged the barely submerged mooring lines in the small boat basin, I noticed with dismay that it was low tide. That meant I had to climb up the 30-degree sloping, slimy-with-green-algae, basin wall. With Paul, and his extra set of hands, that wasn't a big deal. But now I had Jessica strapped to my chest, a backpack on my back, and I had to hold the dinghy's line while I climbed. Slipping once, I struggled up the wall one-handed and tied the dinghy's line to a nearby tree. I nodded to the cross-legged old men who had passively watched my ascent from the shade of a coconut tree and walked into town.

I bought some over-the-counter codeine-coated aspirin at the local store and called Crystal, one of the hospital's two

Western doctors. We had met her at Svilen's birthday party. She was an ear, nose and throat specialist.

Crystal didn't think Paul had a sinus infection, but because he had already started a course of amoxicillin, he should continue it. If his headache was still raging on Monday, I should bring him to the hospital. Disappointed that there wasn't anything else I could do to help my honey, I trudged back to the slippery walls of the boat basin and dinghied home.

That night, Paul was fiery to the touch and I took his temperature: 103 degrees. I dragged him to the head where I showered him with room temperature water. Shivering, Paul cried in protest, but I ignored him. Trying to cool down a feverish man in the equatorial heat – Tarawa was located at zero degrees latitude – was a challenge. I filled a spritz bottle with water, set it on the bookshelf by our bed and collapsed next to Paul. I spritzed him whenever he, Jess or Rosie woke me up, which was way too often.

Paul was out of action, but the demands of living on a boat, and of parenthood, didn't stop just because he had. On two nights the wind kicked up, forcing me to set our GPS anchor alarm and keep anchor watches. That was in addition to Jessica's five-times-a-night bottle feedings, and to playing Florence Nightingale to my moaning Paul.

During the day, I sterilized Jess' bottles, boiled her water, disinfected and washed her diapers. I played with Jessica, read to her and carried her around the boat while I hung the diapers to dry, washed dishes, and made meals. In my spare time, I ran the engine to charge the batteries, made water with an incoming tide, checked our snubber and stowed loose items whenever the boat see-sawed, which was often in bumpy Betio.

Saturday afternoon, Paul's temperature dropped a degree and I fervently hoped that he was recovering.

I was exhausted, I was worried, and I was wrong.

That night, he moaned in pain, rocking himself backward and forward as if he were kowtowing to God, begging for his pain to go away. From our first aid kit, I pulled out the only narcotic painkiller we had on board. It was reputedly seven times stronger than morphine but we had avoided using the addictive drug. We were now willing to risk addiction if it helped ease Paul's suffering. His pain subsided for a couple of hours, but at a cost. The medicine caused insomnia so Paul couldn't sleep.

As soon as Jessica fell asleep for her usual 45-minute nap the next day, I bolted off the boat. I updated Crystal on Paul's condition. She said it sounded like Dengue Fever, a viral infection caused by certain mosquitoes. It could kill, and there was no cure for it. I had two options. I could keep Paul on the boat, making him as comfortable as possible, or an ambulance could take him to the hospital for an overnight stay.

Paul and I had previously checked out the hospital, and its grounds, when Jessica had developed a wheezing cough. The cinderblock hospital buildings were clustered together. Only some of their windows had glass or screens; some were simply gaping holes. Everything was open-air. In the middle of these buildings was the tuberculosis wing. TB was common on the island.

Years ago, I had sold laboratory instruments to analyze tuberculosis and knew that it was an air-borne disease. The fact that the trade winds blew over, and through, the hospital complex was not comforting. I could just imagine microscopic droplets of someone's infected cough blowing into Paul's wing. Nope, there was no way I was going to check my honey into the hospital overnight.

I gave Crystal my decision, set an appointment for Paul to see her the next day, and thanked her. As I rushed back to the dinghy, I bumped into Dolly and Svilen. I told them that Paul might have Dengue Fever. Concerned, they offered to drive us to the hospital the next morning and I gratefully accepted. I doubted that Paul, with his unbearable headache, would survive the 45-minute boom-ba-da-boom minivan ride there.

The next morning, Paul got out of bed for the first time in eight days. He felt fine. I looked at him in disbelief. His temperature was almost normal and he insisted his head didn't ache. He flatly refused to go to the hospital.

Because we didn't have a phone, there was no way of contacting Dolly and Svilen. We got dressed and went ashore to meet them on the strangely bustling street,. Dolly smiled as we approached and explained that the supply ship had arrived last night.

I had been so preoccupied with Paul and Jess that I hadn't noticed the small boats ferrying containers ashore from the supply ship. The ship was anchored near the lagoon's ocean pass.

"Well, let's go shopping," I exclaimed; we had devoured our supply of fresh fruit and veggies in Abaiang, which seemed like years ago.

"But what about Paul's appointment?"

Paul explained that he felt fine and wasn't going. I shrugged.

"Okay, then we shop," Dolly said with her Bulgarian accent

The supply boat was big news. It came once a month, bringing fresh fruit, vegetables, refrigerated goods like cheese – glorious cheese – and yogurt. It also brought general food items and household merchandise. After the ship unloaded its refrigerated containers, we pounced on the three biggest stores in Betio. I bought enough cheese to line the bottom of our fridge, as well as cauliflower, cabbage, carrots and apples. That was the extent of the ship's produce offering and I took some of each.

At US$12 per head of cabbage, prices were not cheap, but this was a clear case of feast-or-famine. In a couple of days, there wouldn't be any cabbage to buy, regardless of its price. I stocked up on cans of powdered baby formula. Prior to the ship's arrival, there had been an island-wide shortage of formula and I couldn't afford to run out. I also bought rice cereal and bags of frozen vegetables to transform into baby food.

A couple of hours later, we returned to Rosie when Paul complained that he was tired. As he climbed into bed, we saw that a rash covered his elbows, confirming that he had Dengue Fever. Where had he gotten it? And how come I didn't have it?

Paul confessed that mosquitoes had assaulted his bare back while he had been climbing a coconut tree in Abaiang at dusk. Because both of his hands were clinging to the tree, he couldn't swat them away.

After a week of daily naps, Paul recovered enough to be functional. It would take nearly two months before he was back to Tigger-ific form.

After celebrating Christmas Day with Dolly and Svilen – Jessica's first Christmas – we motored to our calmer anchorage off the Otintaii Hotel. News of the tsunami in Thailand on December 26th shattered our holiday spirit.

Many cruisers who sail around the world spend

December and January in Thailand, waiting for warmer weather to arrive in the Mediterranean before crossing the Indian Ocean. If Paul and I hadn't decided to take the "road less traveled" and if we hadn't met Jessica, we would have been in Thailand for the tsunami. Solvent Venture had invited us to join them there.

We flipped on our satellite e-mail system and, concerned for our friends' well-being, e-mailed them. Enchanté replied; they were spending the current South Pacific cyclone season in Australia. Safely moored in Singapore, Scott Free didn't feel the tsunami. There was no word from Carol and Alex on Solent Venture.

With dread, we sent them another message the next day. Still no reply. Thinking perhaps their system was down, or their batteries were shot, we sent Solent Venture periodic messages. No response. None of our friends had heard from them either. It was difficult to grieve for Carole and Alex without some confirmation that they were dead. Remembering how our boat rose to the top of giant waves in Panama, I hoped that they had been on board their boat when the tsunami hit and somehow survived.

The tsunami confirmed my unspoken belief that Paul and I were supposed to be in Kiribati; that this was part of our destiny. Who could ignore the serendipitous chain of events that had led us here, and to Jessica?

If Howie hadn't died en route – and coincidentally off Jessica's ancestral island of Onotao -- we wouldn't have stopped in Tarawa. If we hadn't chatted with David and Utara, we wouldn't have considered adoption in Kiribati. If we hadn't met Dolly and Svilen, we wouldn't have found Jessica. Short of a neon sign pointing the way, our path had been clearly laid out. And now, thanks to Jessica, we were safely anchored in the lagoon, and not battling a tsunami with Solent Venture.

Perhaps this sense of a higher order to life made me relax. Or perhaps the fact that hurricanes and cyclones don't strike near the equator made Paul and I complacent. In either case, we were totally unprepared for what would later be termed the "worse gale to hit Tarawa in 40 years."

Late one afternoon, dark clouds tumbled across the sky and the wind started to blow unusually from the west. Still anchored by the hotel, Rosie swung around her anchor until she was facing toward Betio and the open, unprotected portion of the atoll's "greater than sign" shape. Paul and I noticed the unusual change of scenery out of Rosie's windows and climbed on deck to evaluate the situation.

The westerly wind was picking up. What had been a safe anchorage in easterly winds was now the most dangerous anchorage we could be in, with a catcher's mitt of land and coral reefs behind us and on both sides of us. Being at sea, away from land, was the safest place for us but we couldn't get there. With the gathering clouds, it was already too dark to navigate the coral-strewn lagoon. Even with our previous GPS tracks, the risk of hitting a submerged coral head or running aground was too great. We had no choice but to prepare Rosie to face the storm at anchor.

Paul attached two rope snubber lines to the anchor chain to act as primary and backup shock absorbers for the anchor chain. If the waves grew bigger, these rope lines would flex and take some strain off the stainless steel anchor chain.

Down below, I fed Jessica her dinnertime bottle and tucked her into her new bed in the quarter berth. With high lee cloths around two sides of her bed and a homemade pillow bumper around the other walled sides, she would be safe as long as Rosie was safe. I hastily stowed loose items into lockers, and set up our lee cloths around our sea berths in the salon. Dinner was cancelled.

The wind strengthened to 40 knots and the waves surged to eight feet. We were anchored in 15 feet, and a couple of times Rosie bumped. Was her keel hitting the ground when we were in the trough of some of these waves? There was no way of knowing, and nothing we could do about it if she were.

Paul turned on our radar, and set two GPS anchor alarms. With the waves and wind pushing Rosie relentlessly toward the coral reefs behind us, we had to know immediately if our anchor was dragging. We started anchor watches. At 2 a.m., the wind howled at 60-plus knots and the waves grew to 10 feet.

Beep, beep, beep.

We were dragging!

I leapt out of my berth and sprinted to the cockpit, shouting to wake Paul.

Suddenly there was a tremendous bang! on the bow. It was our anchor chain snapping taut. Our two snubbers must have been ripped apart!

I fired up Rosie's engine, threw her into fully-throttled forward gear and motored into the waves to release the stress on our anchor and chain. Paul flipped on our spreader lights to illuminate our decks before dashing forward in the blinding rain – no time for a harness– to check on our anchor.

Twenty feet of anchor chain free-wheeled into the lagoon as Rosie's bow dipped in a trough. Paul stomped on the gypsy to stop the chain from spilling overboard. He grabbed the bow pulpit as a wave crashed over him. I gazed fixedly at the spot I had last seen Paul and was relieved to see him still on deck when the wave passed.

As the bow rode up the next wave, the chain grew taut without the snubber's elasticity and ripped the hefty windlass from its mounts, shearing three of the four five-inch long stainless steel bolts. Fifty more feet of chain fell into the water as Paul watched helplessly. The distance between Rosie and the coral reefs behind us had just shrunk considerably.

As Rosie's nose dove into the next trough, the chain stopped free-wheeling for just an instant. Paul whipped a rolling hitch, a type of knot, around the chain and cleated it off. Between the waves that crashed over him, he rigged five new snubbers, four of which he secured to cleats and one which he wrapped around Rosie's keel-stepped mast. The force of the waves might rip out our cleats, as it had our windlass, but it wouldn't pull down our mast. Hopefully.

Seasick and shivering uncontrollably, despite the equatorial heat, I continued to drive Rosie forward into the wind and the waves, trying to help Paul. But it was no use. Our 48-horsepower engine was no match for the nearly hurricane-force winds. Dripping wet, Paul returned to the cockpit and analyzed our situation. There was nothing else we could do. He said we should turn off the engine and go down below. I refused. How could we do nothing when, in an instant, we might be smashed on the coral reef behind us?

But I couldn't think of anything else we should be doing. I reluctantly turned off the engine.

We went down below, reset the GPS anchor alarms, dried off and crawled into our lee beds. I couldn't sleep. I lay in bed with my eyes open and my ears perked, waiting for the next emergency.

Jessica, on the other hand, slept blissfully through all of the commotion. She woke up at dawn while the storm was still raging. If she noticed the violent motion, she gave no indication of it. She was perky and ready for a bottle and playtime.

Exhausted, scared and still seasick, I moaned. How could I play with our baby at a time like this? The boat was pitching wildly, and at any second, it might be all-hands-on-deck again. Somehow, Paul and I managed.

From our lee beds, we played pass-the-baby for three long days as the wind continued to howl at 40-knots and Rosie see-sawed in the 6-foot waves. I fed us snacks from the locker that was adjacent to my lee bed, once again the "rollover chef" as Janet and Blaine on Charbonneau had nicknamed me in the Bahamas.

When the weather finally calmed, we saw that Rosie was only 10 feet away from a coral reef. If Paul hadn't tied the fastest rolling hitch of his life and if 10 more feet of chain had free-wheeled off the boat, we wouldn't be here. The coral reef would have smashed Rosie, and us, to bits.

But we had survived. And we were suffering from cabin fever. Once we re-anchored Rosie a safe distance from the coral reef, we dinghied ashore. The hotel's floating dock had disappeared along with fifteen feet of the hotel's waterfront retaining wall..

On land, thatched huts had lost their roofs; trees and branches blocked the roads, and debris littered the atoll. The ocean had swept away sections of the primary road - an unavoidable hazard when living on an island that was nearly at sea level. In Betio, two fishing boats sank during the storm. After its anchor had dragged, a large commercial fishing boat crashed into the town's stone loading dock and gouged a 20-foot hole in the stone structure.

While the atoll rebuilt itself after the storm, the island's only New Zealand certified social worker interviewed us for our home study on the boat. Shortly after receiving his report, we secured Rosie and flew to Fiji to file our adoption paperwork with the US Embassy.

I was surprisingly happy to be back in soggy Suva, where there were green mountains, towering trees, blooming flowers and, oh joy, fresh mangoes for sale on every corner. But our fun was limited to eating mangoes and taking Jessica for her first dip in a swimming pool.

We spent three full days at the Embassy, filing Jessica's paperwork as well as applying for a Returning Resident visa for Paul. Our consular officer remarked that this was the first

Kiribati adoption case she had. The Attorney General in Tarawa had similarly told us that none of the Kiribati adoptions had been finalized in the United States despite several attempts. I didn't understand why. These adoption petitions seemed fairly straightforward. Well, as straightforward as two inches of paperwork could be.

In our minds, there was only one reason why Uncle Sam might refuse our petition: our lack of income. Had we not been through the recent gale, that issue would have thwarted us.

Thanks to the gale, my thoughts of cruising with Jessica had crashed as heavily as the storm's 10-foot waves. I could not be a mother and a first mate simultaneously. During the gale, First Mate me had been wrestling with how I might rescue Paul if the waves washed him overboard; Mother me had been wondering how I could best save my baby if we had an emergency evacuation.

Once I started to doubt the wisdom of cruising with Jessica, I remembered Paul's bout of Dengue Fever. Under the nearly ideal conditions of being safely anchored near a hospital and helpful friends, I had barely managed to juggle the needs of Rosie, Jess and Paul while he had been sick. What if Paul became sick on passage?

The storm also reminded me that cruising was more than just passages from one place to the next. Danger lurked all the time. Honestly, what had I been thinking? Had I been thinking at all?

Our cruising days were over.

Paul agreed with my assessment, not so much by his words but by his actions. Paul contacted his previous employer. Despite the four years that had passed since Paul's resignation, his boss in Philadelphia faxed him a job offer; it was a testament to Paul's valuable work history with the company. This was our ace-in-the-hole for Paul's returning resident visa, which he was granted, and for Jessica's pending adoption petition. We flew back to Tarawa to wait for a decision on Jessica's case and to prepare Rosie for crossing the Pacific again.

We would return to America. We chose San Francisco as our port of entry because it lies safely north of the region affected by the eastern North Pacific hurricanes. Most hurricanes had been recorded between June and October, so we hoped to have Rosie snugly docked in the shadow of the

Golden Gate Bridge before then.

Our boat to-do list was long. But trying to work around Jessica's nap schedule was impossible. Svilen generously offered us the vacant, furnished house next door to them while we worked on the boat. We accepted and anchored Rosie within sight of our beachfront temporary house. Paul worked tirelessly on Rosie for weeks while I took care of Jess.

Living on land, in dust-free accommodations, was nice but strange. Packs of wild dogs barked, yelped and howled at all hours of the night; a couple of roosters confused 3 a.m. for dawn; and security guards eerily patrolled our house's perimeter at Svilen's insistence. How could anyone sleep with so much activity going on outside?

In the house, a strange, gooey liquid oozed out of the ground between the laminate floor tiles and, as Jess was now starting to crawl, I felt compelled to disinfect our floors nightly. Mosquitoes – an annoyance that we had experienced only on land -- found their way into the house and buzzed around us.

I missed goo-free, bug-free Cherokee Rose. I missed being rocked to sleep and seeing the stars twinkle through the open hatch over our bed. I missed the constant caress of a sea breeze.

Most of all, I missed our safe drinking water as hundreds of children suddenly became infected with the bacterium Escherichia coli (E. coli). A man had forgotten to treat the public drinking water, thus creating this island-wide epidemic. I thought we were safe because we used Rosie's water for our cooking and drinking, but somehow – maybe from accidentally swallowing some of her bath water? – our eight-month-old daughter got it.

She couldn't keep down any food or formula. Over the next couple of days, she lost weight and slept all the time. She had yellow, watery diarrhea, and her temperature rose to and remained at 103 degrees. She regurgitated the fever-reducing baby Tylenol syrup I gave her. She screamed in agony every time I plunged her fiery little body into disinfected, tepid water. She quit eating and drinking anything I gave her. I was frantic.

Dolly gave me some of her pediatric acetaminophen suppositories and suggested I try the local rehydration remedies of coconut water and rice water. I went home and immediately filled baby bottles with each; this was in addition to her usual bottles of water and formula. Paul brought home UNICEF sachets of oral rehydration salts that the hospital was giving away and I made up a fifth bottle for Jessica.

Paul grimly told me that a dozen children had already died from this outbreak.

What were we doing on this god-forsaken island?

I couldn't lose Jessica. She was my baby.

I called Crystal, our doctor friend. She explained that many I-Kiribati still trusted their traditional medicine man more than modern medical science. According to the medicine man, when a child had diarrhea and vomiting, the child should not be given anything to eat or drink. She concluded that these children were dying of dehydration, not some killer bacterial infection.

I hung up the phone with a different conclusion. Without proper care, this E. coli outbreak *was* a killer.

This was not the first time we had heard about Kiribati traditional medicine. Crystal's husband was a volunteer anesthesiologist at the hospital. He said that it was common for fishermen to come to the hospital with a highly infected cut on one of their toes. The doctor would recommend amputating the toe before the infection spread. Afraid of losing a toe, the fisherman returned to his village to consult the medicine man. Inevitably the man would return to the hospital sometime later to have his leg amputated – if he was lucky, below his knee – because, sure enough, the infection had spread.

Because hydration was the key to surviving this E. coli outbreak, we pushed a bottle into Jessica's slack mouth every 10 minutes. If she didn't sip the flavor we had given her, we swapped bottles until all five had been tried. Her fever continued to rage for days and she continued to sleep.

Fearing that she might die, I was ready to be airlifted off the island so that my daughter could get proper medical treatment. But I couldn't hop on a plane and whisk her. She didn't have a visa.

When the roosters crowed at 3 a.m., I called the Philadelphia-based Immigration officer who was handling our adoption petition. I explained that children were dying from a bacterial epidemic – the count was now higher than 20 infant deaths – and that our daughter was very sick, and at risk. Would she put an emergency rush on our paperwork so that we could fly Jessica home to a hospital?

The Immigration officer replied that our fingerprints were stamped on the wrong form, a mistake made by the US Embassy in Fiji. We needed get them redone before she would consider approving our petition.

I couldn't believe it. Jessica might die and this woman was complaining about a wrong form? She had the necessary data – our fingerprints – in front of her! I hung up, angry and disgusted.

We carried on with forced bottle feedings, suppository administration and copious diaper changes. A couple of days later, after a week of illness, Jessica woke up. We were through the worst of it. Others hadn't fared as well; we heard that more than 30 babies had died.

I telephoned our consular officer at the US Embassy in Fiji. Could we be fingerprinted in Majuro, the capital of the Marshall Islands that lay a mere 300 miles – a three-day sail – north of Tarawa? There was a US Consulate there. Majuro was a tiny step toward San Francisco; Fiji was not. She consented.

I agreed to let Paul sail single-handed to Majuro. He was overjoyed. As we had cruised through the Pacific, he had commented several times that he'd like to have a solo passage. This was an ideal one for two reasons. As far as passages went, 300 miles was nothing and the weather in this area was typically calm. It would be a short and easy trip.

Jess and I would fly to Majuro, meet Paul there and get fingerprinted. Then he, along with a crewmate we had yet to find, would sail to San Francisco before hurricane season started. Jess and I would stay and wait for her visa to be approved.

But first we had to go to court in Betio to complete Jessica's adoption in Kiribati. I smiled as the judge walked in, wearing a powdered white wig and a black robe in spite of the tropical heat. The Attorney General, and Jennifer, our lawyer, were also sporting wigs and robes. Kiribati had evidently inherited more than just their adoption law from the British!

Like a church service, everyone knew their lines and 15 minutes later, the adoption was approved as far as Kiribati was concerned. We returned to our beachfront home in Betio, popped open a ridiculously priced bottle of mediocre champagne and celebrated with Jess, Dolly, Svilen, Crystal and her husband.

When Paul was ready to set sail for Majuro, we held

hands as we walked to the dinghy, which was beached near our house. Dolly was babysitting Jessica so we could say our goodbyes. We hugged. I fastened Dad's St. Christopher medallion around his neck for around-the-clock coverage. Then we launched the dinghy.

"Be safe," I said to my best friend.

Excited to start his trip, Paul smiled and hugged me again. "See you in three days!" Then he hopped into the dinghy and motored to Rosie.

From shore, I watched him climb aboard our home of nearly four years. He winched the dinghy on deck and lifted the anchor.

We had started this trip together, and had been side-by-side ever since, battling the weather, fixing the boat, visiting remote islands and raising our daughter. Now we were ending it apart. He was sailing without me. Tears unexpectedly welled up.

This sailing adventure had become our life, our dream. And now my dream was over while Paul's continued.

I started sobbing. At that moment I'd have given anything to be Paul's first mate again.

Lurking Hazards and Insufferable Delays

Kiribati, May 2005

Half-blinded by my tears, I started running along the exposed reef that extended halfway to Rosie. Anything to be closer to her and Paul.

A fisherman, startled by my sobs, asked if I was all right. I glumly nodded; how could I explain the grief of saying good-bye to a dream?

Unaware of my turmoil, Paul waved to me as he put Rosie into forward gear and turned her bow toward the ocean pass, leaving me to stare forlornly at Rosie's stern. I stopped running.

I wiped my tears away and walked back to the beach, trying to regain my composure. I couldn't face anyone yet. I wanted to hear Paul's friendly voice again, but I didn't have a VHF radio. Then I remembered that the Tarawa Radio office was nearby.

I half-ran, half-walked to the Betio office, where I asked if I could use their radio to call my husband. The woman invited me into the narrow office and passed me the handset. I pushed the transmit button but it didn't work. Understanding the problem, the woman grabbed the handset and, using one of her very long, polished nails, wiggled the button until it popped out.

Aahhh, this is why Tarawa Radio was always jammed, I thought and smiled at the unexpected revelation.

"Cherokee Rose, Cherokee Rose" I called.

"Kel?" Paul answered, surprised. "Switch to Channel 68?"

We switched channels and chatted briefly. Paul cheered me up and I felt better for having made the call. I passed the handset back to the woman, after ensuring that the transmit button was no longer depressed. Until someone else pushed the sticking button, Tarawa Radio would be operational.

Walking home, I reflected on our journey. Here I was, grief-stricken that Paul was sailing without me; that, despite having come all this way, I wouldn't finish our trip.

But I was wrong.

How had I forgotten the underlying point of our trip? It wasn't about sailing around the world, or to San Francisco. We had been searching for some meaning to our lives; some way to overcome our infertility-induced life crisis.

We had been sailing to Jessica.

And together Paul and I had reached our destination.

My sailing trip might be over but my adventure wasn't. Jess and I were still in Tarawa. And her adoption visa was still pending.

As soon as I entered Dolly and Svilen's house, I scooped up my beautiful daughter and hugged her tightly. I kissed her head while silently praying for Paul and his single-handed passage. I was grateful that I didn't have to simultaneously be first mate and mother again.

Frankly the next couple of days would have been easier if I had been first mate. At least I would have known what was happening. On the second day of this piece-of-cake passage, the blip of our satellite email system disappeared off Purplefinder.com. Purplefinder was what dad had used to track us to New Zealand, and to Tarawa. Now I was using it to track Rosie and Paul.

On this website, an icon of a little white boat marked Rosie's exact position in the Pacific Ocean. If I moved my cursor over the boat icon, a pop-up window appeared with our current wind conditions, coordinates, speed-over-ground and direction. Except there wasn't a little white boat.

Where was Rosie? What had happened? There were two possibilities. First, there was a power shortage on the boat, forcing Paul to turn off the satellite system. In the past, we always sent a quick update email to Dad before we flipped off the system. Surely Paul would have sent me a message if that was the case, knowing how worried I'd be if the little white boat simply disappeared off the screen. The other possibility was that the boat sank.

Damn it, Paul!

My mind raced. Had he crashed into a submerged coral reef? Had he hit a submerged container? Had there been a fire on board? I just didn't know. The only thing I could do was stick to our current plan.

As Jess and I boarded the plane to Majuro the next day, I stopped at the cockpit door and poked my head in. The pilot and co-pilot were going through their preflight checklist.

"Excuse me, but do you have a VHF radio on board?" I asked

The slightly graying pilot twisted in his seat to look at me.

"My husband is lost at sea," I explained. "I was hoping that once we were airborne, you might call him on Channel 16." Because VHF worked for vessels that were in line-of-sight, being hailed from an aircraft would cover a lot of ground or ocean.

The pilot was willing to help. "What megahertz frequency is Channel 16?" he asked.

I didn't know. Until that moment, I hadn't known that Channel 16 was an assigned name for a radio frequency. I was also surprised that aircraft didn't use the same channel system as boats because we had been hailed by two airplanes in the Pacific.

There was nothing he could do to help me without the frequency and no way for me to quickly look it up inside the air terminal; its only modern convenience was a metal detector.

For the entire flight, I vainly searched the ocean from my window seat, looking for a pinprick of white that might be Rosie. I saw just the vast, dark blue sea studded with the occasional turquoise lagoon, the mark of an atoll.

Once we arrived in Majuro, I checked Jess and I into one of the island's larger hotels. Five sailboats were moored off the hotel. Because two inflatable dinghies were tied at the dock, I knew that there were some cruisers on land, roaming around town. Hope swelled. If I found them, they would call Cherokee Rose for me. With Jess snoozing in her baby carrier, we loitered near the dinghy dock.

Within 15 minutes, I spotted a sailor walking purposefully toward the dinghy dock. Once I explained my situation, he took me and Jess to his boat so I could call Rosie. There was no response to my hails. The man returned us to the dinghy dock, promising that he would keep trying.

Two days later, Paul responded to his hail. He was alive! Saltwater had permeated the engine's crankcase so he had shut off the engine. Before he could update me, the satellite email system mysteriously died. Without the engine and without any wind he and Rosie wallowed at sea, doubling the time for this passage. He sailed into Majuro the next day. Jess and I were on shore, waiting to hug him and whisk him off to the US Consulate for our fingerprinting appointment.

With our adoption petition hopefully complete, and on its way to being approved, we started our next task: finding a crew mate for Paul. We emailed our friends and family, hoping that someone might want a high-seas adventure to San Francisco. There were no volunteers for a trip that would last over a month. The recommended route of sailing to 40 degrees north before turning east toward San Francisco was 4,400 miles, or roughly 44 days at sea.

Along our travels, we had met several licensed captains so we e-mailed them about their availability and pricing. Some wanted $20,000 to sail with Paul. We didn't need that skill level; after all, we already had a captain on Rosie. We broadened our search to include sailing forums. We finally found an experienced sailor who was willing to sail with Paul if we paid for airfare and expenses. But he was a she.

I had emphatically ruled out women as possible crew mates. The close quarters on a boat bred instant familiarity and I was not about to share my man with some Suzie Sailor. However, when it came to price, no one compared. After four years of spending without an income, price mattered.

Helen had sailed in the Caribbean and had even been rescued by a Coast Guard helicopter when a boat she had been crewing began to sink due to mechanical failure.

With Paul breathing down my neck to hire someone, I e-mailed Helen with some logistical questions. Hoping she had a sense of humor, I also asked her if she had any facial hair. I laughed when she replied; she enclosed a photo of herself entitled "Many Chins." I promptly emailed her a contract and hired her.

She arrived in Majuro a week later from Honolulu, bringing a new antenna that we had ordered for our broken satellite system, as well as her own sailing gear. Paul installed the antennae and changed the engine oil for the third time, in an attempt to remove any leftover salt water in the crankcase. While he worked, Helen and I went provisioning.

She said she was a gourmet cook. After savoring Helen's fine cooking at sea, I figured that Paul would feel cheated by the gruel-equivalent passage meals I had been feeding him for the past four years. Thus I was secretly relieved that this was Paul's last passage; I couldn't compete. She started filling our grocery cart with pasta, canned New Zealand butter, frozen meat and 144 single-serving portions of Jello Pudding Snacks.

Gourmet? Hmm.

Paul was a "savory" man. I doubted he'd eat more than a single serving of pudding on the entire trip. But who was I to argue with her quantities or choices? This was her passage, not mine. I rounded out her groceries with carrots, apples and cabbage, as well as passage basics such as cheese, crackers, canned soup, ultra long-life milk, breakfast cereal and Paul's watch-time weakness, Pringle's potato chips.

Once the provisions were stored and the repairs were complete, she and Paul left Majuro for San Francisco on May 26, 2005. As they turned Rosie toward the ocean pass, Jess and I waved and blew kisses before returning to our hotel room. I had shed my tears in Tarawa. I was now on autopilot and my destination was Cincinnati.

My sister, Suzanne and her husband, Kevin, lived in Cincinnati. They wanted Jess and I to stay with them while we waited for Paul to return on Cherokee Rose. Hopefully, Jess would receive her visa long before Paul arrived, and we'd have several weeks to visit with Su and Kevin before flying to Philadelphia for Paul's new job.

I emailed our Immigration officer in Philadelphia and Kevin made numerous phone calls to her on our behalf, but we both got the same message. Nothing was happening on Jessica's adoption petition. Yes, our paperwork was complete. Yes, everything looked fine. And yet there was this invisible hold-up that blocked our ability to fly to Cincinnati. As the weeks ticked by, this hold-up was expensive. Our hotel room cost us US$80 a night - a lot of money for people without an income.

While I was livid, thankfully Suzanne was logical. She suggested that I contact my congresswoman in Philadelphia and explain our situation. My congresswoman assigned Tom, a member of her staff, to our case. He pursued our Immigration officer relentlessly, copying me on his e-mail correspondence and summarizing his phone calls. Upon the lack of any apparent obstacles, he, too, became discouraged with the lack of progress. Watching him lose enthusiasm for our case was disheartening.

A thousand miles away, Paul was losing enthusiasm for his new crewmate. An accomplished sailor, Helen's background was racing, not cruising, and she eagerly suggested ways to make Rosie sail faster. After all, she had a lot of experience on a variety of boats. Paul patiently explained and sometimes demonstrated why her suggestions wouldn't work for Rosie, whose cruising design did not resemble that of a racing yacht. Paul's experience was limited to Rosie and, on board her, he was the authority.

After awhile, Helen stopped make suggestions and barely spoke. Worse yet, she quit cooking for Paul.

Paul didn't miss her cooking; he preferred more variety than pasta tossed in butter with a hunk of meat beside it. But she had also stopped washing the dishes. So between fridge repairs, changing the engine filter, fixing a broken water pump, rewiring the wind vane as well as sailing and keeping watch, Paul had to cook and clean three times a day.

Over the phone, I complained about his situation to my girlfriend Claire. She replied, "Well, Kel, it's better than the alternative."

"What do you mean?" I asked, confused.

"Would you prefer that Paul loved her cooking, her conversation and her company?

No, I didn't want that. But I would have preferred some middle ground, like she was sulking but still pitching in with the cooking, cleaning and repairs.

One windless day, as they motored north, Paul cast his fishing line.

Zzzziinnng!

He grabbed his rod and fought the enormous fish for over an hour. Just as he was reeling it to the side of the boat, the fish stopped fighting. Blood stained the water around the boat and dripped off his catch as he yanked it aboard. Only there was no catch; a shark had eaten Paul's tuna. Based on the uneaten head dangling from his hook, the tuna had been sizeable.

As Paul tossed the head overboard, the engine's usual

noise sped up, as if the engine was revving, before suddenly dropping to a low mean hum. Something was straining the engine! Paul quickly turned it off and started searching for the problem. Rosie had run over a mid-ocean commercial fishing net. The net wrapped itself around the engine's propeller, overloading the engine's transmission in the process.

Paul and Helen discussed their only option: dive in the water and cut the fishing net off the propeller. But the water was still bloody – and evidently full of hungry sharks. Because there was no wind, they couldn't sail out of the area. They wallowed for two hours, waiting for the water to clear before Paul mustered up the courage to dive in.

As he was getting ready to jump overboard, Helen suggested tying a rope around Paul's waist for safety. In an emergency, she would pull him in. Sharing a similar plight – hanging on the end of a line in shark-infested water – to the tuna he had just reeled in was hardly comforting.

Once the propeller was free, and Paul was safely on board, they altered course to Midway Island. Located west of the Hawaiian Islands, Midway was off limits to cruisers except for emergency stops. Paul hailed the island and explained that he was nearly out of fuel; did they have any fuel he could buy? The radio controller gave him permission to anchor and come ashore. Before the atoll was in sight, flocks of albatrosses flew alongside Rosie, leading the way to land.

It didn't take more than a couple of steps on land to realize that Midway was a bird sanctuary. There was a roosting bird every couple of feet. Stepping around hundreds of birds, Paul and Helen followed their guide as he led them to Immigration. As a remote national wildlife refuge, a small group of researchers lived on the island in a university-campus setting. Everyone slept in dormitory rooms and ate at the central cafeteria. For entertainment, there was a free movie theater and bowling alley; there were also a couple of social clubs where alcohol was served.

Paul and Helen were invited for dinner at the cafeteria. Having been at sea for 14 long days - days made longer by their differing views on sailing - they were both ready for some friendly conversation. So were the scientists and researchers.

When it was time to return to Rosie, they discovered they couldn't see a thing. The moonless night was eerily black and noisy with roosting birds. Paul couldn't see his hand when he held out his arm. How would they find their way home? There were no lights along the footpaths. After borrowing a flashlight, Paul and Helen picked their way down the hillside, trying to leave the feathered residents alone but getting angry squawks nonetheless.

The next day, Paul motored Rosie to the fuel dock where the attendant filled up Rosie's tanks with high quality airplane-grade diesel. The dock wasn't designed for paying patrons, so Paul gave the man a case of Victoria Bitter as a small thank you. Both men were thrilled with the exchange.

Two days later, On-the-Nose-Cherokee-Rose was pounding into the waves with the apparent wind only 16 degrees off her bow. Surrounded by unending rows of four-foot-high, gray waves and an equally gray blanket of clouds overhead, there were 2,600 miles of ocean between them and San Francisco.

Up and down Rosie went; up, down, up, CRASH!

Rosie shuddered to a stop. Startled, Paul bolted out of his seat in the cockpit and raced toward the sound. On Rosie's port side, the once sapphire water was rust-colored.

Paul's heart raced. Rosie had hit a submerged container.

He dashed back to the cockpit, past Helen, and flew down the companionway steps. He yanked up the floorboard in the bow, then the next one and the next, searching for any sign of a leak or a hole in the boat. There was nothing. Paul decided that Rosie's lead keel must have landed squarely on the submerged metal container as she crashed down one of the waves.

Slowly Rosie's momentum, and the wind, pulled her forward and soon she was pounding along as if nothing had happened. Except that it had raised the stress level on board; hitting a container at sea was every sailor's nightmare. Where there was one container, there might be another. In a bad storm, a ship could lose 50 containers at a time.

Estimates range from 675 to 10,000 containers fall overboard every year, usually due to heavy weather. The containers are nearly, but not fully, airtight so once they hit the water, it takes them a long time to sink. Even after they are submerged, they are still buoyant until water displaces all of the air. That's what makes them so deadly. They can't be seen and they lurk under the surface of the water, just waiting to sink an unlucky boat.

I felt frustrated. I couldn't help Paul as he dealt with

unforeseeable hazards like mid-ocean fishing nets and submerged containers. I couldn't even help him with the usual stuff, like passing tools, reading from the repair book or fixing meals. Equally frustrating, I couldn't seem to help Jessica either.

There was still no word on her visa. In a case of déjà vu, Jessica caught a milder form of e-coli poisoning again – I would recognize those yellow watery diapers anywhere -- which was confirmed as a community outbreak by the local paper a couple of days later. Enough of this lingering-in-limbo. Immigration needed a little motivation.

My dad's business partner was politically well-connected on the state- and federal- level. I hoped a squawk from his office might encourage some action from our Immigration officer, or her boss, or her boss' boss. Sure enough, within days of his office's involvement, Jessica's adoption petition was approved. Another 10 days later, her visa arrived from the US Embassy in Manila, the Philippines, which handled the Marshall Islands.

With Paul – knock on wood – safely sailing without any more incidents, and Jessica's visa finally on its way, I relaxed and took pleasure in my daughter's development. She said, "dada?" for the first time, obviously noticing that her daddy was gone. Now 11 months old, she started crawling in earnest and pulling herself up on the legs of a chair to stand. She smiled at me, and drooled on me. She was so cute, I considered adopting another Pacific Island baby, not immediately as our life was in transition but in the future.

Wondering what the adoption procedure was in the Marshall Islands, I called the Marshallese government's Central Adoption Agency. When the director learned that I didn't live in the Marshall Islands, he said he couldn't help me. But there was one adoption agency in the United States that could facilitate a Marshallese adoption and he suggested that I contact them. I mentally filed the information. It would be sensible to complete our first adoption, and obtain Jessica's visa, before I started a second one.

Through a stroke of luck, a Filipino woman was returning to Majuro from Manila and she hand-carried Jessica's visa, passport and approval papers, with her. I greeted her at the airport with a big smile and gratefully collected our paperwork. We were on a tight schedule as our flight departed that afternoon, in four hours. I raced back to our room, packed and paid our massive hotel bill. Then we were finally off, with a 5-hour flight to Hawaii, a 20-hour layover in Honolulu and then a 9-hour non-stop flight to Cincinnati.

Airplanes traveled so fast! After a total of 22 days at sea, Paul was only halfway to San Francisco. Fifteen hours of flight-time put me in Cincinnati. It was no wonder that sailboats were considered obsolete as a means of transportation.

Suzanne and Kevin greeted us at the airport with a bouquet of balloons from Dad and Lynn as well as a large sparkly banner that read "Welcome home Jessica!"

Cincinnati is a cute town, with quaint gingerbread-house neighborhoods, hills that slope down to the winding Ohio River and neighborhood shopping squares. Every evening, while I waited for Paul, I would carry Jess through Mount Lookout and Hyde Park, admiring the homes and gardens. After living on a sea of blue, I was dazzled by the sight of so much green.

One day Suzanne suggested that we not move to Philadelphia, but stay in Cincinnati. The British marketing company she worked for was young, hip and in need of good project managers. She would be happy to submit Paul's resume with her recommendation.

I, too, had been wondering about our decision to move back to Philadelphia. We had just been on a major adventure. We had grown. How would it feel to return to the same town, to the same jobs, that we had left four years – and a lifetime – ago? It seemed as though we were wimping out, taking a safe step backward rather than an unknown step forward.

Without mentioning it to Paul, I gave Suzanne his resume. If there wasn't any interest, there wouldn't be any reason to bother Paul. A couple of days later, Paul received a note in our joint email account from one of the company's data directors. He asked Paul to elaborate on some of his prior experience.

I confessed what I had done to Paul via satellite email and summarized the director's questions. Paul's first email was brief: What are you doing, Kel? Several hours later a second e-mail followed, addressing the questions. And that was how, sailing toward San Francisco, Paul initially interviewed with dunnhumby, USA. I forwarded two more questioning emails from dunnhumby to Paul who willingly replied. I could just imagine these businessmen's faces when they read his latest e-mail, which stated that a gale was approaching and that he would reply after he had battened down the hatches and ridden out the storm.

Paul was nearing the northern California coastline and I had been tracking the weather. Storms seemed to march easterly across these waters every four or five days. I could only hope, and pray, that Rosie would get them through the bad weather.

Go, Rosie, go! Bring home my honey.

And, like the faithful friend she was, Rosie did. On July 4th, 2005, Paul sailed under the Golden Gate Bridge. He hailed the Coast Guard and announced that he had just arrived from Majuro, the Marshall Islands.

"Welcome home," the Coast Guard officer said.

Paul flew to Cincinnati and I leapt into his arms as soon as he exited baggage claim, squashing Jessica between us. Paul's 42-day sailing ordeal was over and so was mine. We were together once more.

We had started this journey searching for some purpose to our lives. In the process, we gained more than we could've imagined. As a couple, we had learned how to sail Rosie and repair her. We had battled severe storms and the equally severe challenges of infertility. We had adopted our daughter and adapted to parenthood. We had started as a couple and miraculously ended as a family.

Sandwiched between us, Jessica looked up at us with curiosity. Paul beamed at her, overjoyed to see her after his time at sea. I smiled at the sight of both of them. I knew another adventure awaited us.

While Paul had been sailing, I had plotted our future. He would get the job in Cincinnati; we would sell Rosie, buy a house, adopt another baby and save our money. When the kids were older, we would complete our circumnavigation. It was a fine plan.

And it could wait a day or two. For now, it was enough to simply be with my family.

Final Passage

Paul got the job in Cincinnati and we started the paperwork process to adopt another child from the Pacific Islands. We bought a gingerbread house and, because we hadn't sold Rosie yet, took out a second mortgage to pay for the down payment. For nearly a year, there was scant interest in Rosie. According to our boat broker, the market for ocean-going yachts was soft. If that was the case, we figured Rosie needed a competitive edge. She needed an interior makeover.

On one of our quarterly trips to San Francisco to check up on Rosie, Mavis came with us. She had volunteered to look after Jessica so Paul and I could do boat work. I rented a work shed at the marina with the thought that we'd sleep on Rosie and work in the shed. The opposite occurred. Because all of our tools and materials were on Rosie, it was easier to work on her and sleep in the shed.

With one window, and a functional bathroom, Mavis cheerfully dubbed the shed "the chalet." She scoured and disinfected it from top to bottom, transforming the chalet into Jessica's nursery by day and our communal sleeping room at night.

On board Rosie, Paul retiled the galley with shimmering turquoise glass tiles and installed a new white kitchen countertop. I recovered our vinyl ceiling headliner and painted the interior fiberglass walls. Paul and I sanded, stained and varnished our teak-and-holly floor. While Jessica napped, Mavis sewed new cushion covers. It was hardly the way we wanted to spend our precious few weeks of annual vacation, but when we were finished, Rosie looked beautiful. And, finally, someone else thought so, too.

Before Mike offered to buy her, we told him about the endless engine problems we had experienced and recommended that he install a new engine. Mike appreciated our honesty and made a fair offer on her. We accepted.

Like the day we bought Rosie, the day we sold her was a happy one. Not because we wanted to part with Rosie, but because it was impossible to maintain her in California while we lived halfway across the country in Ohio. It was time to move on.

With our past behind us, we eagerly awaited our future. According to our adoption agency, our paperwork had been approved by the Marshall Islands' Central Adoption Agency; the agency would call us when it received more news. We held our breath every time the phone rang, hoping that the caller would announce that we were parents. Three months later, Paul and I hugged and danced with joy after receiving the special phone call: we had a 2-month old Marshallese son!

Not all of our phone calls were as joyful. One day, prior to our son's birth, the phone rang while I was working in my home office. It was Mike, the man who had bought Rosie. While he came from a family of sailors, he himself had very little sailing experience so occasionally he would call us with questions. As seasoned cruisers to a soon-to-be cruiser, we were happy to help.

I set aside the scouting slides I was reviewing and listened attentively as he described the work he was having done on Rosie. He had hired a company to install a new, larger diesel engine in Rosie. Once the engine was installed, he and three friends – one who was an experienced sailor – would fly down to San Francisco and sail Rosie back to Seattle.

"Did they have to install a new prop shaft?" I asked.

"Yes, and they had to make a bigger exhaust system."

"That makes sense," I said, nodding to myself. I cautioned him to test the engine before they set sail; these were not minor changes.

"We'll try. We intend to cast off two days after we arrive."

"You're setting sail after spending only two days on the boat?" Surely I had misheard him.

Yep.

That didn't give him much time to test the engine and learn the boat's complicated systems.

"Well, I have only one week off work," he explained.

He sounded just like us, when we had first purchased Rosie and tried to sail her to Philadelphia. But now I knew how ignorant we had been, leaving on a boat we didn't know according to a date marked in our calendar. We had been foolish.

"Most experienced sailors only set sail when there is a favorable weather window. You should probably start watching the weather across the Pacific Northwest," I advised him, adding, "Storms seem to march across that area every four or five days."

"I will," he said. "But we have to leave on that date so that we are back in time for work."

I shook my head and bit my tongue. He owned Cherokee Rose. He was her new captain. Besides, what could I say? We had done the same thing.

"You sound worried," he said, breaking the silence that had fallen in our conversation.

"I am."

Mike and his friends were motoring out of San Francisco Harbor when he called Paul at work. He wanted to know how to use the radar. As Paul started to talk him through it, a loud alarm resonated from the boat. Even through the phone, Paul knew that distinctive sound. It was the high water alarm on our – no, Mike's – backup bilge pump. This alarm sounded if the primary bilge pump couldn't keep up the intake of water.

"How do I turn it off?" Mike shouted over the alarm.

"Flip off the switch on the electric panel behind you," Paul said. "It's in the second column of switches, toward the bottom."

A couple of seconds passed then the alarm ceased.

"Okay," Mike said, returning immediately to their conversation. "Now where were we...?"

On the second day of their passage, they were hit by a gale. With 10-foot seas and strong winds, they pounded their way north with Rosie flying off the tops of the waves and slamming into the trenches.

In the middle of the night, Mike went down below to get some sleep during his off-watch. He dreamt that Rosie was taking on water and, startled, woke suddenly. He pulled up the closest floorboard. Water lapped at the base of the floor!

It wasn't a dream; it was a nightmare.

There was a leak, except he didn't know where the water was coming from. And because the water level had overflowed Rosie's six-foot deep bilge and permeated every nook and cranny under the floorboards, he didn't have any clues in the form of leaks or dribbles. To make matters worse, he didn't know where Rosie's eleven through-hulls were so he couldn't check to see that they were closed. The batteries were wet so the electric bilge pumps didn't work. They pulled the hose off the engine's saltwater intake valve and, using the engine as a massive bilge pump, tried to suck the water out of the boat. For some reason, that didn't work.

At 1:30 a.m. on the second day of their journey, 12 miles southwest of Point Arena, Mike got on the radio, "Mayday, Mayday, this is sailing vessel Cherokee Rose." He and the crew were preparing to abandon ship into the life raft.

The Coast Guard dispatched a helicopter and 47-foot motor lifeboat to search for the men. At nearly 4 a.m. the two rescue vehicles spied the life raft when Mike set off an emergency flare. The helicopter lowered a basket and a rescue swimmer who retrieved two of the men before the helicopter needed to refuel. The Coast Guard crew aboard the motor lifeboat rescued the other two men, and Rosie's life raft. All four men were reported to be in good condition.

Rosie sank.

Glossary

ACCIDENTAL JIBE

If a boat is turning downwind through the wind, but has forgotten to take in the slack in the mainsail sheet, the wind can catch the sail on its back side. That will cause the sail, and the boom to slam across the deck unexpectedly. The force of the swinging boom can break the rigging or hit (and possibly kill) a crew member. Accidental jibes are BAD.

ALTERNATOR

A cylindrical-shaped device which generates electricity from an engine.

APPARENT WIND

The wind on a moving boat. This term can refer to the apparent wind speed or the apparent wind direction which differ from the true (land-based) wind. For example, if the true wind direction is exactly 90-degrees to the direction that the boat is sailing, the apparent wind direction will be less...because the boat is moving forward, there is now a forward component to the wind that isn't there when standing still, and that decreases the wind angle. By the way, zero degrees is on the nose of a boat and 180-degrees is directly behind the boat.

APPARENT WIND SPEED

The wind speed on a moving boat (as opposed to true wind speed which is the wind speed when not moving). For example, if the boat is moving 5 knots into the wind and the true wind speed is 20 knots, the apparent wind speed - the wind felt on the boat - is 15 knots.

ATOLL

A coral island which encloses a lagoon.

AUTOPILOT

A handy device which steers the boat according to wind direction (the same principal of our wind vane) or according to a compass setting. We nicknamed our Robertson autopilot "Bob" and he was a valued member of our team. Imagine having to steer the boat by hand, day and night for 22 days?! No thanks...

BEAM

At right angle to the boat, or off to the side of it. Usually used to refer to the wind direction. For example, sailing with the wind on our beam means that we are sailing across the wind; the wind is perpendicular to our direction. This is a good wind direction for sailing.

BEAUFORT WIND SCALE

A means of relating observed conditions at sea or on land to wind speed. Before wind measuring instruments were available, sailors still described their conditions at sea, but one man's "stiff breeze" was another man's "light breeze." This scale helped standardize these weather observations. For example, a flat sea covered with ripples but without crests is considered "light air" on the Beaufort Wind Scale with a corresponding wind speed of 1 - 3 knots. Small waves with breaking crests is a "moderate breeze" with winds of 11 - 16 knots.

BECALMED

Occurs when there is no wind which means a sailboat won't go very far or very fast (unless someone turns on the engine!).

BILGE

The lowest part of a boat's interior where any water dribbles or leaks on board will collect. On Rosie, we had a six-foot deep bilge under the floor (which turned out to be very handy when Paul needed to access the bottom of the engine, which was suspended over this deep recess).

BILGE PUMPS

A pump whose purpose is to suck water out of the bilge. We had two electric pumps and two manual pumps for Rosie's bilge. Resting on the bottom of our deep bilge was one electric pump, which took care of the little everyday dribbles of water that collected there. About six-inches higher, and mounted to the bilge wall, was a second bilge pump. If the everyday bilge pump couldn't keep the water out of the bilge - for example, if we had a fair- sized leak on the boat - the second, back-up pump would activate when the water level reached it. This pump also sounded a very loud alarm, thereby alerting us to a potential problem.

BIMINI

An awning used to shelter the cockpit from the sun and sometimes from the rain. Our bimini had a clear plastic window in it, like a car's sun roof, which enabled us to see the mainsail and mast head above us. We also had a canvas cover for the plastic window so we could fully shade the cockpit when at anchor.

BLOCK

A pulley on a boat. We used a block-and-tackle (several pulleys and a long rope) to hoist the engine out of the boat and onto the deck.

BOAT DOCUMENTATION

This is similar to a car's registration...in our case, our boat was federally registered as we knew we going to sail around the world, and not just within a certain state.

BOB

Our nickname for our Robertson autopilot.

BOOM

The spar (or metal pole) that is attached, and is perpendicular, to the mast and extends towards the back of the boat. The bottom of the mainsail is attached to the boom.

BOW

The forward part of the boat.

BOW PULPIT

The stainless steel guardrail at the front of the boat. While anchoring the boat or retrieving the anchor, Paul held onto this guardrail whenever Rosie pitched up and down due to the waves.

CAPSIZE

To tip or turn a boat over.

CHOCKED

In my book, this verb refers to a boat which is supported by metal braces while being on land for repairs. There is a similar word with a different meaning...a chock (a noun) is a deck-mounted guide though which lines are run.

CIRCUMNAVIGATION

To sail around the world.

CLEATS

A metal fitting on deck that is used to secure (tie off) lines. Most of the cleats I have seen are shaped like a pi symbol (as in pi equals 3.14...) and the ropes are wrapped under and around the flat top in a figure 8 shape.

CLOSE-HAULED

Sailing as close as possible into the wind. Obviously a boat cannot sail directly into the wind (which is considered to be at zero degrees), but if it bears off about 45-degrees or more, it can sail nearly upwind. We were close-hauled sailing to the Bahamas from Florida which is why Charbonneau dubbed us "On-the-Nose-Cherokee-Rose" - because the wind was on our nose. The motion on a boat sailing this close to upwind is uncomfortable and can get quite rough if the waves are big. Not my favorite point-of-sail.

CLUTCH

A device through which a line is strung and, when a lever is pressed, keeps the line from slipping.

COMPANIONWAY

Steps or ladder leading from the deck or cockpit of a boat to its cabin. I also use "companionway" to refer to the doorway which separates the cabin from the cockpit.

CRUISE, CRUISER, CRUISING...

To cruise simply means to visit the islands or ports in the area by boat; a cruiser is a person who does this.
At one point in the book, I say that we had become cruisers but not sailors...there is a difference. (Disclaimer: this is my definition and/or opinion; it may be different from someone else's.) A sailor is a person who knows tons about sailing and how to tweak the performance of a boat, given the wind and sea conditions, until it is fully maximized. A sailor will sit in the cockpit and analyze slight changes in the wind and happily readjust the sails accordingly for hours. Sailing is not a means: it is the purpose of the journey.

A cruiser sets the sails, flips on the autopilot, and then leaves the boat to sail itself while he/she does something else...read a book, repair the fridge, make some water, or plot the next route. If the wind changes enough to merit an adjustment in sail configuration, then the cruiser will tend to the sails. For a cruiser, sailing is usually a means to visit exotic ports, not an end.

On our trip, most of our friends were simply cruisers like Paul and I. Surprisingly, only a couple of boats were manned by sailors who happened to be cruisers, too.

DEPTH INDICATOR

A two-piece instrument that measures the depth of the water under the boat. It consists of an instrument panel that flashes the depth on a screen for crew to consult as well as an underwater transducer, fitted under the hull, to measure the depth.

DODGER

A canvas (or fiberglass in the case of a hard dodger) protective covering at the front of the cockpit designed to shield the crew from ocean spray and splashes. It also provides some protection from the wind.

DORADES

An air vent that prevents water from going into the cabin but allows air to circulate in the cabin. While Rosie had hatches, similar to opening skylights in a house, there were many times that we couldn't open them, for example, on a rough passage or when it rained. In those situations, the dorades were the only means to get fresh air below.

FORESTAY

The metal shroud (part of the boat's standing rigging) that runs from the bow of the boat to the top of the mast, to which the jib is hanked (or attached).

FOUL-WEATHER JACKET

A jacket that is designed to keep a person dry and warm on wet, cold days. Typically a foul-weather jacket is bright yellow, has velcro closures around the wrists to keep dripping water out, and flaps that cover its many pockets.

FURLED

Refers to when a sail (usually the jib or staysail) is rolled up around its headstay. A sail can be fully furled - entirely rolled up - or partially furled. The advantage of furling a sail is that you can make the sail any size you want for the given wind conditions by rolling it up a little bit or a lot. After our maiden voyage, we installed roller furling on both our jib and staysail so that we could control the size of the sail from the safety of the cockpit. Running around on deck during a gale can be dangerous!

GOOSENECK

The fitting which connects the boom to the mast.

GPS

Global Positioning System is a satellite navigation system which provides one's location (in longitude and latitude), provided one has a receiver and an unobstructed line-of-sight to four or more GPS satellites in space.

GULF STREAM

A swift and warm Atlantic Ocean current that originates at the southern tip of Florida and runs north and parallel with America's eastern coastline before crossing the Atlantic Ocean.

GYPSY

A toothed-wheel on the windlass that engages the anchor chain. If the toothed-wheel doesn't match the chain size closely, the chain can cause undue wear on the wheel and/or cause the chain to jump uncontrollably off the windless when the winch is operating. Paul referred to this runaway condition as freewheeling.

HALYARD

A line used to hoist or lower a sail.

HARNESS

Strong rope or webbing, sometimes with a built-in inflatable life vest, worn around the chest and tethered to the boat to prevent a crew member from being separated from the boat.

HEADLINER

The drop-down ceiling inside the cabin. On Rosie, the vinyl headliner could be removed to access the deck hardware that was below deck, like the nuts to the numerous bolts which held cleats, clutches, stanchions, etc on deck.

HEADWIND

Wind that comes from directly in front of you; on a boat that means when the bow is pointed dead into the wind.

HEAVE-TO

The act of setting the sail(s) and the rudder to counter each other, thereby "stalling" the boat so that it holds its position. This technique is used in storm conditions to make the motion on board bearable or when any speed could jeopardize the boat/crew. We also used this technique in good weather when we wanted to hold our position until daybreak, for example, before entering the pass to Minerva Reef.

HEAVY WEATHER

Yuck. When there is strong wind and big waves.

HOVE-TO

Past tense of heave-to.

HULL

The main body of the boat, not including its rigging, sails or its keel.

IMPELLER

According to Nigel Calder, this is "a rotating fitting that imparts motion to a fluid in a rotating pump." In our story, the impeller moves coolant around the engine to cool it. If the impeller doesn't work, the engine overheats...

JIB

The forward sail which is attached to the forestay.

JIBE

The act of turning the boat through the wind while the wind is behind you.

KEEL

The heavy fin beneath the water that is attached to the boat's hull and designed to keep the boat upright as well as preventing it from slipping sideways in the water. On Rosie, our lead keel extended six-feet underwater.

KNOT

A measure of speed. One knot equals one nautical mile per hour. A nautical mile is 6076 feet and equals one minute of the earth's latitude. For comparison, a mile on land is 5280 feet.

LAND SPITS

A deposit of sediment and sand along coastal areas that

eventually forms land, similar to how a sand bar is created. For a more technical definition, check out http://en.wikipedia.org/wiki/Spit_(landform).

LEE CLOTH

A strong piece of fabric or mesh used to keep a crew member from rolling out of bed while sailing.

LINE

A line refers to any rope on a boat. Why isn't "rope" used? I have no idea.

LOCK

A means of raising or lowering a boat. Here's my simple definition: A lock consists of a basin of water enclosed at opposite ends by water-tight gates. A boat enters one side of the basin, the gates close and water is either pumped into the basin, or drained out of the basin, thereby lifting or lowering the boat. Then the other gate is opened and the boat leaves the lock.
In the Panama Canal, the water in the Pacific Ocean is higher than in the Atlantic so Rosie needed to be raised. It turns out that Gatun Lake is higher than either ocean so Rosie needed to be lifted up on the Atlantic-side of Gatun Lake and then lowered slightly on the Pacific-side before entering the Pacific Ocean.

MAINSAIL

The sail that is hoisted on the mast (and is usually attached to the boom). Our mainsail had battens sewn into it to give it better sail shape. It also had three reefing points, which enabled us to lower the sail to any of these points and thereby decrease our sail size. During storms, our mainsail was triple-reefed which meant that it was as small as it could be, just short of taking it down altogether.

MAST

The towering aluminum or wood pole in the middle of the

boat from which the mainsail is hoisted. Most (if not all) of the metal shrouds on a boat and its standing rigging is attached to the mast, too.

MAST FOOT

This is the base that the bottom of the mast sits on.

MAST-HEAD

The top of the mast. On Rosie, we had one light on top of the mast as well as a wind direction indicator, an anemometer (which measures wind speed) and an antenna for our VHF radio.

MAYDAY

There are three internationally recognized distress signals that are used in certain situations:
   Mayday - only for a life-threatening emergency
   Pan-Pan - an urgent, but not life-threatening situation
   Securite - a signal to warn others of a hazard or dangerous situation

MOORING BALL

In particularly deep anchorages or in anchorages where the current is strong, sometimes marinas or yacht clubs will permanently anchor balls or buoys so that boats can tie up to them. Then the boat doesn't have to set its own anchor. Mooring balls are also used where careless anchoring has ruined coral reefs to minimize further damage.

NAV STATION

Usually referred to simply as the nav station. This is the desk area on a boat, designed so that crew can plot their position on large, bulky paper charts. With the increasing use of electronic charts, this is where the computer might be located as well as other electronics. See website to see Rosie's nav station. Mounted in the wall you will see: Fuse box, Inmarsat C Satellite E-Mail System, MP3/radio, Single Side Band radio and VHF Radio. Then mounted on the desk: GPS, secondary Autopilot control and Radar. Then a laptop (plus 2 spares) for electronic charts, satellite e-mail, etc.

OBSERVATION PORT

On board, the tanks - for diesel, drinking water, gray water, etc - have hoses which lead to small exterior holes to fill or empty them as the case may be. In order to clean the inside of the tanks or to check for leaks, the tanks also had large holes on top of them that are usually bolted shut with a tight-fitting lid.

When Rosie went aground in Charleston and subsequently laid down on her side, we discovered that one of our diesel observation ports had NOT been tightly sealed so diesel leaked out of this top access point. Talk about being heeled over!

OUTBOARD

A portable engine with a propeller that is mounted on the transom (the back) of a dinghy or boat.

PEAK FLOW

When a tidal current reaches its maximum speed.
In the USA, there are typically two high tides and two low tides per day, with six hours between each one. As the tide ebbs (falls) or floods (rises), the movement of water creates a current. The current is approximately its strongest three hours after slack tide (when there is no current at all, at the precise moment of high or low tide); this is peak flow.

PILINGS

A wood post driven into the seabed to support docks or to form a breakwater.

POOPED

Yes, this is a sailing term. Being pooped is when a wave crashes over the stern of your boat and fills the cockpit with water. This happened to us numerous times on our passage to Panama and it is scary!

PORT

1. The left-hand side of your boat as you face forward
2. A window in the cabin of a boat
3. A harbor

PREVENTER

A block-and-tackle system used to stop the boom from swinging across the cockpit in the case of an accidental jibe. We used ours every time we were sailing downwind.

QUARANTINE

When a boat arrives in a new country, the boat is expected to hoist a yellow flag, sometimes called a Q flag. This lets onshore officials know that the boat has just arrived and will be coming ashore to clear in. Crew members are supposed to stay on board as part of a quarantine while the captain of the vessel goes ashore to check in with customs and immigration. If all goes well, the captain returns to the boat and the Q flag is lowered. Then the flag of that country is hoisted as a sign of respect (also called a courtesy flag) and the crew is allowed ashore. In several cases, Paul returned to Rosie with officials who wanted to check our food, cigarettes and alcohol stores before clearing us in.

RAFT UP

When two boats tie up together, usually at anchor.

REDUCED SAIL

When the overall sail area on a boat is decreased. When there is too much wind for the sails (for example, the boat is steeply heeled or is going too fast for the wave conditions), smaller sails are needed. The area of most forward sails can be decreased by simply furling them, or rolling them up. Mainsails are typically lowered a notch or two, ie reefed, to reduce their sail area.

REEFED, REEF

A way of reducing sail area. The front sails on Rosie are furled, or rolled up, to the desired size while the mainsail is lowered to one of three different points or dropped altogether. See Mainsail for more details.

REVERSE OSMOSIS WATER MAKER

A machine that converts salt water into drinking water.

RIGGING

There are two types of rigging on a sailboat: the standing rigging and the running rigging. The standing - or permanent - rigging is the mast, boom and all of the metal shrouds that support the mast. The running rigging is all of the lines (ropes) that are attached to the sails, including the halyards and sheets.

ROGUE WAVE

I just checked Wikipedia's definition of a rogue wave and it differs from my mine.
Here's what I mean when I refer to a rogue wave: waves typically travel in the same direction, have roughly the same size and go roughly the same speed. A rogue wave is one that comes unexpectedly from a different angle, might be larger than the rest of them and travel faster or slower than the others.
In Panama, most of the walls of waves came from behind us, but every once in a while, a rogue wave would hit us from the side.

ROLLER FURLING

A way of rolling up the front sail around its forestay to decrease its sail area or to roll it up entirely at the end of a passage or in strong winds.

RUDDER

The underwater fin that is controlled by the tiller, the wheel and/or the autopilot and steers the boat by deflecting water. Water has to be moving past the rudder in order to steer the boat.

RUNNING

Sailing with the wind directly behind the boat. In these conditions, the sails are usually set for wing-on-wing or the spinnaker is hoisted. Because waves usually come from the same direction as the wind, running is more comfortable than pounding into the wind and waves. Running, however, can be dangerous due to the risk of an accidental jibe which is why Paul rigged preventers.

SEA ANCHOR

A parachute- or cone-shaped piece of fabric that is tossed into the water off the bow of the boat in heavy weather. Floating just under the surface of the water, the parachute slows the boat down. It also keeps the bow of the boat facing into the wind and breaking seas. If the waves are large, it is dangerous for a boat to be sideways to the breaking waves as the boat might roll over. Keeping the bow of the boat into the waves exposes less of the boat to the force of plummeting water and helps the boat ride up and down the waves instead of being tossed around.

SEA COCKS

A valve which opens or closes an underwater hole in the hull. Some sea cocks allow salt water to come in, such as for cooling the engine, while other sea cocks are designed to let water out, such as from the kitchen sink.

SEXTANT

An instrument used for celestial navigation and for getting one's position before GPS became prevalent.

SHEETS

The lines which are used to control a sail, and its shape, by taking them in or easing them out.

SHIP'S LOG

The boat's log book which contains information about one's position, time and date at sea. If all electronics failed, this log could be used to estimate one's location and to make educated course adjustments as needed. On passage, we made a new log entry every hour, including date and time, latitude, longitude, distance to go, speed over ground, compass bearing, wind direction and speed, engine hours, whose watch it was, sail configuration and any comments. As I write this, looking in our log book, I see a couple of notes: did 2 loads laundry; saw meteor(!?) within 10 feet of boat...oops, I might give away part of our story...You get the idea.

SHOALS

Shallow water that may be dangerous to a boat.

SHROUDS

I refer to all of the metal wires which extend down from the mast as "shrouds." The ones in front are also called headstays or forestays; the ones in the rear are also called backstays. The ones at the side of the mast are simply called shrouds.

SLACK TIDE

The moment when there is no tidal current, which occurs at exactly high and low tides.

SNUBBER

A piece of rope used to reduce the strain on the anchor chain and windlass; it acts like a shock absorber.

SPEEDOMETER

The instrument which measures our speed through the water.

SPINNAKER

A large billowing front sail which is used when sailing downwind.

SPREADER LIGHTS

A spreader is a vertical support placed high on the mast and used to guide the shrouds from the the top of the mast to the deck. On Rosie, we had 2 flood lights attached to the underside of the spreader, one on either side of the mast, that illuminate the deck at night when switched on.

SQUALLS

A typically short storm which starts when the wind suddenly picks up and is followed by rain, thunderstorms and/or lightening.

STARBOARD

The right side of the boat when looking forward to the bow.

STAYSAIL

Cherokee Rose was a cutter, which meant that she had three sails: a higher- cut forward jib; a secondary smaller "jib" that was between the main jib and the mast; as well as the mainsail. This secondary front sail is the staysail.

STERN

The back end of a boat.

STERN PULPIT

The stainless steel guardrail at the stern of the boat. Our barbecue grill and two outboard motors were attached to this guard rail.

TACKING

The act of turning the boat through the wind, while heading into the wind.

THROUGH-HULL FITTING

This refers to a nylon or metal piece which is inserted into and securely fastened around an underwater hole in the hull of the boat. Sea cocks and/or hoses are then attached to these fittings.

TOE RAIL

A wooden or metal rail around the the outer edges of the boat's deck.

TRAVEL LIFT

A special crane fitted with slings used to hoist a boat from the water or lower a boat back into the water.

TRUE WIND SPEED

The actual speed of the wind when standing still.

TURNBUCKLE

A mechanical fitting attached to the bottom ends of the metal shrouds and stays. These fittings can be tightened or released to adjust the tension of the standing rigging.

VHF RADIO

Very High Frequency two-way radio typically used for boats within line-of-sight.

WINCH

When the load on a line is too much to haul in by hand, the line is wrapped around a drum and, using the drum's handle, is turned, thereby pulling in the line. This drum, or winch, is also helpful for releasing a line under strain in a controlled manner. Winches are usually used for hoisting the sails and trimming them.

WIND GENERATOR

A fan-shaped device which rotates when the wind blows and generates electricity. Unfortunately, it doesn't generate wind for the sails as a friend mistakenly, but understandably, thought...

WIND VANE

A device that steers the boat relative to the wind direction.

WINDLASS

An electric or hydraulic machine which raises or lowers the anchor and its chain on the boat. On Rosie, our windlass was at the bow, and in a locker to protect it from salt spray, waves and rain.

WING-ON-WING

A sail configuration used when sailing downwind...the mainsail and boom are pushed out over the water (not quite perpendicular to the boat) on one side of the boat while the front jib is held out over the other side of the boat, usually with the help of a pole. This maximizes the sail area that is exposed to the wind.

Acknowledgements

Boy, where to start?!
Let's start at the beginning...thank you to everyone who helped Paul and I as we set off to sail around the world. Dad, Mavis and Suzanne were honorary crew members, helping us every step of way, in person and via e-mail and phone. Thank you to Kevin for his tireless help on our adoption paperwork. And a big hug to Mom, Lynn and Claire who cheered us on.

Bruce, who unexpectedly died a couple of years ago of a heart attack, thank you for sailing with us on our maiden voyage and for your constant encouragement. We miss you.

Thank you to *all* of the cruisers we met along the way who took the time to teach us, guide us, fix us dinner and help us with the endless repairs. We count Charbonneau, Acclaim, Free Spirit, Scott Free, Solent Venture, Sueno, Enchante, Spirit, and Kela as life-long friends, no matter how great our distance or elapsed time. We include Dolly and Svilen in this group of friends; thank you for your guidance and friendship in Tarawa.

Lastly, a special thank you to our children's birth moms for sharing Jessica and Nick with us. I am so proud to be their mom, too.

Writing this book turned out to be another journey. A huge thank you to my editors, Nancy J. Stohs and Christine Tawtel Hendricks who generously read (and reread) my manuscript, offered suggestions to improve and clarify the story and encouraged me along the way. Thanks, too, for your suggestions on my website...you are the best!

Dad, Lynn and Mavis, thank you for your input on the various drafts. Thanks to Dad, for pushing all the buttons on my website and thoroughly testing it; Suzanne, for your input as well; and Mom, for your help with the videos. Lastly, a special thank you to my Nana, whose kind words kept me going at a tough time.

Paul, honey, thank you for holding my hand through both journeys. Anything *is* possible with you.

For additional photos, emails and information about our trip, please visit the Book Supplement section of www.sailingtojessica.com.